Escape, Escapism, Escapology

ESCAPE, ESCAPISM, ESCAPOLOGY

American Novels of the Early Twenty-First Century

John K. Limon

BLOOMSBURY ACADEMIC
NEW YORK · LONDON · OXFORD · NEW DELHI · SYDNEY

BLOOMSBURY ACADEMIC
Bloomsbury Publishing Inc
1385 Broadway, New York, NY 10018, USA
50 Bedford Square, London, WC1B 3DP, UK
29 Earlsfort Terrace, Dublin 2, Ireland

BLOOMSBURY, BLOOMSBURY ACADEMIC and the Diana logo are
trademarks of Bloomsbury Publishing Plc

First published in the United States of America 2022

An earlier version of Chapter 2, "I Flit, I Float, I Fleetly Flee, I Fly," was
published previously as, "Escapism, or, The Soul of Globalization," in *Genre*,
John Limon, pp. 51-77, Copyright © 2016, Duke University Press. All rights
reserved. Republished by permission of the publisher. www.dukeupress.edu.

For legal purposes the Acknowledgments on p. 229 constitute an extension
of this copyright page.

Cover design: Eleanor Rose
Cover image: Cover shows a detail from Frisbee by Kate Vita Vander Wende.
Courtesy of Michael McCafferty

Bloomsbury Publishing Inc does not have any control over, or responsibility
for, any third-party websites referred to or in this book. All internet addresses
given in this book were correct at the time of going to press. The author and
publisher regret any inconvenience caused if addresses have changed or sites
have ceased to exist, but can accept no responsibility for any such changes.

Library of Congress Cataloging-in-Publication Data
A catalog record for this book is available from the Library of Congress

ISBN: HB: 978-1-5013-9111-8
PB: 978-1-5013-9110-1
ePDF: 978-1-5013-9108-8
eBook: 978-1-5013-9109-5

Typeset by Deanta Global Publishing Services, Chennai, India

To find out more about our authors and books visit www.bloomsbury.com
and sign up for our newsletters.

CONTENTS

Part III
FOREIGN CORRESPONDENTS

Part IV
PREQUEL

INTRODUCTION

I need to apologize for my first epigraph. I once read an anecdote, presumably in a newspaper or magazine, that made an impression. I cannot think how to track it down. The only part of the anecdote about which I am certain, its final seven words, is a cliché, which means that a Google search is hopeless. I will insert the name of a Hollywood mogul into the story because the story needs a name, but I am unlikely to have the correct one. The mogul was down on his luck: perhaps he was a producer on a string of flops; perhaps he had notoriously sacrificed his reputation to hackery; perhaps he had just been through an unsightly divorce; probably all of these. Here is the anecdote with everything reinvented by me except its spirit and closing quotation.

Two friends had gone to Hollywood with hopes of writing screenplays. They were attracted to the glamour of Hollywood, but they also had standards, and they hoped to write films that would not make them ashamed. It did not go well for them, at least at first; they were unemployed or misemployed. There seemed to be few prospects for a life of creativity with an aesthetic conscience. Meeting at a restaurant for lunch, the two writers looked on as Robert Evans was seated at a table across the room. One of the writers commented to his friend, "This is as good as it gets."

> "But you can't just turn your back on all your responsibilities and run away from them," Major Danby insisted. "It's such a negative move. It's escapist." Yossarian laughed with buoyant scorn and shook his head. "I'm not running *away* from my responsibilities. I'm running *to* them. . . . You know who the escapists are, don't you, Danby? Not me and Orr." (Joseph Heller, *Catch-22*, 451)

> If I had to put it to words I'd say that what she wanted, more than anything, was what she'd always wanted throughout her Lost Childhood: to escape. *From what* was easy to enumerate: the bakery, her school, dull-ass Baní, sharing a bed with her madre, the inability to buy the dresses she wanted, having to wait until fifteen to straighten her hair, the impossible expectations of La Inca, the fact

that her long-gone parents had died when she was one, the whispers that Trujillo had done it, those first years of her life when she'd been an orphan, the horrible scars from that time, her own despised black skin. But where she wanted to escape *to* she could not tell you. . . . Beli had the inchoate longings of nearly every adolescent escapist. (Junot Díaz, *The Brief Wondrous Life of Oscar Wao* 79–80)

"Forget what you are escaping *from*," he said, quoting an old maxim of Kornblum's. "Reserve your anxiety for what you are escaping *to*." (Michael Chabon, *The Amazing Adventures of Kavalier & Clay* 21)

As if in the world there were no places to escape to, only places to flee. (Colson Whitehead, *The Underground Railroad* 257)

Ubi fracassorium, ibi fuggitorium. (Pulcinella, in Giorgio Agamben, *Pulcinella*, epigraph)

Part I

ESCAPE, ESCAPISM, ESCAPOLOGY

Chapter 1

NOTES FROM NEVERLAND

The first inkling of an escapism project came to me while reading Junot Díaz's *The Brief Wondrous Life of Oscar Wao*, comparing it as I read to Michael Chabon's *The Amazing Adventures of Kavalier & Clay*. What had stumped me about Chabon's book was its almost scholastic interlacing of escapology, escapism, and escape: a one-time escapologist (Kavalier, former apprentice in Houdini's line of entertainment) escapes Nazi-occupied Prague to America, where he cocreates a comic book hero called The Escapist. I was defeated by the epic scope of a narrative that was unified, obscurely to my mind, by mutually exclusive concepts. Escape is one way of dealing with real dangers, escapism is a failure to deal with real dangers, and escapology invents techniques to deal with artificial dangers.

What set off my escapism project was a sense of something similarly perplexing in Díaz's *Oscar Wao*. Díaz's novel, like Chabon's, concerns an escape from a totalitarian state—in Díaz's case, Trujillo's Dominican Republic, still informed by Trujillo long after his assassination. Once again, the escape is in some relation to escapism: Oscar Wao is not only a devotee of comic books such as Kavalier might illustrate; he is also a cognoscente of fantasy and sci-fi genre literature, as well as fantasy and sci-fi films and video games. Above all, he is a fan of J. R. R. Tolkien, whose saga *The Lord of the Rings*, centered on the hobbit Frodo, is in intimate relation to the picaro-hagiography of Oscar Wao—but what intimate relation? Tolkien's book has no influence on Díaz's naturalism, politics, tonal flamboyance, or wit.

Chabon and Díaz are masterful writers, and the two books in question may be their masterpieces. It wouldn't be absurd to begin assembling a sub-canon of novels from the last quarter century with these two books. In a "BBC Culture" poll of 2015, twelve novels were named best of the twenty-first century. *Kavalier & Clay* finished sixth; *Oscar Wao* finished first (Ciabattari, n.p.). We might add several more novels to the sub-canon, taxonomized not only by their acclaim but also by the extravagance of their titles: Dave Eggers's *A Heartbreaking Work of Staggering Genius*, Jonathan Safran Foer's *Everything is Illuminated* and *Extremely Loud and Incredibly Close*, and Arundhati Roy's *The God of Small Things* and *The Ministry of Utmost Happiness*.

After their hyperbole, here is the second thing to notice about these titles: in all cases, they are misleading. I am not chiding these works, which are, in part, *about* the misdirection of their titles. *The Amazing Adventures of Kavalier & Clay* mimics the hyping of The Escapist superhero radio program; by the end of the novel, the two cousins are antiheroically amazed in blind pathways of sexuality and love. The wondrousness of *The Brief Wondrous Life of Oscar Wao* ups the ante on the happiness of "The Short Happy Life of Francis Macomber," with the paradoxical consequence that we may read more irony into the novel's title than is, finally, appropriate. Eggers himself challenges the uniqueness of the heartbreak of his semi-fictional memoir (he acknowledges that other siblings have been orphaned) and its genius (he admits that some passages of the book are skippable). In Foer's *Everything is Illuminated*, much is purposely dim. One begins by guessing that the phrase *Extremely Loud and Incredibly Close* will refer to the intensity of the sensuous experience of 9/11, but it turns out to be easy to overlook what local imaginary post-9/11 phenomenon it does refer to.

Many of Roy's titles play sly games with hyperbole. *The God of Small Things* miniaturizes and then qualifies the apotheosis of its title character. *The Algebra of Infinite Justice*, the title of a collection of essays, is a parody, which only reveals itself to readers when they are reminded that the first official name for the US Global War on Terror was "Operation Infinite Justice" (renamed "Operation Enduring Freedom"). If you anticipate that *The Ministry of Utmost Happiness* will be a dystopian fiction in which a government agency provides opiates for the masses, on the model of Orwell's Ministry of Truth or Peace, you will be surprised that there is a nongovernmental administering of happiness in the book, which the book itself, at its most optimistic, hopes to take as a model. Nevertheless, the novel is unsure that even threadbare happiness is a possibility for its characters.

All of these works suggest a subgenre, a telltale stirring in a corner of the world of ambitious contemporary fiction, and the thing to explain is not merely the self-conscious hyperbole or the self-conscious bathos, but their unlikely coexistence. These novels are about an entanglement of innocence and experience. Their disappointment is built into their display. They are inflated and deflationary. If it is possible to preserve the double-edgedness of "This is as good as it gets," leaving it to its positive colloquial deadness (things can never improve on this) but reviving it simultaneously with negative literalist energy (things will never improve), it will capture my most essential thesis about the contemporary blurring of escapism, escapology, and escape.

Here is the second phase of the undertaking of this escapism project: the story of how it began to generate a literary theory. I know of three serious books explicitly on the subject of escapism: the psychoanalyst Adam Phillips (*Houdini's Box: On the Arts of Escape*) believes we are escaping the risks of our desires; the cultural geographer Yi-Fu Tuan (*Escapism*), our animality; the philosopher Emmanuel Levinas (*De l'évasion*), the shame of naked being.

You might begin a project on the literary form of escapism by trying to assimilate these three nonliterary works. What they argue in concert is that escapism implies trying to evade the scandal of the self, the split of its aspirations, instincts, or ontology, or their division from one another. They disagree about the particulars of the scandal, but for my purposes, the enviable fact is their shared confidence about the relation (however vexed) of self (however split) and reality (however variably understood), as revealed by their shared assurance that they can establish what it means for selves to *escape* reality.

When I wonder whether my own book has a worthwhile subject, I hold onto its pathos, which is my incapacity for sharing the assurance of Phillips, Tuan, or Levinas about which way we turn from reality and which way to face it. It would be enough to know one and infer the other. This is also the pathos of the novels I've been reading. I am not invoking a postmodern skepticism about the apprehension of reality in general—its hiddenness in or behind language, ideology, fantasy, or simulacra. In the books that form the core of this study, on the contrary, reality is vivid in every direction; there is a surfeit of unproblematic reference (mixed, occasionally, with problematic reference). Without exception, Chabon, Díaz, Foer, Eggers, Donoghue, Morrison, Groff, Butler, Whitehead, Saunders, Ward, Grossman, Roy, and Gass seem capable of describing anything, on any level of analysis, with a specialist's precision. They are observant, polymathic, and eloquent. What it seems to me they don't know is how to motivate their vision, how to conceive not only what their characters are escaping *from* but also what they are escaping *to* (the italics are inevitable), which equals not knowing the direction of their freedom or redemption.

It is too obvious to need proving that in contemporary literary theory there is a competition for centrality that entails correlative charges of evasion, which might mean not to home one's attention on textuality, power, history, data, affect, evolution, or the Real. *All* of this can seem escapist, however, to those who work practically on problems on the scale of world health, or racial injustice, or climate change, or on local, community problems. Those who work on large- or small-scale political issues can seem evasive to one another. And acting on the largest or smallest political issues can seem evasive in relation to the fact that your childhood friend is addicted to fentanyl, or your father does not remember your name, or your job no longer commands your own respect. All courage not your own is cowardice; it doesn't face the reality *you* face.

If I cannot produce my own theory of which aspects of life are central and which are peripheral, and if some important novelists have the same disability, how can I write a book on escapism, on their escapism? Anyone with confidence in the truth and virtue of his or her propositions can readily produce a theory of escapism by way of contrast and find texts to support it. The opposite approach will have the strength and weakness of being a literary approach, that is, one not committed to a version of reality imported from a politics, philosophy, or science that demands uniformity of premises and consistency of inferences.

Two works dedicated to meeting the charge of escapism where it has been leveled came to my aid at this juncture (rationalized retroactively) of my project: Stanley Cavell's *Pursuits of Happiness* and Rodgers and Hammerstein's *The Sound of Music*. *Pursuits of Happiness* takes up the charge of escapism brought against Cavell's favorite American film comedies of the 1930s and 1940s, emblems of film in general: "A colloquial version of the idea of comedy as reprieve is the idea of film as providing 'escape,' which seems to be the common public understanding of what film is good for, though I have not heard it said what the escape is from, nor where it is to, nor what its method is" (Cavell 186). Cavell, clearly, does not expect to hear a codification of the rules of escapism because he takes it to be mindless—not the so-called escapist work itself but its reception—as opposed to the noncolloquial reprieve, which allows you to be "free to stop and think." What you are free to reflect on is the inescapability of the heartlessness of the world, which may be the only heartening distance you get from it. But escapism for adults is not mindless, which does not mean it is reflective; it is precisely in the imprecision of the line between thought and thoughtlessness, as between maturely grasping the necessity of escape and childishly grasping at evasions of it, that adult escapism flourishes.

Adapting Northrop Frye's nomenclature, Cavell presents most of his seven favorite classic film comedies as "green world" romances, sophisticated fantasies of the potential for conversation and adventure on the part of men and women in the post-suffrage phase of twentieth-century feminism. But Cavell notes that two of his comedies marked by a "terrible darkness," *It Happened One Night* and *His Girl Friday*, don't debouch to the green world that, Cavell observes, is always called Connecticut in films of the 1930s and 1940s, and *His Girl Friday* is sufficiently grim to be denominated a "black world" comedy (Cavell 172, 182). Surely these two films are the least susceptible to the charge of escapism.

Let us make the charge, anyway, by comparison with William Faulkner's short story, "Pantaloon in Black," the narrative of a Black man, Rider, whose young wife Mannie has mysteriously died, told first by an omnipresent and almost omniscient (if superficial) narrator, then by an uncomprehending deputy sheriff to his willfully oblivious wife. What the deputy cannot understand and his wife refuses to contemplate is why Rider, jailed for killing a white gambler whose cheating at dice serves the unjust God who took Mannie, breaks out of jail only to submit to a lynching. What troubles both the sheriff and his own wife, comfortable assuming the brainlessness of African Americans, is that Rider is tormented by his consciousness and self-consciousness: he keeps repeating, "Hit look lack Ah just can't quit thinking" (Faulkner 154). Nor can the sheriff fathom why Rider did not take the death of his wife as a liberation, a wonderment the sheriff's wife presumably takes in. Hearing enough that discomfits her, she leaves the house and ends the story to go to "the picture show" (Faulkner 154).

It is possible she flees to *His Girl Friday*. Faulkner was writing "Pantaloon in Black" in 1940; *His Girl Friday* was released that January. This, too, is the story of an escape from prison, but the deputy's wife will prefer it: because the escapee, Earl Williams, is a white man who killed a Black man, he won't be lynched. He won't be legally executed, either, because Walter Burns (Cary Grant) and Hildy Johnson (Rosalind Russell) revive their mutual excitation by keeping Earl from his scheduled hanging. (Walter is a newspaperman, but Hildy is about to give up her calling in journalism to marry a dullard when Walter wins her back to champion Earl's cause.) Like "Pantaloon in Black," the film features an actual escape from mortal danger—a legal hanging—the consequence of an interracial homicide. But as in *Kavalier & Clay* and *Oscar Wao*, the film puts that actual escape in relation to simple escapism—Walter's disgorgement of Hildy from a looming domesticity on behalf of the audience's (e.g., the deputy's wife's) fantasy of a sexually glamorous, verbally dexterous, egalitarian romance. For the purpose of theorizing escapism, the crucial question is: What is the relation of Earl's jailbreak and Walter's home-wrecking? Eventually, Hildy wins Earl a reprieve by reason of insanity. Cavell is interested in Earl only insofar as he stands for Hildy's own need for a reprieve by reason of insanity (his working definition of comedy) from the world's brutal corruption. Cavell does not otherwise pay attention to Earl's actual, one-time, witless escape from jail.

Cavell is also uninterested in Earl's crime, which happens to be shooting (for addled reasons) a Black policeman, unseen and unnamed. There is a second invisible Black character in *His Girl Friday*: when Earl is on the loose, a reporter jokes that the befuddled police have interviewed a newborn baby to see if "the pickaninny is Earl Williams." It's a multiply bizarre joke, for one thing because Earl Williams is played by John Qualen, a character actor almost always employed to play Scandinavians.

The film is intermittently about the invisibility of babies, including the imaginary Black one: one of its first lines, spoken by an advice columnist to Hildy before she enters Walter's office to announce her departure, is, "my cat just had kittens again," a fact without consequences but implicit advice for Hildy, who claims to want to get married to breed. The evoked kittens and the joke Black baby fail to appear in the film alongside the one deceased invisible man. Giving birth, being born, and dying are ceded to Blacks and animals; it is by the power of Grant and Russell's immortal stardom that the cycles of generation can be sloughed. We catch the claim of self-generating immortality in progress when the mayor, who needs Earl's execution to secure "the colored vote" (a pure demography) in an upcoming election, threatens Walter lamely—"You're through"—and Walter returns a threat: "The last man to say that to me was Archie Leach, just a while before he cut his throat." Walter's purported homicide disguised as Leach's suicide enables the homicidal and suicidal self-fashioning of Cary Grant, *né* Archibald Leach. What is killed off is mortality itself. Film stardom makes it thinkable that Blacks can do the dying for whites—a Black man is murdered off-screen, jeopardizing the vote of unseen Black masses, but dead Archie Leach is resurrected as immortal Cary Grant on-screen to save the murderer from reciprocal death—a point near to Faulkner's in *The Sound and the Fury*, in which Southern white children believe that only Blacks and animals can die.

This much is close to territory surveyed in *Playing in the Dark*, where Toni Morrison argues that whiteness needs Blackness to have any shape at all. According to Morrison, whiteness without Blackness is summarized collectively by white authors themselves this way: "mute, meaningless, unfathomable, pointless, frozen, veiled, curtained, dreaded, senseless, implacable" (Morrison, *Playing* 59). In particular, white men invent a binary with Blacks to define their own control, and white women, their own virtue. In *His Girl Friday*, Blackness is born and dies at the margins so that whiteness can stake a claim to transcendence of the animal body. After Earl escapes his cell, Walter and Hildy hide him in a rollaway desk as if in a womb to be c-sectioned outside the Criminal Courts Building, so that Grant and Russell, free of childbirth, can be born again to eternal life. The film, more than a mechanism for Hildy's reprieve, is an entire escapist contraption involving characters, actors, and audience: a real escape (Earl Johnson's from death row by way of police ineptitude and Walter and Hildy's manipulations) enables an escapist fantasy (Faulkner's sheriff's wife's, by means of Walter and Hildy's mutual invigoration), which enables an escapological fantasy (Grant and Russell's immortal stardom, grace of Johnson's reprieve from the law, and the racist outsourcing of mortality).

His Girl Friday needs Earl Johnson because it needs an infantile, innocent beneficiary of a journalistic crusade not to seek justice for mortal Blackness, paying for immortal whiteness. In *It Happened One Night*, there are no significant Black people to begin with (a few may be glimpsed at train depots), a notable omission in view of the fact that the plot is an escape from South to North by a woman whose dollar value can be ascertained and on whom a bounty has been placed in newspapers by her master, her father, who has sent out the contemporary version of patrollers to recapture her. Whiteness doesn't need Blackness for contrast here because it has usurped its history, its Underground Railroad, neo-slave narrative. In this respect, *It Happened One Night* represents a technical improvement in escapism over *His Girl Friday* insofar as the difficulty of the real physical escape (from South to North) has been conjoined with the difficulty of the escapist relationship of Peter Warne (Clark Gable) and Ellie Andrews (Claudette Colbert), unlike the escapist relationship of Walter and Hildy, which requires the escape of Earl Williams as surrogate.

If race and history surface, they barely do so at the typological moment of the film, when Peter and Ellie are crossing a stream; Peter slings Ellie over his back, which Ellie confuses with piggybacking. A screwball discussion of piggybacking ensues, an interlude when Peter and Ellie almost openly admit to enjoying their verbal sparring. Ellie brags that her father was a great piggybacker, which Peter denies. Then Peter, freely descending to Ellie's level of self-infantilism, asserts that Lincoln was a great piggybacker. Why does Lincoln appear at the river-crossing moment of a story about escape from South to North? The film turns to screwball dialogue to conjure him; it makes its reference to history in a comically ahistorical and regressive way. Insofar as the typology depends on Blackness, it is not Blackness made visible as contrast to white self-definition, or Blackness kept invisible as sacrifice to screen apotheosis: the notion that freedom has a direction, as it did for slaves, elicits the historical envy of whites who had been, if Peter and Ellie are any indication, existentially, if not physically, enchained.

The problem is that freedom isn't in fact northward for Peter and Ellie. They know whence they are escaping but not whither. For most of the film, they approach Ellie's formal wedding ceremony in New York to her cad fortune-hunting husband (with whom she had previously eloped); Peter is escorting her in return for the sensational tabloid story of her flight from her father. They continue northward together toward a second incarceration, unable to synchronize their growing consciousness of having fallen in love. Peter, however, has dreamed of escaping America altogether—his fantasy is of a Pacific island and "nights when you and the moon and the water all become one." The newspaperman Peter Warne is reminiscent of the newspaperman Jake Barnes in *The Sun Also Rises*, who periodically escapes femaleness for fishing or swimming—dreams of an all-male or one-man oceanic feeling, so sensuous and nonsensual that it feels like eternal life and oblivion at once.

Both Warne and Barnes are logophobic newspapermen whose mission is to protect aristocratic women from their own impulses; like Barnes, courtier of Lady Brett Ashley, Warne finds himself delivering the aristocratic woman (whom he calls Brat, which almost always sounds like Brett) to another man. But Ellie, unlike Brett, comes to share her deliverer's dream of unity with wordless oceanic nature, asking, "Have you ever been in love, Peter?" and entreating him, "Take me with you, Peter! Take me to your island! . . . We can run away." She is Wendy Darling rather than Brett Ashley at such moments, while Peter Warne morphs from Jake Barnes to Peter Pan, and their dream is never to grow corrupt in the adult world of ownership and the commercial exchange of humans.

A comedy of remarriage transposes into a comedy of re-parenting, ancestor of the re-parenting novels of my study, but not quite before our eyes. Whether Wendy/Ellie can play the role of Peter's mother as well as lover (and, if Cavell is right, daughter) is not directly raised by the film, but his need of a mother seems to be suggested near its beginning: before he assumes the role of paternal Lincolnesque liberator of Ellie, Peter drunkenly gets himself fired from his newspaper job; he seems motherless before he takes on the role of substitute father. We might indulge Freud's diagnosis that the sensation of unity with the universe, Romain Rolland's oceanic feeling, is a reminiscence of oneness with the maternal body (Freud 11–15). We do not see Ellie and Peter in their Neverland; when we last hear of them, they are embarked on a honeymoon to the interior of the North American continent. Yet we have glimpsed a perfecting of the trinity of escape (from the enslaving South and commodifying North), consubstantial with simple escapism (from loneliness and lovelessness to egalitarian glamorous cinematic romance), consubstantial with escapology (self-loss in oceanic immortality), at the expense of time and American history. It is not that Blackness defines the social and historical virtues of whiteness, otherwise without shape, by way of binary distinctions, lending form to the separate identities of white maleness and white femaleness. On the contrary, the removal of Blackness from its own history means that whiteness can redefine formless oceanic unity as rebirth and re-infancy that preclude racial, sexual, or economic difference.

Cavell argues that his favorite classic American comedies offer not an escape but a reprieve from darkness (not noticing that the darkness of Blackness had to dissolve into their comedy). *The Sound of Music* denies the charge for itself and for musicals (not acknowledging that the Holocaust must be absorbed into its harmony). Twice in *The Sound of Music*, one character instructs another not to run from her troubles. On the first occasion, the Mother Abbess of the convent where Maria is a postulant advises her to follow her dream toward Captain von Trapp; Maria in turn advises Liesl not to run away from her dream of Rolf. The advice is identical, but the Mother Abbess's advice is superior: Rolf turns out to be an up-and-coming Nazi, and the whole von Trapp family must literally run away from him and his associates. The only consistency, at least at first glance, is that the film is keen to denounce escapism, on behalf of the realism of dreams.

The importance of the film of *The Sound of Music* (more than the stage musical) for my study is this disavowed self-knowledge of its escapism, along with its universal acknowledgment. When Lars von Trier wishes to exhibit a form of manipulation antithetical to his own melodramatic manipulations in *Dancer in the Dark*, he inserts a stunted performance of *The Sound of Music* into his anti-musical. When Arundhati Roy wishes to introduce a Western stereotype of patriarchal cleanliness into *The God of Small Things*, she brings her child protagonists to the film, where one of them is contaminated by a pederast in the lobby. *The Sound of Music* had been assigned the role of paradigm of escapism, and had denied it in advance, before I took up the theme; the film's escapism is inescapable across several continents and eras.

This does not imply that its escapism is easy to pinpoint: *The Sound of Music* coordinates the same trinity of cognates that stumped me upon first reading *The Amazing Adventures of Kavalier & Clay*. First is the actual escape: from Nazi-occupied Eastern Europe in both cases. Nazism or slavery supplies the escape-alibi (or escape nostalgia) of most contemporary American escapism. Second is the simple escapism: in *The Sound of Music*, Maria's, from self-dissonance to a literally, figuratively harmonious husband and family, on behalf of any family dysfunction among filmgoers. Third is the escapology: with the help of the trickery of nuns, out of the silent convent graveyard (in the film) and over the Alps, alive with the sound of music. The family escapism and quasi-Christian escapology do not merely make the presence of Nazism more palatable; they distract us from the strangeness that the escape from Nazism is entirely played out within one ethnicity, an escape of whiteness from whiteness.

The self-knowledge and global recognition of the escapism of *The Sound of Music* are sufficiently critical to protecting my own study against the circularity of tendentious theories of escapism that I shall devote a chapter to the film, though it does not belong to the period or genre of my archive. I am pushing my analysis as far as I can toward a kind of structuralist abstraction, on the model of Tzvetan Todorov's study of the fantastic, to quarantine escapism from its usual function as an insult to those who do not see oppressive reality as clearly as we do, or who obscure it for commercial purposes. Of course, there is no helping the discovery of avoidance in escapist works, as in Cavell's comedies and *The Sound of Music*. My intention, however, is not to deploy a special mode of critical knowingness to define the reality that escapism escapes; it's to locate the purpose of escapism amid alternative alternatives to the world, especially Utopianism and messianism. Unlike Cavell's comedies, all the novels of this study face historical reality. To acknowledge the reality of slavery or Nazism is to face something in the world worth escaping from, but not to claim knowledge, like messianists and Utopians, of where to escape it to. I do not assign myself the authority to know better.

Todorov defines the "verbal" aspect of the fantastic as its obliging readers to "hesitate between a natural and supernatural explanation of the events described"; the "syntactical" aspect (formerly known as point of view) involves entrusting the reader's hesitation to a character; the "semantic" aspect, so called because it thematizes perception, is defined by the reader's rejection "of allegorical as well as 'poetic' interpretations of the text" (Todorov 33–4). Todorov's three aspects of the fantastic align with the aspects of *The Sound of Music*'s tripartite escapism this way. The verbal aspect of the film is its obliging audiences to hesitate between experiencing the film as historical escape (from annexed Austria) and escapism (from loneliness and family dysfunction) and escapology (from the convent cemetery). The syntactic aspect of the film is this hesitation as experienced and overcome by Maria, whose function is to reconcile a historical flight from mortal political danger with both childish adventure and the restoration of paradise. The semantic aspect of the film is its vanquishing of death, the thematizing of the film's own immortality by way of its music.

There is a curious similarity on the verbal level of the fantastic and the escapist: an ambiguity of the natural and supernatural in the fantastic and an ambiguity of escape, escapology, and simple escapism in complex escapism. Todorov's ambiguity follows from his identifying the fantastic by way of its placement between the uncanny (natural explanations) and the marvelous (supernatural explanations), and escapism can be understood by its Venn overlap with Utopianism and messianism.

The escape aspect of escapism (e.g., the von Trapp's flight to Switzerland) takes on attributes of Utopian travel; the escapological aspect of escapism (e.g., the von Trapp's emergence from the graveyard) resembles messianic return, resurrection, and redemption. The third part of escapism is a consequence of the recursiveness of its escapist aspect (escapism insofar as it turns not toward messianism or Utopianism but toward its audience), effected by placing texts or models of escapism within escapist texts: *The Lord of the Rings* within Díaz's *Oscar Wao*; *Gulliver's Travels* within Whitehead's *The Underground Railroad*; *Peter Pan* within *It Happened One Night* or Grossman's *The Book of Intimate Grammar* or Foer's *Here I Am* or Eggers's *Heartbreaking Work*; *Grimms' Fairy Tales* within Groff's *Arcadia*, the musical performance of family harmony within *The Sound of Music*; and *The Sound of Music* within Roy's *The God of Small Things*. Scope is always a central escapist theme, manifest most acutely in the embedding of *Alice in Wonderland* in Emma Donoghue's *Room*: the relation of expansive *Alice in Wonderland* within *Room* mimics expansive Alice's relation to the White Rabbit's house in

Wonderland, which mimics macrocosmic theoretical interpretations of *Room* within microcosmic *Room*. Insofar as escapism uses the escapes of characters from tyrants to disguise authorial escapes from readers (mass audiences as well as theorists) with rival powers, contemporary escapism, in its purely escapist dimension, turns inevitably to a kind of fractal meta-escapism.

Escapism Today, like Messianism Today or Utopianism Today, is a function of the globalized imagination. That is why it is merely a heuristic first approximation to state these slogans: messianism is about a history-redeeming return from lostness to recognition; Utopianism is about a history-redirecting exploration from familiarity to strangeness; and escapism is about *this* place, the place we already inhabit, in costume. It is not messianic: this is *as good as it gets*. It is not Utopian: *this* is as good as it gets. It is not about leaving home or the restoration of a homeland. It is about neither a promised return nor a promising future; its time and place are here and now.

Of course, the von Trapps leave Austria for Switzerland and eventually (it is not in the musical, but the musical depends on our knowing it) America. More precisely, they are fleeing Austria not so much for the United States as for international markets, centered in the United States but borderless, which means that there is no longer such a thing as radically leaving or returning home. This is a hypothesis well known to Arundhati Roy, who will, in a late chapter of my book, finally make explicit its globalization themes from an incorporated homeland, where the von Trapps make a guest appearance.

It is not the case that escapism is superior to contemporary messianism and Utopianism in registering the imaginative effects of globalization. That would be a nice irony but it is not true: though messianism is in the first instance a return home and Utopianism an exploration diametrically away from home, both messianists and Utopianists now take globalization, the impossibility of any physical distinction of there and here, of a Utopian community or messianic kingdom materially separable from the obscene or profane world, as their problem. And their global problem becomes a double bind when that indifference of home and away is presented as itself Utopian or messianic, as in Thomas Friedman's account of the electronically interconnected, collaborative, increasingly democratic global economy that he calls the flat world.

I do not vouch for the accuracy of Friedman's book or its superiority to other accounts of globalization—instead of a flat globe, equally open everywhere to the clever ideas of individual entrepreneurs, Joseph E.

Stiglitz's globalized world is dominated by the short-sighted interests of US corporations and, especially after the Great Recession of 2007–9 (in the shadow of Friedman's third edition), the long-term national interests of China (Stiglitz 79–100). From Stiglitz's point of view, Friedman's flattened globe is a Utopian vision that we can approach by more enlightened social and trade policies, including the calling off of Trump's trade war with China; it is neither present reality nor the inevitable future.

Friedman's flatland serves my project by explicitly stating, near the start of the twenty-first century and for a huge international audience, the globalized meaning of imagination, the aspect of globalization that registers as the greatest challenge to the escapist (messianic- or Utopian-inflected) novel. I do not use the fact of globalization, however understood, as the socioeconomic explanation of my literary phenomenon, but I do not use it merely to name the phenomenon, either. The point is to connect one aesthetic with another. Friedman's book ends with his hoping to inspire a new generation that "wakes up each morning imagining and not only imagines that things can be better but also acts on that imagination every day" (Friedman 635). But a hallmark of the global yet individual imagination, in Friedman's preaching, is its tribute to inescapability: he warns businesses and nations that they must acquire the "leadership, flexibility, and imagination to adapt" to the "speed of change" that will otherwise "simply [overwhelm] them" (Friedman 49). What Friedman calls imagination is clear in his endorsement of the humanities, almost entirely on the grounds that the creative imagination serves technological or technical innovation, which cyclically determines the imagination that serves it (Friedman 316–20).

Though he acknowledges that it has been flattening for centuries and is not yet absolutely flat, Friedman's relatively leveled world has its putative origin at the fall of the Berlin Wall; now the binary with communism has been replaced by one with globalized terror, which means that a choice has been replaced by a nonchoice. (Even terrorism, not a reasonable option, exists according to the letter, though not the spirit, of nonoptional globalization.) Friedman finds dramatically more evidence for economic world flatness in India than in any other nation (the doubly ironic comparison is with Columbus); he was heartened of course by the turn of India away from socialism toward global capitalism after 1989 (Friedman 552) and by (so he argues) the consequent fact that the huge Muslim population of India has not participated in international terror (Friedman 622–6). Arundhati Roy's tracking of the soul of India also pivots on the fall of communism and India's resultant privatization; her account, unlike Friedman's, features catastrophes, repression, and violence, but for my purposes the important distinction is that all Indian change testifies to world historical sameness:

> Is the last stop of every revolution advanced capitalism? Think about it—the French Revolution, the Russian Revolution, the Chinese Revolution, the Vietnam War, the anti-apartheid struggle, the supposedly Gandhian freedom struggle in India . . . what's the last station they all pull in at? Is this the end of imagination? (Roy, *Beast* 225)

Roy's dystopian pessimism about the history of imagination is nearly identical with Friedman's Utopian or messianic optimism. Messianism Now and Utopianism Now search for something reversible within the globalized imagination; Escapism Now lives on nostalgia for the possibility of eluding the inevitable.

Messianism Now means messianism after Walter Benjamin's elucidation of what he calls the "weak messianic power" of a kingdom of God without gods or kingdoms (Benjamin 254). His messianism is immanent, entirely human and fallible. Weak messianism takes place when the present, in crisis, compels the irruption of a past moment. Such interventions do not occur in time but construct it, insofar as time is not an empty vessel containing events. Empty time is a vacuum, open to windstorms of progress, which evacuate the mounting tragedies of the past and present for the illusion of an improved future (technical improvements substituted for existential improvements), such as the one now envisaged by Friedman. In contrast, "there is historical time," as Werner Hamacher summarizes Benjamin, "only insofar as there is an excess of the unactualized, the unfinished, failed, thwarted, which leaps beyond its particular Now and demands from another Now its settlement, correction and fulfilment" (Hamacher 164).

In the tradition of weak messianism, two of the most influential texts are Jacques Derrida's *Specters of Marx* and Giorgio Agamben's *The Time that Remains*. Their similarities will help define the escapism frontier with current messianism. The best way to conceive how they differ is by contrasting what happens at the interruptions of temporal linearity, of the procession of identical and self-identical moments, which makes the influx of messianism possible.

For Derrida the present is haunted, our post-Soviet world by Marx as Shakespeare's Denmark by the ghost of the dead King Hamlet; the return of the unjust past puts the present out of joint, which invites the messianic to spook it symmetrically from the future (Derrida, *Specters* 10). But the messianic future, unlike Hamlet *père*, does not insist on revenge, which would prolong the past. It promises an unlimited hospitality to every Other (Derrida, *Specters* 26–9, 81–2), an open-ended and all-inclusive homecoming to the homeless. Because this hospitality is always in excess of demands, it is perpetually indefinite. Derrida refers to this featureless messianic time, without the Messiah or even messianism (he prefers to retain the adjective only), as a desert (Derrida, *Specters* 33, 74, 210–12).

It is not a desert in Agamben; it's a garden. It's *the* garden, Eden. Agamben's messianism starts not with Hamlet and the unburied dead, but with Paul and perpetual renewal. Paul's hermeneutical challenge was to unite pre-messianic history, through the resurrection, with apocalyptic history, the imminent future: the history of Jews and the law with faith and the Parousia. The time between the resurrection and return when histories overlap is called "messianic time" or "the time of the now" or (as opposed to the end of time) "the time of the end" (Agamben, *Remains* 61–2). The doubling of epochs is inferred by means of typology and recapitulation (Agamben 71–8), as when a figure from the Old Testament is revised (Christ for Adam) or a doctrine summarized (loving your neighbor for all the commandments) in the New Testament. But Agamben sees in Paul's messianic time not any particular doubling from era to era, nor the awaiting of a Parousia, rather in the always-available doubling of *Chronos* (passing time) and *Kairos* (gathering time), which equals the ever presence of Eden. The ostensibly completed past requires completing in every present moment; the evanescent present carries the past's fullness to term.

The anti-Christ of the out-of-jointness of the present, in *Specters of Marx*, is Francis Fukuyama. Derrida calls on Marx, or the spirit of Marx (shorn of his particular political or historical doctrines), to devastate Fukuyama's pronouncement, after the fall of Soviet communism, that liberal democracy is the end of history. Derrida argues that Fukuyama's grand narrative is sustained by toggling between two half-claims, the falseness of one sustained by the wishfulness of the other: liberal democracy has now defeated all contenders for historical dominance, and victory belongs to an ideal of liberal democracy still historically unrealized (Derrida, *Specters* 78–81). Yet if we apply Derrida's diagnosis of Marx's preoccupation with Stirner—Marx struggles with an all-too-similar ghost of himself (Derrida, *Specters* 175)—to Derrida's own obsession with Fukuyama, we might see in Fukuyama's toggling a disjointedness of time, a present haunted by its unjust past and visited by its future. Derrida's spectralization of Marx entails that he cannot spell out a practical alternative to Fukuyama's capitalism's implicitly out-of-joint time, though liberal democracy is incapable of disproportionate messianic liberality.

The part of Fukuyama in Agamben's *The Time That Remains* is played by Carl Schmitt (Agamben, *Remains* 104–8). Schmitt's axiom is that the sovereign's sovereignty is equal to his legal right to declare an emergency, which entails a state of exception to law. At such a crisis, laws are anything the sovereign proclaims; at the end of the history of this logic, citizens cannot be certain of the laws they must obey or the severity of punishment for disobeying, including death camps (Agamben, *Remains* 106). All of life, everything outside the law, becomes its inside; the state of exception is normalized. The puzzle for Agamben is that this condition resembles Paul's abrogation of the law, which Paul claims to be the fulfillment of the law: inside and outside the law are indistinct; the state of exception is universal. Agamben's solution is almost literally to consider Schmitt the anti-Christ in Paul's technical sense, a negative prophet of the state of exception, precursor of messianic time. The messianic state of exception, Agamben writes, is the *Aufhebung* of the sovereign's state of exception, which implies, for example, not that death camps could ignore the commandment against killing, but that not killing would survive as a free expression (say, in Paul, of love) rather than as submission to a commandment (Agamben, *Remains* 106–8).

For my purposes, what is most useful in Derrida and Agamben's mirror arrival at messianism is their capacity to define escapism's messianic border. First: both their essential messianism books take as their historical problem a totalized globe—dominated in Derrida's account by liberal democracy (ideology expanding and conquering in advance of actual democratizing), in Agamben's by the general state of exception, which justifies, among other examples of rogue state-ism anywhere in the world, Guantánamo (Agamben, *State* 3–4). It is the reach of globalization in its unbounded corporate and military form that makes their updated messianism both necessary and conceivable, as anti-Christ to Christ.

Second: both books are (nonetheless) theses of nondenominational messianism. Derrida's book elaborates a primordial messianism, based in what is anterior to religions. Agamben's welcomes Jewish and Islamic scholars into the polylogue, and though his book is centered on Paul, it opposes any institutionalized Christian church whose self-perpetuation would indefinitely postpone Paul's "time of the end." But the time of the end is not the end of time: neither Derrida nor Agamben attempts to prophesy what a revelation would reveal, as if it could reveal the final truth and the last judgment. The past, by way of Agamben's remnant and Derrida's revenant, invoked by Agamben's doubled time and Derrida's disjointed time, inhabits and fractures the present; it does not predict. This keeps contemporary messianism clear of the catastrophic grand narratives of the twentieth century, but it means that the antagonism of Christ and anti-Christ will always be a matter of close contingent unauthorized interpretation. In this way, current messianism is both stronger and weaker than traditional and current Utopianism, whose weakness and strength consists in its commitment to programs with rationales.

I do not argue that reflecting this kind of immanent messianism is unthinkable for fiction. Ben Lerner has taken from Agamben the Hasidic formula of the messianic relayed by Gershom Scholem to Benjamin to Ernst Bloch—"everything will be as it is now, just a little different"—as his epigraph in *10:04*. He takes a typically Agambenian tack in producing his slightly altered world, presenting a cultural economy in which the nadir of vacuity has been reached so transparently that a transformed world can show through, minimally but distinctly. Lerner's New York, in Lerner's America, has been sufficiently monetized that it reaches into the work we are reading, which seems approximately to be the novel for which his fictional avatar has been given what is called a healthy six-figure advance. And through that meta-monetization, every value in the novel is priced: the health problems of Lerner and his friends are treatable because of the advance, and the artificial production of a child by Lerner and a friend is affordable because of the monetization of the writing we are reading, according to the writing we are reading.

In Derridean fashion, the past makes its appearance in the present, as if from the future demanding salvation, by virtue of Lerner's present's out-of-jointedness, and the Lerneresque narrator's Marfan syndrome, one of whose symptoms is double-jointedness. It is generally by way of illness and other bodily malfunctions—or often, by possible illness and the threat of bodily malfunctions—that the world takes shape for Lerner or his narrative namesake in a new configuration, as if on Benjamin's description of messianic history-making: when "thinking suddenly stops in a configuration pregnant with tensions, it gives that configuration a shock, by which it crystallizes into a monad" (Benjamin 262–3).

The question one asks reading *10:04* is what makes the new configuration, the monad crystallized at 10:04, messianic, though one case of notional disfigurement accomplishes the specifically messianic task of demonetizing the world. Alena, a friend of the fictional Lerner, gains possession of an apparently perfect diptych by Cartier-Bresson. It is in fact conceptually disjointed—its two photographs had once been components of a triptych—and therefore has lost its total sale value. The narrator writes:

> This was a reversal of the kind of recontextualization associated with Marcel Duchamp, still—unfortunately, in my opinion—the tutelary spirit of the art world; this was the opposite of the "readymade" whereby an object of utility—a urinal, a shovel—was transformed into an object of art and an art commodity by the artist's fiat, by his signature. . . . It was as if I could register in my hands a subtle but momentous transfer of weight: the twenty-one grams of the market's soul had fled; it was no longer a commodity fetish; it was art before or after capital. Not the shattered or slashed works to which Alena thrilled, but those objects in the archive that both were and weren't different moved me: they had been redeemed, both in the sense that the fetish had been converted back into cash, the claim paid out, but also in the messianic sense of being saved from something, saved for something. (Lerner 133–4)

This is part of a much longer paragraph, but even quoted at fractional length, Lerner is doing a lot of discoursing, even more than usual: Would anyone capable of admiring his book need an explanation or illustration of the readymade? The passage is useful to quote because it is so explicit, so prosaic, a textbook example of telling rather than showing: Does Lerner have to invoke commodity fetishism by name? The problem for novelists of the messianic in secular form is that without tutoring we may not recognize it. If Duchamp is the anti-Christ of this passage, the Schmittian sovereign who determines by fiat the state of exception to laws for what is inside or outside the museum, plus the Fukuyaman prophet of the triumph of the commodity, then "recontextualization" alone does not achieve the messianic, and a more desirable form of recontextualization than Duchamp's must be preached. In a messianic kingdom devoid of dogma, theology, church, or apocalypse—the Cartier-Bresson "diptych" is saved from *what*, saved for *what*?—it may be impossible to distinguish Christ from anti-Christ. Perhaps Lerner's narrator's overexplaining of the wounded de-commodified artifact helps to monetize this anti-capitalist passage. Lerner's agent had advised him to justify his advance by making his next book more reader-friendly.

That is not the only difficulty for a novelist who recognizes and regrets the market pressure of a well-formed narrative, which Lerner may register in two ways: the book needs some development (even without a definite outcome) in the story of his alter ego's attempt to impregnate his friend, and it needs some sort of inconclusive climax to his cowriting of a children's book on dinosaurs with a boy, Roberto, whom the alter ego is tutoring. It isn't accidental that both stories concern generations. Almost all the books I treat in this study center on the attempted saving of a child, who is meant to save an adult in return.

In nearly every case of what I call escapism, the book involves an interim, a moment that does not redeem time but fends it off: when the innocence of the prematurely wise child meets the experience of the heroically childlike adult. That time is not fixed, that the clock only hesitates for a chiasmic moment, is the principal difference between messianism (including Lerner's, successful or not) and escapism.

The mirror cases of Dave Eggers and Emma Donoghue illustrate the temporality of an ersatz escapist salvation most succinctly. In Eggers's masterpiece of envisaged salvation, *A Heartbreaking Work of Staggering Genius*, the older brother, Dave, manages to save his younger brother, Toph, for a time by way of his heroic dedication to relieving Toph of the burden of their parents' death, taking on re-parenting responsibilities within a fraternal program of obscurantist fun. (Some scenes from the relationship of Dave and Toph are nearly quoted in the relationship of Ben and Roberto, as when each pseudo-parent, almost losing his charge, loses his equanimity: one hope for the messianic capacity to defeat death is predicated on the capacity to re-parent.) "For a time" means from Toph's childhood through his early adolescence, the era of Dave's increasingly threatened power to protect him, metaphorized as the passing moment that a Frisbee between Dave and Toph seems to rest at the apex of its flight.

In *Room*, Emma Donoghue conducts an experiment in a specifically female messianism, something like Eggers's insofar as a young person is given sole responsibility for the doggedly ludic salvation of a younger person, but descended most profoundly from the experimental messianism of Toni Morrison in *Beloved*. Female messianism is based on the liquefaction of the female body at its margin: Ma's prolonged commitment to nursing her son Jack in *Room* is anticipated by Sethe's confidence, during her moment of freedom in antebellum Ohio, that she has "milk enough for all" (Morrison, *Beloved* 100). This is the form communion takes within female messianism; yet the courage of both Morrison and Donoghue is in taking their own re-parenting experiments seriously enough to falsify them. In Eggers, the tragedy of the escapist version of salvation is that Chronos overpowers it; in Donoghue, the tragedy of the escapist version of salvation is that Chronos exposes it. This represents the surfacing of the critique of escapism within escapism, increasingly visible in my tracking of the subgenre.

*   *   *

The preeminent theoretical defense of Utopianism in recent years is Fredric Jameson's exhaustive *Archaeologies of the Future*, whose ramifying dialectical structure follows from the thesis that Utopianism is a necessary form but all Utopian content ultimately fails. The problem, which Jameson never lets go of, despite his sympathy for the speculative alterities of any Utopia, is the conceptual distance that needs to be traversed to arrive there. If the distance is too great, Utopia seemingly loses touch with human life, however it is conceived at the moment, and the speculative adventurousness of the narrative will be experienced by readers as boredom (Jameson, *Archaeologies* 97). If it is too small, and a particular Utopia unwittingly represents the premises of its own era, then all its political and social rationalization, however attractive and diagnostic, will amount to ideology (Jameson, *Archaeologies* 168 ff.).

It is the latter danger that obsesses Jameson: every particular Utopia is wedded to its historical moment and manifests, despite itself, symptoms of its epoch's political unconscious. In the face of this inevitable generic crisis, what saves the genre for Jameson is no uniquely convincing Utopia but Utopianism as an endlessly self-critical form: Utopianism, not any single Utopia, manifests the essential flaws of any system whatever, including Utopian ones. The value of Utopianism does not consist primarily in the fictionally illustrated achievement of an ideal yet workable system; it consists in tireless "disruption," disruption by way of its generic form manifested in the disputatious singularities of its content. In Jameson's view, this (as he calls it) "eleventh hour" salvaging of the Utopian project is, strangely, empowered by globalization, its nemesis (Jameson, *Archaeology* 211). If globalization by definition makes alternative social structures unthinkable—if, as Jameson quotes "someone" as saying, it is easier to imagine the end of the world than the end of capitalism (Jameson, *Archaeologies*, 199; *American Utopia* 3)— then any particular Utopia must be fatally unconvincing, and only the adversarial spirit of Utopia—each Utopia against not only the current system but also every other Utopia—can have any purchase on our postmodern decentered interest.

Archaeologies of the Future does not predict a meta-future when Utopianism might take on a positive task beyond disruption, when some Utopia might provide a convincing alternative to globalization. How could it? Jameson mentions only a few times, though it is crucial, the perennial Utopian paradox of the vanishing mediator (Jameson, *Archaeologies* 86): if Utopian systems to have any truly Utopian force must escape ideology's gravity, erring on the side of exorbitant distance, they must challenge the reigning idea of human potential, which in turn apparently requires a supernatural originality on the part of their founders. To the extent that their Utopias, however, are intended for ordinary humans, and insofar as their Utopias typically have a socialist program, exceptional mediators must vanish from their societies. How then does Jameson come to write a Utopian text, and make a socialist argument, himself? The answer is that he discovers a possible place for the Utopian not sighted in *Archaeologies*. This means that he has discovered another approach to the dilemma of the distance of Utopia, hitherto defined as too far or too near. This must entail a different account of its invention and establishment.

Jameson's model society, as described in *An American Utopia*, is centered on the US army, an already-existing provider of socialized education, health care, and housing, an established venue of identity-ranging solidarity without sameness. The army is the most promising US example of Lenin's "dual power": a recognized font of social power apart from governmental power, beyond the conservatism of constitutional federalism. One of the virtues of this model of Utopia is that it does not take for granted the army's grounding in inevitable human aggressivity or find in the military the privileged outlet of such aggressivity as it exists (*American Utopia* 60), but suggests all sorts of social objectives for the military deployment of all manner of human passions, by way of a computer matching of jobs and psyches. Another virtue is that if universal conscription takes care of the medical, educational, and housing requirements of all citizens, they won't need to work at their military jobs for more than a few hours per day or months per year, which leaves ample free time for all the desires, pleasures, and perversions each decentered self, on our current conception of selfhood, might indulge. In this way the army Utopia accepts the imperfect humanness—including the inevitable envy that humans feel from what Lacanians call the theft of their *jouissance*—of a reformed humanity (Jameson, *Archaeology* 73–7). Octavia E. Butler's story "The Book of Martha" takes the opposite tack, centering Utopia on the hedonic dream life that Jameson removes from the military, socialist side of his Utopia, though the premise of irreconcilable human self-division is the same (Butler, *Bloodchild* 203–4). The dominant trope of Jameson's Utopia might be the oxymoron: between adjective (nonviolent, American) and contradictory noun (army, Utopia), there is no new element. The question of change must be, as ever, how the elements realign.

If the traditional dilemma of the Utopian scheme is that it is either too near or too far, Jameson solves the problem by finding his Utopia at no distance at all. This is the required move of any true Utopia in the age of globalization: as the disillusioned traveling Utopianist of Junot Díaz's *The Brief Wondrous Life of Oscar Wao* concludes, "the only way out is in." Utopia to be neither redundant (ideological) nor irrelevant (inhuman) must be discovered not beyond human societies but hidden, like the purloined letter, by blinding social visibility.

It is what makes possible a transvaluation of societal values, by way of reversing of a mechanism of global violence to an agent of national community, that is invisible. Recall that Jameson's first brilliant deployment of the idea of the "vanishing mediator" is his characterization of Max Weber's invariant mode of analysis, most famously concerning the Reformation: to the extent that Calvin sought to extend monastic Christianity beyond the monastery, he unleashed its asceticism and temporal regimentation into all Europe, enabling capitalist modernity. Protestantism is the vanishing mediator between the medieval and the modern, feudalism and capitalism. Just as "religionization" as the end of Protestantism becomes the means of modernity (Jameson "Vanishing Mediator," 71–4), "militarization" as the means of army recruitment and social organization for the sake of war might come to redefine the peacetime national purpose. (Though Jameson does not refer in *An American Utopia* to his Weber essay and the vanishing mediator, he alludes to it by his analogy of the army and the monastery [Jameson, *American Utopia* 29–30].) As for Weber's nostalgia for the prophet, an integration of means and ends, charisma and rationality, vanishing mediator between magicians and priests: Jameson models a less-divine authority. He remembers discovering his Utopian idea in a cartoon from his childhood, in which Eisenhower responds to the enticement and threat of socialism by pointing out its presence in his own military background (Jameson, *American Utopia* 19). From Republican president to cartoonist to literary theorist is a casual nonhierarchical metonymy, with no apparent need for a belated charismatic intervention. It is unclear to me who is responsible for the apothegm that it is easier to imagine the end of the world than the end of capitalism, but Jameson can do so, and perhaps Jameson's repeated attribution of the brief, dry, yet apocalyptic condemnation to "someone" is a case of prophetic self-vanishing.

Ecotopia, which Jameson sometimes considers the last great Utopian production (Jameson, *American Utopia* 1), would also prefer a transition from United States to Utopia without the intervention of a prophet, but it does not take the vanishing of the vanishing mediator quite as blithely, because it faces the problem of romantic love. From Jameson's point of view, the romantic interest of any Utopian plot only testifies to the understandable failure of Utopian novels to interest bourgeois readers in egalitarian systems populated by smug contented citizens endlessly willing to itemize the most minute technical advances of their societies. But the romance of Will and Marissa in *Ecotopia*, the sort of romance that Jameson deems "perfunctory" (Jameson, *Archaeologies* 188), is not external to the essence of its Utopian narrative, a sop to conservative or conventional readers, but represents the most persistently troubled and telltale aspect of Ecotopian life in general, and Utopian life in general.

One way to put the fundamental meta-question posed by *Ecotopia* is: Where in Utopianism is the Utopian located? Is it in the adventurous sailing away from one's own land and preconceptions or in the adventurous return with heretical views? Or is it centered in the smugness of the inhabitants of Utopia themselves, who find their contentment in diminishing the adventure of ever-nearing horizons? This question is about not the boredom of Utopian narratives but the boredom of Utopian existence, which concerns Jameson as well (Jameson, *Archaeologies* 188). The narrator Van Jennings writes in *Herland* that "it was no use for me to try to piece out this account with adventures. . . . There were no adventures because there was nothing to fight" (Gilman 49). In *Ecotopia*, adventure is deprecated at the beginning by its narrator: anticipating his departure from his superficial lover, Francine, Will knows that when he returns she'll be "all charged up by some adventure or other" (Callenbach 3). Insofar as the book has any adventure at all, it is Will's exploration of Ecotopian love with Marissa, a love whose frankness and naturalness seem exotic to him until they seem merely frank and natural, as they do to Ecotopians. It may be impossible to establish a perfect society, but trying to do so is not an adventure if perfection is approached by acclimatizing.

The love of Will and Marissa reflects both the conceptual and narrative challenges of a graduated Parousia. They are excited by their gender differences, the source of their primary mutual attraction, but they are also intrigued by their growing affective affinities. The

Utopian dilemma of too near or too far focuses on their desire. The Utopian future promises more alignment, but in that case, what will happen to the joy of their desiring? Does romantic love have to vanish in the process of Utopianization? In such instances, the question-begging formula of *Ecotopia* is "almost religious," a phrase applied, for example, to the Ecotopian devotion to trees and wood (Callenbach 61, 116), which is the book's central example of the convergence of nature worship and political economy, the environmental correlative of the asymptotic approach of romantic love to general human sociability.

The first use of the phrase "almost religious" is revealing: Ecotopians "sacrifice . . . present consumption, . . . [to] ensure future survival—which became an almost religious objective, perhaps akin to an earlier doctrine of 'salvation'" (Callenbach 47). This is the point at which Utopianism pretends, tentatively, to do the work of messianism. It makes the attempt again in Arundhati Roy's *The Ministry of Utmost Happiness*, which winds up at a cemetery in India that has been developed by unclassifiable Indians to include an inn for the desperate, a school, an animal hospital, and a burial service for those refused burial elsewhere. In these two novels, the messianic aspect of their Utopianism consists in the repudiation of progress in empty time, in the anti-consumerist, anti-presentist communion of the living and the unborn (Callenbach) or the living and the dead (Roy).

The problem, acknowledged in Roy but not in Callenbach, is how to make Chronos do the work of Kairos, or progressive time do the work of messianic return, or history do the work of the primordial: the phrase "almost religious" only marks the site of the crux. Invoking the Utopian problem of the vanishing mediator allows us to define the distinction between Utopianism and messianism as the difference between the repression and the return of the mediator. The return of the mediator in all cases of messianism (of the unredeemed past, of the messiah, of Israel as the messianic nation) always consists in making visible the return of prophecy. "Almost religious" seems to refer to the geometry of the asymptote, but there is no sacred or profane math to justify it. What enables messianism but not Utopianism is the equation of timelessness and time, of the sacred and the profane.

That there is no outside to corruption, perversion, power, and brutality is the premise of what I have nominated as a paradigm of complex American escapism: *His Girl Friday*. But the paradoxes of escapism that does not have a Green World to escape to are yet more intense in the era of globalized labor, capital, supply chains, information, communication, military violence, environmental disaster, American popular culture, and disease. The project, in short, is to sustain the possibility of adventure, as in *It Happened One Night*, that cannot rely on a shared dream of a place beyond the United States, or outside markets, or after dysfunction, where people can feel at one with oceanic undying nature. The problem is the closing of the world frontier; the problem is locating Utopianism not in the smugness of Utopians, who don't exist, but in the adventurousness of the flight to Utopia, when there is nowhere to find it.

An unexpectedly instantiated Utopia in contemporary American fiction is the Valentine farm in Colson Whitehead's *The Underground Railroad*, which welcomes runaway slaves to its freedom and democracy. (Both Roy's India and Whitehead's Indiana locate contemporary Utopianism as the community of the casteless.) But the Valentine farm, suffering from the Utopian conceptual impossibility of separating itself from history within untransformed time, is undermined from within and without—like Arcadia in Lauren Groff's meta-Utopian *Arcadia*—and insofar as *The Underground Railroad* has a sustained Utopian impulse, it needs to attempt something other than positing an approach to justice inside Indiana, in the achievement of a home.

Once the Valentine farm is destroyed, in a chapter of the book entitled "The North," Cora, the runaway heroine of the book, heads north and then west. Why is the chapter not called "North and West"? (The improbable likeness is with the flight north and unexpectedly west in the whitened neo-slave narrative, *It Happened One Night*.) At the end of Chabon's *The Amazing Adventures of Kavalier & Clay*, Sammy Clay is last seen moving in the direction of California. Clay had experienced a Utopian interlude on a Jersey Shore estate with his lover, Tracy Bacon, and Bacon's uniformly beautiful, athletic, and cultivated gay friends, who welcome Clay democratically, though he is not beautiful, athletic, or cultivated. But Bacon is killed in the Second World War, and Clay seems intent, at the end of the novel, not on finding a similar Utopia at the California shore but in making a liberating run for it. It is Clay's last amazing adventure, but, like Cora's flight, or Peter and Ellie's, we do not see where it arrives. It heads into the heart of the continent, but it may not make it out.

This is to say that when the Utopian impulse hits escapist novelists, they insist on its adventurousness over its programmatic complacency. It is a perpetual sailing away in a world without any ocean to sail on. There can be no place in untransformed time that is within reach of perfection. The Utopian distance problem is momentarily solved by perpetual distancing: the Jamesonian answer to inescapability is already here; the novelistic answer is never here but nowhere else. When California fails as the direction for adventures, characters may take off for Alaska—northward once again. In Eggers's *Heroes of the Frontier*, a mother with her two children flees the entrapments of Ohio to Alaska, testing (or creating in the first place) their frontier heroism in a place already corrupted. In Chabon's *The Yiddish Policeman's Union*, a novel explicitly concerned with a false messiah, a divorced couple, Meyer Landsman and Bina Gelbfish, reunite to solve a murder mystery, as if inspired by Cary Grant and Rosalind Russell. Their personal adventure inhabits the corruption of Alaska as fully as Grant and Russell's inhabits the corruption of New York; it is the setting of a retread trailblazing, a "black world" comedy, a Utopian adventure only insofar as an unsettling adventure within the closed frontier must take the place of a settled smug separate Utopia.

What precisely is an adventure? For my texts, it is a special variant on Utopianism, on-the-road Utopianism in the midst of intractable imperfection. It is no place in the sense that it transpires in undefined territory, at the interstices of corrupt spaces rather than apart from them, as, for example, between immoral laws and amoral lawlessness in *The Adventures of Huckleberry Finn*. Observing that *It Happened One Night* does not retreat to the Green World of Connecticut, Cavell explains that the picaresque from Florida to New York gives "*adventurousness . . .* the scope it requires in order to win out" (Cavell, his emphasis 105). In the interim of their starting and ending, Colbert and Gable, like Huck and Jim, create a new possibility for human relations, not so much by way of indifference, as in *Ecotopia*, as by way of the liquidation of difference, as in *Huck Finn*, while drifting between the enslaving South and commodifying North.

Agamben brings out a dimension of adventure implicit in Cavell: adventure, on his philology, is a paradoxical remarriage of retrospect and contingency (Cavell might say, recognition and improvisation) in events that are both events and the tales of events: "*Ici commence l'aventure*" at the beginning of a *lai* means that the events of the story and the story of the events begin at once (Agamben, *Adventure* 27). An adventure is a segment of your life that contains your biography, a summation of past wayward journeys in a present accounting of them, Chronos and Kairos in the tale and telling. Agamben recognizes in that use of adventure a corollary of his version of messianism, and provides the necessary etymology. Adventure derives from *eventus* or *adventus*: it's a marvel, an advent, a messianic recapitulation within time (Agamben, *Adventure* 23). This is the hope of the vicar Panicker in Chabon's *The Final Solution*: "How many rude and shoeless young men, he wondered, set off in search of adventure, believing with all their hearts that they were answering a summons from God?" (Chabon, *Final Solution* 107).

But in almost all the novels I am collecting under the escapist rubric, the simultaneity of the unfolding and the enfolding of adventure results from the self-conscious performing of a performative. Panicker answers a summons from his creator Chabon by researching his destiny not in his domestic life but in a Sherlock Holmes novel. We are encouraged to wonder what it means to consider the lives of Kavalier and Clay as "amazing adventures"—in whose generic judgment are their lives adventures at all, and not an oscillating open-ended series of good and tragic breaks? The effect is to divide the contingency from its formalization; the unity of the American *lai*, its concentering of events and narratives of events, though often advertised in book titles, thus their hyperbole, is always belated rather than always in time, thus their bathos.

The novels that I call escapist are very nearly all aftermaths of aftermaths of catastrophes; the unifying in stories comes only at the end of that bathetic series, and the story is never about the achievement of a form. In the aftermath of the Holocaust, Israel fails as a messianic homeland; in the aftermath of slavery, California and Alaska fail for Utopian homesteading. The American Utopian adventure, in the midst of irredeemable corruption, finds failure at every location. Just as messianic synchronicity of past and future in the present reduces in escapist fiction to a novelized interim between adulthood and childhood, alternative Utopian social movements located elsewhere are personalized in performative removals to closed frontiers. The name of the cause of these twin contractions of imaginary time and space is globalization.

Once California and Alaska have been settled and corrupted, there is no longer a proximate space for the American Utopian imagination. The benefit of this closing of the frontier is the forestalling of smugness: no programs are itemized, no circularities of cause and effect are recycled, and no laurels are rested on. The penalty paid by this kind of adventure is that no reality ever projects an ideal; unconventional truths have no potential purchase on conventions. When narratives conclude, space-time looks the same as ever, with protagonists either reabsorbed into it or lost to view. The escapist adventure, by its connection to the advent, is a kind of escapology: a novelist's illusion for the purpose of escaping space-time personally and momentarily. You escape from the heartbreaking (work-as-life) to the staggering (work-as-writing) by virtue of the escapology of a performative performance, by the literary art of escape. "Superheroism," Chabon writes, is the story "of our rebirth into the world of adventure, of story itself" (Chabon, *Maps*, postscript 15). Storytelling doesn't concentrate the adventure; it *is* the adventure. Messianic rebirth or Utopian revolution are escapist arts you learn to perform if you cannot surmount the deathwardness of your life on the flat earth.

*   *   *

What does Dystopia look like to escapism? Jameson distinguishes dystopias that are based on human fallibility (thus resistant to the possibility of original innocence) and those based on revulsion to currently seductive Utopias (Jameson, *Archaeologies*, 198). Though specialists on the Utopian identify this latter model as "anti-utopian" rather than dystopian (Claeys 3), in any case it is the model of *The Circle*, whose Utopia of perfect social visibility, transparent accountability, and interactive democracy is shown to be a dystopia of perfect social visibility, transparent accountability, and interactive democracy. His dystopia is a refusal of the Utopianism of capitalist globalization in the tradition of dystopian refusals of socialism: Friedman makes an appearance in Jameson for his demonstration that "literary Utopists have scarcely kept pace with the businessmen in the process of imagination and construction"; Jameson cites Friedman's praise of Walmart's centralized planning as mooting the fear of socialist centralization (Jameson, *Archaeologies* 153). But Friedman's Utopia is both centralized and dispersed: it is a circle, like Eggers's, whose circumference is nowhere and whose center may be anywhere. Its vision is of an absolute Hegelian unity of the individual and the world imagination.

None of the writers of my study is Utopian or messianic. You feel, however, the pull of Utopian visibility or messianic illumination in the sheer maximalist bulk of many of their books, their will to describe. I began by arguing that that descriptive capaciousness is congruent with ignorance of where the center of reality dwells; the ignorance entails the capaciousness. But the capaciousness, though a public display, is also a mode of private disappearance. My paradigmatic films, *His Girl Friday*, *It Happened One Night*, and *The Sound of Music*, are about saving by publicity or saving from publicity, or both. Hildy, in *His Girl Friday*, finally prefers the public newspaper world to domestic privacy, but her implication in the amorality of journalism requires a reprieve by reason of insanity. Peter, in *It Happened One Night*, uses newspaper publicity as the precondition for his disappearance with Ellie. In *The Sound of Music*, Captain von Trapp equates all public viewing with Nazi surveillance, yet the family escapes Nazism by submitting itself to a public music festival with Nazis in attendance. Dave Eggers's *A Heartbreaking Work of Staggering Genius* can be approximated as an oscillation between the dream of invisibility and the craving for fame; Emma Donoghue's *Room* features an escape from hateful privacy to hateful publicity. This pervasive theme is the consequence of the collapse of messianism and Utopianism into escapism, the super-genre of inescapability.

Augustine writes in Book Ten of *Confessions* that "the human mind, blind and inert, vile and ill-behaved, desire[s] to keep itself concealed, yet desire[s] that nothing should be concealed from itself. But the contrary happens to it—it cannot be hidden from truth, but only truth from it" (Augustine 209). The desire to be veiled in a transparent world is the professional ambition of novelists, whose disaster, as Eggers and Donoghue illustrate, is to expose themselves to an opaque world. "I often dreamed of watching without being seen," writes the narrator of Olga Tokarczuk's succinctly named novel, *Flights*, one of whose spokeswomen concludes her prophetic rant with an escapist benediction: "Move. Get going. Blessed is he who leaves" (Tokarczuk, 179, 260). (In Tokarczuk's most vivid story in *Flights*, the destination of a wife's flight is called Kairos, where she is out of view of both her husband and the minimum of narration. No chance of uniting it with narratable Chronos.) Repeatedly in the works I examine, authors identify with their characters hiding from tyrants; repeatedly, the tyrants are, most immediately, readers and audiences. Authors may wish to imitate the God "which seeth in secret" (*King James Version*. Matt. 6:4), but they inevitably share their secrets with the world. Escapism falsifies historical escape, but it does not falsify the escapist wish of authors; historical escapism disguises the author's attempted escape. The false escapes of characters enabling the escapism of audiences camouflage the real escapes of authors *from* audiences. This turns escapism into meta-escapism.

I want to try out this updating of Augustine's definition of sin, which is the desire to usurp the power and prerogatives of God: that messianism without a second coming, the sacred fully dissolved in the secular, is a usurpation of one of God's two primary functions, salvation; and that Utopianism, which is the secular doing the work of the sacred, is a usurpation of God's other primary function, creation (Agamben, *Nudities* 1–9). Messianism today promises redemption without God; Utopianism re-creates by speech acts a flawed but unfallen human nature within an unalienated nature. Creation manifests the goodness of God's greatness. He pronounces a satisfied judgment on each day's prodigious creativity: and it was good; and it was very good. Salvation manifests the greatness of God's goodness. He saves what is finite and undeserving of eternal salvation by way of goodness that is infinitely countervailing. Literary escapism does not know the direction or meaning of Utopian greatness and messianic goodness. Escapism on the model of Phillips, Tuan, or Levinas begins with knowledge of the essence of human reality (its desires or animality or being) and how it is evaded. But what is being escaped in sophisticated literary escapism is *ignorance* of the essence of human reality and therefore of how to redeem or free globalized humanity. This means that humanity, which needs freeing or saving from tyrants, cannot be distinguished from the dispersed tyranny: escapist novels cannot decide whether they are saving us or seeking salvation from us. The alternative worlds of contemporary escapism are not qualitatively superior to our own; they are our inescapable world at momentary fictional frontier outposts or short-lived performative Zions. This is as good as it gets; this is as great as it gets.

*   *   *

Bathos: this book comes in four sections. A chapter on *The Sound of Music*, universally taken as the paradigm of an escapist work of art and therefore not conducive to the circularity that all diagnoses of escapism exploit, will complement the present chapter as introduction to my premises. This is unfair to the novels I examine, which are not solely intended as popular entertainments; nevertheless, the musical is self-conscious about its escapism in ways that will clarify the super-genre (escapism) and subgenre (escapist novels of the twenty-first century) as a whole. The super-genre and subgenre are the concentric objects of my study.

Part II, "Family Likenesses," is a series of essays on American novelists of the last twenty years or so: Michael Chabon, Junot Díaz, Dave Eggers, Jonathan Safran Foer, Emma Donoghue, Lauren Groff, Colson Whitehead, George Saunders, and Jesmyn Ward. (For the sake of my project, the Irish-Canadian writer Emma Donoghue will be considered an American writer, as in one sense of American, she literally is. I devote a chapter to *Room*, which takes place in the United States.) Octavia E. Butler and Toni Morrison are touchstones. All the authors I dub escapist are importantly different from one another, and some of the difference is a function of sex, race, religion, or ethnicity, easy to predict if the two primary escapes of escapism are from slavery and Nazism. Yet we should notice that both escaping from Nazism and escaping from slavery (and in part escaping from colonialism) center on the question of race. And it is worth reprising the fact that *It Happened One Night* is an escapist paradigm of escape envy, whites trying to escape over the route blazed by the Underground Railroad, that *The Sound of Music* is based on escape envy, whites featuring their own escape from whiteness, and that "Pantaloon in Black" opposes itself to "picture show" escapism paradigmatically by demonstrating the futility of even a physical escape from racial incarceration. The escape aspect of escapist novels is not their realistic aspect, as opposed to their escapism and escapology. All escapism that begins with a specific historical escape is escape envy or escape nostalgia: seventy-five years after the establishment of Israel and India, and twice as long after the emancipation of American slaves, and invariably a short time after the deaths of empires and dictators, we dream collectively of escape as a lost historical possibility. On her escape northward, the escaping slave Cora finds in South Carolina an attractive stop, yet reality there is anachronistically summarized as a "changing display in a shop window" (Whitehead, *Railroad* 116). She heads west, but we are not told whether she finds there a less commodified reality.

All my authors comprise a kind of mixed family, expanded by intermarriages, in a sense defined by Wittgenstein and modified by Cavell. Cavell defined his family of films in *Pursuits of Happiness* by attending to the way one film called to another—absences in one invoking presences in another; potentialities in one finding actualities in another.

It was the mixed hyperbole and bathos of *The Amazing Adventures of Kavalier & Clay* and *The Brief Wondrous Life of Oscar Wao* that sent me to *A Heartbreaking Work of Staggering Genius*—and eventually to *The Ministry of Utmost Happiness*. But the theme common to *Oscar Wao* and *Kavalier & Clay* (can experienced x save innocent y so that innocent y can save experienced x?) also brought into the subgeneric family multiple works by Dave Eggers and Jonathan Safran Foer, though Eggers and Foer are in some ways antithetical writers, one Jewish, oriented backward in time and eastward in space, the other "not even Jewish" (as he jokes) and oriented forward and westward. It is the limited power of x to save or free y, the largeness of the Utopian or messianic ambition and the severe limitation of means and range, that is manifest in the bathos of the hyperbole of the titles. Eggers's project of saving his innocent younger brother from the tragedy of his orphanhood suggested Emma Donoghue's *Room*, though *Room*—featuring a mother who, unlike Eggers, does not wish to postpone her full adulthood—concerns saving the child both within his artificial escapist life and from it. Donoghue's *Room*, about a mother's creation of an escapist world for her son, obliged a postscript on Lauren Groff's *Arcadia*, which may be read as a failed Utopian version of Donoghue's failed messianism. The theme of escape from incarceration brought Colson Whitehead into the fold, though in the case of actual slavery or its aftermath, innocence is not centrally at issue, and accordingly there are very few children in the novels of his that I examine before *The Nickel Boys*, though their absence is marked and regretted. The paradox of whiteness in *The Sound of Music*—the emblem of escape from Nazism is edelweiss—comes into play throughout this study and needed to find its way to the escape from slavery of *The Underground Railroad*.

Jesmyn Ward's *Sing, Unburied, Sing* and George Saunders's *Lincoln in the Bardo* pick up motifs from escapist books: Ward's novel like Eggers's novel-memoir centers on a child caring for a younger child; Saunders's novel implies the necessity of escape from an entombed escapism, like *Room*. Most of all they resume the focus of Whitehead's *Zone One* on undeath rather than salvation or rejuvenation. The fact that they were both published in 2017 may indicate the end of escapism as the dominant American fictional mode of the twenty-first century (neither book features an interior fantasy text); insofar as both books refuse to premise an innocence that precedes experience, they may resemble the oeuvres of David Grossman and Arundhati Roy (whose latest novel is from 2017) more than the fiction of their American cohort whose canonization seemed underway in the 2015 BBC poll cited at the outset of this chapter.

Part III, "Foreign Correspondents," takes up world analogues to American themes as tokens of globalization. According to the Cavellian protocol, my attention to two post-messianic American novels that posit the failure of Israel led me to the novels of the Israeli writer David Grossman, who must take the scenario literally. The centrality of *The Sound of Music* to Arundhati Roy's *The God of Small Things* led me to her work one way, her titular extravagance another. I might have otherwise been led to *The God of Small Things* as a precursor of *Oscar Wao*, whose title character is also a god of small things, also assassinated when he violates the love laws, and also bequeaths to his book a concluding posthumous vision of short-lived antinomian love. There is, furthermore, a continuing investigation into the informing of the present by the shape of past absences that defines the feminist escapism of Donoghue, Groff, and Roy.

Both Grossman and Roy try out desperate, secular, even post-human, Utopian inventions to replace routinized, weaponized divine missions. Both take up the theme of the salvific child in similarly non-American ways; the fact that no innocence naturally precedes experience in either author raises of necessity the question of how real choice might enter a world already fatally experienced in advance. (The history of the Warsaw Ghetto drives even an American writer to wonder how children could retain their rights of childhood; it might be possible to consider a new line of American writing on escape by comparing Jim Shepard's *The Book of Aron* to Grossman's *The Book of Intimate Grammar*, whose hero happens to be named Aron, respectively an American and an Israeli novel, which decouple the bookish imagination from childhood innocence, *pace* Michael Chabon at his most ingenuous.) Grossman and Roy in tandem are meant to clarify my interior examination of the early twenty-first-century American novel in relation to my exterior theorization of the time of escapism in globalized space.

Part IV, a prequel, consists of a few pages devoted to the many hundreds of pages of *The Tunnel*, by William H. Gass, a novel that predicts from the end of the twentieth century almost all the fiction of my book, and summarizes them in one prolonged enactment of escape, escapism, and escapology. There is no re-parenting, however, of an innocent precocious child: from Gass's epic novel summarizing the twentieth century in 1995, the twenty-first-century escapist novel is prepared for its flight.

Chapter 2

I FLIT, I FLOAT, I FLEETLY FLEE, I FLY

Begin again with the consensus that Rodgers and Hammerstein's *The Sound of Music* is the epitome of escapism, the role it plays as foil to Lars von Trier's *Dancer in the Dark* and Arundhati Roy's *The God of Small Things*. More evidence: when philanthropists treat a few kids to a month of relief from the slums of Mumbai, the method is rehearsal for a single performance of songs from *The Sound of Music* with the Bombay Chamber Orchestra at the National Centre for the Performing Arts. One doesn't know quite how to tabulate the escapism of that intention, as recorded by the documentary, *The Sound of Mumbai: A Musical*. Gay and lesbian *Sound of Music* Sing-a-Long festivals on two other continents discover the campy escapist potential of the musical's Anschluss.

It is not self-evident that the escapism of *The Sound of Music* needs to be exposed. *The Sound of Music* is aware of it. When Maria Rainer, postulant of the Nonnberg Abbey near Captain Georg von Trapp's Salzburg estate, falls in love with the Captain at the expense of the designing Baroness Elsa Schraeder, she retreats to the Abbey for a regimen of nonstop praying. The Mother Abbess summons Maria for a lecture, the lesson of which is that "our Abbey is not to be used as an escape" from "what . . . you can't face." One side of the equation is not implausible: self-commitment to a convent may be a form of escapism, an allegory of Adam Phillips's claim that what escapism escapes is the fear of our desires. But what Maria cannot face on the other side of the equation is following her rainbow back to the handsomest, richest, bravest, truest, and eventually kindest widower in Austria, along with his seven uniformly talented and adoring children. What is purported, perhaps rightly, to be an overcoming of the heroine's escapism is itself an escapist fantasy.

Encouraged by the Mother Abbess, Maria returns to the von Trapp villa to find Liesl, the oldest child, unhappy in her adolescent romance with Rolf. Rolf has not yet revealed himself as a young Nazi; Liesl is merely despondent that he has not visited for a while. In view of his neglect, Liesl laments, she'll be "glad when school begins." We hadn't heard much about the formal education of the von Trapp children. The raising of the inconsequential theme enables Maria to parrot the lesson of the Mother Abbess: "Liesl, you can't use school to escape your problems. You have to face them." The inference is that Liesl should devote herself to Rolf as Maria to Captain von Trapp, not using school as her convent. But Rolf is no Captain von Trapp. Maria is uniquely glib, proud to relay the lesson she has learned without wondering if it is apt, possibly to allow her to reiterate the musical's self-incriminating opposition to escapism. Alternatively, this is the film's chance to make the more sophisticated meta-escapist defense that if reality is obscure— could anyone have anticipated that boyish Rolf was more prone to fascism than authoritarian Captain von Trapp?—so is the means of escaping it.

Escaping Rolf is not escapism in the Adam Phillips sense of evading dangerous desires; it is escape in the sense of fleeing Nazism. Rolf is the last impediment to the von Trapp family's escape from Austria, which takes the form of literally running away from real dangers. The point is not that it is impossible to make a distinction between escapism and life-saving escape. The point is that the essence of the appeal of escapism for adults is the obfuscating of the escapism-escape border: the impossibility of confidently knowing the direction reality points from slavery and evil to freedom and salvation is what allows us to sit still.

If converting a situation in which escape is necessary for characters into a setting in which escapism is possible for readers and audiences is the methodology of escapism for adults, then the telltale sign of escapism is conceptual repurposing: everything threatening must be translated into something pleasurable. The escapist work of art teaches its audience how to make the translation. Roberto Benigni's *Life is Beautiful*, in which the father, who does not know German, mistranslates the laws of the concentration camp into the rules of the game for his son, is the most lucid example. The father's creation of an escapist fantasy for his boy (the death camp is a game) allows the film's creation of an escapological fantasy for us (the game is a resurrection ritual).

Escapism in *Life is Beautiful* takes place entirely within the camp; the child's ultimate escaping the camp is only represented to pay tribute to escapism inside it. This model sounds plausible enough that I want to argue against appearances that in *The Sound of Music* the von Trapps not only fail to confront Nazism but also stay, in effect, where they are. It is still within Austria that Nazis force upon the von Trapp family the necessity of singing in public. That is where the von Trapp family becomes who they have always been to us. They are escaping (in actuality) to Vermont, but Vermont is merely the home office of their multinational corporation, where the world first encounters what the Austrians had seen. Escapism is not merely available to globalization; it is the sign of globalization, whose motto is: there's only here, here.

Thus, the Alps, apparently the frontier the von Trapps cross to leave Austria behind, are not so much scaled as conceptually repurposed. In the original Broadway production, though not in the Hollywood film, Captain von Trapp, when he hears that the borders have been sealed against his flight, grieves that the Alps are no longer "standing there protecting us" (Crouse 148). The Mother Abbess, in both play and film, reassures the family by way of the Old Testament, quoting Psalms 121:1: "I will lift up mine eyes upon the hills from whence cometh my help." In the Broadway production, she also cites Isaiah 55:12: "For ye shall go out with joy, and be led forth with peace: the mountains and the hills shall break forth before you into singing" (Crouse 148). The Bible passages do not merely restore the mountains from foe to friend; they repeat the Mother Abbess's repurposing of the profane as the sacred. The Isaiah exultation echoes the musical's opening axiom as sung by Maria: in the communion of humans and nature in song, humans are sanctified. "My heart will be blessed/ With the sound of music." What is the meaning of this thorough integration of the sacred and the profane? This is beyond messianism without the messiah; this is messianism without change, even the slight change predicted by Hasidic tradition.

Or consider it Utopianism without travel, centered on the place that is never left behind. Already in Austria, the Utopian potential of musicals in general, and of *The Sound of Music* in particular, is exhibited and scrutinized: the general critical opinion is that the spontaneous dancing and harmonizing of purportedly non-showbiz humans in song is Utopian. Yet the unrehearsed but orchestrated group singing in musicals is Utopian only if it figures, in some way, a more loving, joyful, and improvisatory community elsewhere. My argument, however, will be that inexplicably unified singing in *The Sound of Music* is not Utopian but both escapist and verisimilar, once we take the orchestrated Friedmanesque globe to be its setting. Immobile escapism such as *The Sound of Music* epitomizes is realistic if there is no place for the Utopian imagination to go.

If you call your musical about escaping the Austrian Anschluss *The Sound of Music*, you direct attention from catastrophic history, as well as messianic or Utopian alternatives to catastrophic history, to the genre itself. To put the word "music" into the title of a musical is one recursive step. A second step comes out in the question, what is the difference between music and the sound of music? Here is the beginning of an answer. One of the marks of classic Broadway musicals is the repurposing of songs in a different mood: the song sung radiantly by the heroine when she is first in love, for example, is reprised when she is in despair, though she breaks down in the middle and runs sobbing from the stage.

At such moments, it is as if the music of the musical, formerly tied to a moment of the action, charged by that moment with a particular meaning, recurs as pure sound with another meaning. The professional challenge is to change the mood without altering the notes. After Maria's disappearance, the von Trapp children's dismal singing of "[The Hills Are Alive with] The Sound of Music," a weepy reprise of the musical's anthem, is a case in point. A fine example of repurposing in the optimistic direction is the return of "[How Do You Solve a Problem Like] Maria" as the wedding march of Maria and the Captain. It *almost* makes sense: the wedding approximately solves the problem of Maria's disjunction of free temperament and obedient calling. In the film, Captain von Trapp takes Maria's hands, on his way to taking her hand in marriage, just six or seven seconds after the ostensibly rhetorical, but now plausibly answered, question, "How do you hold a moonbeam in your hand?" Yet the return of the song, with all its lyrics intact, doesn't quite work out: the possibilities for characterizing Maria are no longer "a flibbertigibbet, a will-o'-the wisp, a clown." The arrangement has to be clever to turn that perky song into a processional, but the lyrics return with no clear function except to be evacuated of meaning. The sound of the music is what counts.

The background music of the film is particularly egregious in its repurposing of diegetic melodies and songs. When Captain von Trapp, having dismissed the Baroness, finds Maria near the gazebo and prepares to kiss her, "[The Hills Are Alive with] The Sound of Music" plays faintly in accompaniment. Why? They aren't in the hills. When the von Trapps flee from the music festival pursued by Nazis, an excited "So Long, Farewell" is transformed from its first unctuous diegetic mood (the children performing their goodnights to a grown-up *soirée*) into an element of non-diegetic suspense. (It makes no difference whether the music is inside or outside the action.) This randomizing process becomes so ingrained that it may register as a novelty when the von Trapps arrive at the top of a mountain apparently marking the border between Austria and Switzerland (if they are at the nearest border to

Salzburg, they would be climbing and descending toward Munich, not far from Dachau), and the soundtrack plays "Climb Ev'ry Mountain," literalizing the advice of the Mother Abbess. But the literalism suggests something like a period to the incongruous art. This song may be the end of the musical in the sense that the last line is the end of the poem to Agamben (Agamben, *Poem* 109–18): the moment when the war of sound and sense, or in this case the always imminent triumph of sound over sense, that constitutes the musical is forestalled by a perfect détente.

The motive of a soundtrack's recycling music in contradictory moods is to reinforce, especially at moments of narrative crisis, that we are in attendance at a musical rather than in, for all significant purposes, Austria, Switzerland, the United States, or India. Even if the music is a melancholic reprise, its repurposing serves that escape from time and place. Not merely that there is music in the background, which could be affectively appropriate in the usual way of soundtracks—rather that the background music betrays its contumely for the story it putatively serves. The plot's shape and suspense are undermined by music that can be transposed from one location in the narrative to another.

If it does not matter to the melodies of a musical where in the plot they reappear, it may not matter to the plot of a musical where in history it takes place. The entirety of *The Sound of Music* is a repurposing of an earlier Rodgers and Hammerstein hit, *The King and I*, from another era and corner of helplessly transposable world history. In *The King and I*, an unmarriageable woman finds herself overwhelmed by the exotic opulence of her employer the King's palace. Anna is unmarriageable partly because of her viduity, partly because of her race. In *The Sound of Music*, set in not a palace but a baroque mansion nearly as intimidating, and a fictionalization of world and family history almost as free, Maria seems beyond matrimonial reach by virtue of her class and calling.

Both Anna and Maria, who may as well have only first names, obscuring their marital status, one a widow, one affianced to Christ, are put in charge of offspring not their own. There is an excess of children in both cases, seven von Trapp Austrians and dozens of royal Siamese. In both cases, miscommunication marks the beginning of teaching, but the sympathy and support of their teachers win the adorable children rather quickly. In both cases, an illicit love transpires between the rich, rigid, authoritarian, and hitherto fertile patriarch and the apparently off-limits teacher. In both cases, illicit love gets expressed between the monarchical or aristocratic man and his hired woman in a scene of pedagogy at a dance. Anna teaches the King the polka, and Maria begins by teaching one of the two von Trapp boys the Ländler, before the graceful Captain breaks in. The dance, half cultural and half corporeal, serves in both scenes as the transition from lessons to love, with highly charged looks exchanged between an amorous man and his love-struck dance partner. The political context in both cases is the threatening by foreigners of the patriarch's land, which he had believed to be his inviolable autocracy, but which he newly deserves to run democratically by virtue of his softening under the tutelage of a strong woman, though he cannot go on ruling it.

The book of *The Sound of Music* was written by Howard Lindsay and Russel Crouse, but they worked in close collaboration with Rodgers and Hammerstein on all phases of the storyline. They must have realized that they were rewriting *The King and I*, except without the death of the patriarch at the end. I have speculated elsewhere that it was the splitting of the King of Siam (dictator and paternal disciplinarian) into offstage Hitler and reluctantly onstage Captain von Trapp that allowed the latter to shed his rigidity and learn to live. Thus, the partly tragic *King and I* is repurposed for a particularly upbeat version of the escapist musical.

It does not matter whether a Rodgers and Hammerstein musical takes place in Siam or Salzburg, insofar as the sound of music becomes the diffuse, displaced, atemporal location of the musical. Austria dissolves into a musical setting. If Captain von Trapp can be saved from his autocratic tendencies less tragically than the King of Siam, it is because he can dance and sing and play the guitar; his going on stage to sing is the sign of his redemption. If the children can be taught by Maria how to save him, it is because the pedagogy of the musical starts at the very beginning, with "Do-Re-Mi." That song begins with the notes themselves, then puns on the notes, then celebrates the capacity of notes to form songs, itself its example. But though the song never transcends the song, the setting of the song, switching locales from phrase to phrase, is the first advertisement for the contemporary moment of Salzburg tourism. This means that father and children are fit to survive in the sound of the music of the musical, their new globalized homeland. It's as if the musical is about the founding of a tourist trap, with the von Trapps always in residence.

The process takes some effort to work out—the adult who needs saving is not, as in some of the paradigms of my escapist archive, an older brother or young mother. It is a fertile, authoritarian father, which means that before being saved, he needs to be leveled. I use the term advisedly: the repurposing of the Alps as the profanation of the divine seems to require that they be reconceived as high green hills. It is the hills that are alive with the sound of music, and it is a green hill that the von Trapps scale at the end of the film, though the relevant song pretends that it is a mountain.

Thus, repurposing, when its function is making the autocrat of the family available to the love of his children, takes the form not of castrating so much as phallic downsizing. The King of Siam, shamed into throwing away his whip rather than flog the recaptured concubine Tuptim, begins immediately to die, which turns the musical from comic to sentimental while turning Siam from absolute monarchy toward limited democracy, in the care of the tutored prince, a diminished but not deposed potentate. In *The Sound of Music*, one man in one generation must be both despot and democrat: Captain or Baron von Trapp, aristocrat, war hero, and quasi-military commander of his household, must be transformed in effect into Herr Trapp, domesticated, decommissioned, almost neutered in neutral Switzerland. I say *almost* neutered because of the symptomatic exactitude of the film: his boatswain's whistle, with which he calls family and servants to order at the beginning of the film, prefigures the whistle with which Rolf attests his loyalty to Nazis over friends at the end, when he signals for help in capturing the fleeing von Trapps at the Abbey. The bequeathing of the whistle is a ritual of masculine passage that is both performed and disavowed; the whistle survives in the film as a fetish.

If the whistle is rather too obvious a sign of ridiculous masculinity, it serves a subtler complementarity as the universal gage of infinitesimal difference. It symbolizes the phallus as dieresis; it sorts while signifying nothing. Rolf, especially in the film, is a figure straight from Klaus Theweleit's *Male Fantasies*, a book about proto-Nazis in the *Freikorps*. By way of gun and whistle, Rolf hopes to forestall the wet soft messiness of sexuality, which he has feared since singing to Liesl, the more sexually adventurous of the two, at the gazebo, with a final kiss followed by a panicked flight. Meanwhile, Julie Andrews as Maria is the beautiful heroine as belated tomboy, cherished by many of the escapist audience at gay and lesbian Sing-a-Long festivals. At one point, Captain von Trapp, flustered, calls her "captain."

That the mark of difference is less than an iota makes possible the repurposing that is the musical's method on behalf of all musicals: infinitesimal difference as the bridge of easy translatability across all binaries. Diacritical marks mark the visual sameness of what they segregate. Musicals often pose this conceptual puzzle to critics: how to recognize in conventional marriage plots the nearly undisguised inrushes of gayness. The solution is that all boundaries, including those between sexes and sexual practices, are minimal in the escapist version of a globalized, that is, a defenselessly traversable, world, in which the mountains between countries turn out to be pregnable hills.

Maria and the Captain pass the guitar back and forth; on such a depreciated conception of territorial rights, every stream can be forded. But I have left the children out of the analysis, which is an important omission, since it is the children who will be the saving agency, mediators who vanish by growing up, in almost all the escapist novels I am about to consider. There are plenty of them in the two musicals I've been comparing. The King of Siam has produced scores of children by many concubines; the Captain has produced seven children by one deceased wife. (In reality, Captain von Trapp goes on to father three more children by Maria, but this is alien to the imagination of the musical.) Further procreation seems to be jeopardized by the ambiguity of the sexual status of the woman each now loves. The King is at the point of winning Anna during the increasingly charged "Shall We Dance?" seduction, when they are interrupted by the news of Tuptim's escape and recapture. Soon thereafter, the King begins to die, which is convenient, because Anna's race has been a romantic barrier whose overcoming we are not sure how to envisage. And we have no conception of what might transpire between the post-postulant Maria and the Captain, except to note that the number of his children is already adequate for solfege.

The phallic downsizing of the suddenly non-philoprogenitive patriarch enables the reciprocal, nongenerational salvation of the musical. The father and the children save Maria from burial alive in the Abbey (escapology); the children and Maria save the father from his joylessness (escapism); the father and Maria save the children from Nazism (escape). This is an immobile and poised structure, precursor to the momentary unity of older and younger family members in escapist novels, mutually exempted from time in the midst of death.

The central mystery of minimal difference in *The Sound of Music* is the celebration of edelweiss. Edelweiss as a flower is the sign of Austria in the film; every commentator notes that "Edelweiss" as a song is often taken as an authentic Austrian anthem. In fact, it is the final lyric written by Hammerstein in his life, correspondingly the final song of the festival before the von Trapps flee for their lives. It is the plant one honors in one's uprooting, which has the happy effect of reconciling deracination and dwelling. It allows the von Trapps to bless damned Austria, their eternal homeland, as they leave it. Yet how does one know that "Edelweiss" is not a Nazi folksong—apt efflorescence of the infected land?

As if *The Sound of Music* were a Malevich painting, the question is the relationship of white and white, specifically of edelweiss (and the Captain) as against the Baroness Schraeder. Especially at the scene of the ball, the Baroness is a monstrous frozen sculpture of silvery or gilded white, emblem of the treasures of whiteness, from shoes to gloves to unyielding gilt-platinum hair. The only character in the film as blond as the Baroness is Rolf.

In her blinding whiteness, the Baroness resembles the glaciers of Austria with which the film begins. That opening, which far outdoes the Abbey opening of the stage version of the musical, begins with shots of an inhuman, almost unearthly mountainscape, first only shrouding white clouds, and then icy desolate peaks. The mountains, quite distinctly not inviting surmountable green hills, are not alive, and what they are not alive with is the sound of a ghastly wind. Very deliberately, the world becomes greener and then bluer and then barely human-friendlier, a quick history of the planet after the Ice Age, until at last we see Maria as a spot on the far verge of a green hill. She quickly fills the screen, and by her striding, twirling, and singing into it, she replaces the glacial castrating inhumanness later to be embodied in the icy, chiseled, ghastly Baroness she also replaces. Whiteness is not personified in the Baroness; her whiteness is mineralized in the Alps. The whiteness of the Austrian Baroness is the mirror of German whiteness—she ruthlessly plots to expand her hegemony from Vienna to Salzburg by enlisting and corrupting one true Austrian, whom the Nazis also wish to corrupt and enlist from Berlin.

There is a musical precedent that may have been known to Oscar Hammerstein. Around 1934, representatives of a Berlin women's group greeting Hitler at Anhalter Bahnhof wondered what sort of bouquet to offer him. Albert Speer writes that he was contacted by his friend Karl Hanke in Goebbels's Propaganda Ministry; no one had any idea (Hitler's aesthetics favored the sublime), but they agreed to name edelweiss as a symbolically sensible fiction (Speer 47). Around that time, Harry Steir's song, "Hitler's Favorite Flower is the Simple Edelweiss," became a hit in Germany.

Could this evil twinning of edelweiss anthems indicate the effectiveness of the song in *The Sound of Music*—do the Nazis in the front row of the festival, who are uneasy about the popularity of the von Trapps and particularly about the audience participation in the singing of "Edelweiss," recognize that purity in Austria is Austrian and that German Nazism is its stain? The joke would be that the Nazis are the Jews of Austria, the internal traitorous aliens, but the joke would be discomfiting for non-Nazis as much as Nazis: the best rebuke to the cult of endangered white purity is not to seize control of it. Equivocal edelweiss was the insignia of both the Waffen-SS Mountain Rangers and the anti-militaristic youth group, the Edelweiss Pirates.

What if anything is the difference between the whiteness of glaciers that survives, inhumanly frigid, in the Baroness Schraeder in Vienna, and the whiteness of edelweiss, which may be repurposed as the sign of human grief? What is the diacritical mark that enables a transition from the purity of Germany's flesh to the purity of Austria's soul?

The answer may be nothing; but if so, the musical is not escapist at all. If the musical is escapist, all the escape is predicated on the phrase "blossom of snow." This is not the unmelting, inhuman glacial snow that mineralizes the Baroness Schraeder. Insofar as the blossom of snow is felt by Austrians to greet them, to look happy to meet them, accommodating like the beautiful rather than terrifying like the sublime, repersonification (the flower as snow, the snowflower as friend) is the trope of repurposing at its most urgent: of the mineral as the vegetable as the human. Escapism cannot defeat the inhumanity of the world (mist, mountains, glaciers, baronesses, Nazis), but it can soften it. The method is not to unman superhuman (kingly) or inhuman (military) patriarchs but to discover what melts in them. Among Maria's favorite things are "silver-white winters that melt into springs," which is possible in Captain von Trapp only when the silver-whiteness of the wintry Baroness is succeeded by the greenness of the governess.

It has been suggested that the play of whiteness in *The Sound of Music* exists for the sake of discriminating, at a crux in its history, the United States as a white country from Germany as a white country. The point would be to make sense of a world war on that basis. But *The Sound of Music* is a forestalling of the Second World War, an escape from it in advance, by discovering a virtuous whiteness within Austria, and by a demilitarization of the Austrian war hero who might have faced the problems of his country by fighting them rather than by fleeing them to his familial peace-loving musical destiny. We see the family arrive at an unremarkable—green and roundish—peak with more impressive, snow-topped mountains in the distance, along with green valleys. That is as far into their destiny as we follow them. There is no Utopian arrival or messianic return anywhere, but even as an adventure, this is an adventure without events, precluding the events of the Second World War. We may suspect, however, that though the musical fails to find its climax as the von Trapps descend toward nothing in particular, the film has a more satisfactory destination in mind, at least for Oscar Hammerstein.

Return to the escape scene of *The King and I* for a clue. The Burmese concubine Tuptim is anxious to flee the Siamese palace with her beloved Lun Tha. When English imperialists arrive at the court, the King hopes that demonstrating Siam's aspiration to Western culture is the best method to hold them off; Tuptim is engaged to write a ballet version of *Uncle Tom's Cabin*. Tuptim's ballet is a triumph with the British, who applaud it heartily and cry out for its author, *but Tuptim has escaped.*

Fans of *The Sound of Music* will recognize the ruse. Once the von Trapps have performed at the Salzburg Folk Festival and their first prize has been announced, the Austrian audience, aroused to patriotic pride, applauds at length, *but the von Trapps have escaped.* Tuptim and Lun Tha are not the protagonists of their musical, so one is killed and one captured without fatal danger to the play; the von Trapps, for historical and aesthetic reasons, escape unscathed. This is a perfect repurposing of the escape-during-applause gambit, which must make deep sense, because it makes very little superficial sense. Why try to escape at precisely the moment when your absence will be visible, your point of escape precisely known, your intention immediately inferred? In *The Sound of Music*, it is arranged for there to be no alternative; in *The King and I*, there is every alternative. Tuptim and Lun Tha are punished for the sake of the theatrical device, itself.

What does it mean for performers, at the end of their performances, to receive our applause? All solutions to the actor's applause dilemma (should they humanize or stay in character?) are paradoxes of artifice and naturalness, which is why applause per se is an apt theme of musicals, the locus classicus of such paradoxes. For Tuptim, receiving applause would have been especially ambiguous: as author of the adaptation, she is outside it, though traces of her are everywhere; as narrator, she is at its margin; when she addresses the King to make her appeal to him not to keep her enslaved like the American slaves in the play, she is at the margin of her marginal role as narrator abutting *The King and I*'s reality. Tuptim's removing herself from her art to receive the applause of the imperialists would, in effect, reverse directions and recommit her to her play, only more so: to the grace and playfulness of her play, admired by the Englishmen, but not its politics. To the degree of that re-aestheticization, she would be re-enslaved.

In *The Sound of Music*, there seems at first to be no question of acting. The von Trapp family is on stage, during their climactic performance at the music festival, as themselves, the von Trapp family. Yet there is already a complication: they are delivering a mainly rehearsed, partly improvised performance; but delivering fully rehearsed performances is what they had done, pervasively, in ordinary domestic life, as at their "Lonely Goatherd" puppet show (in the film). The partly improvised performance is slightly less artificial than their stagy off-stage lives.

There are deeper strata of convolution. In a sense, the von Trapp family is pretending to perform at the festival. Captain von Trapp has rescinded his total opposition to the family's singing in public only as an ad hoc tactic for keeping the Nazis from enforcing his immediate departure to the German navy. The von Trapps are actors after all, singing all their songs in roles. When the children perform "So Long, Farewell," they try to contain the meaning that they are not merely leaving the competition; they are leaving the country. When Captain von Trapp introduces "Edelweiss" as his own valedictory, he betrays nothing about where he is going, but Max misinforms the audience that von Trapp departs to the German navy. Their traveling outfits, Maria asserts beforehand to a skeptical Nazi who knows they might intend to flee Austria, are actually costumes, which is equivocal. (Their outfits are meant for traveling and are repurposed as costumes for their performance; but insofar as the von Trapps are only performing performance for the sake of disguising their escape, their outfits are costumes of costumes, or real.) Had the von Trapps returned to the stage to receive their first prize, they would have been adhering to the terms of their performance but not their performance of performance, which means that for von Trapps as for Tuptim, returning to the stage would have equaled returning to captivity.

It is Maria who equivocates to the Nazis that the traveling clothes they are wearing are costumes for the festival, because she stands on the conceptual border of art and nature. Unlike the Captain, she had wanted to perform at the festival, and escaping the country finally necessitates it. If the verbal dimension of escapism is the confusion of escapism and escape, Maria is the character who represents the syntactic obligation (the text's obligation to find a point of view for its verbal ambiguity) to reconcile them. Her escape from the Abbey, which for her would have been an incarceration, brings her to the escapist fantasy of a perfectly harmonious family, whose performance of harmoniousness is its salvation. The escapist fantasy of perfect family harmony, as demonstrated at a festival of national harmony, equals actual escape from Nazis. At the intersection is the impossibility of returning for the applause that the von Trapps have fraudulently, authentically earned.

Oscar Hammerstein II, from the third generation of important theatrical Hammersteins, was so thoroughly immersed in theater that he must have found even a minimal resurfacing to life confusing. Audiences were the place where the honed pseudo-simplicity of his art entangled the sophistication of his commercial acumen. Judging the reactions of audiences was critical, especially when the plays were in preview, but he mistrusted the applause of audiences as an index. Hammerstein "looked for a certain expression on their faces, what he called a 'glow,' a steady smile that stayed there when they were enjoying a show. . . . Applause could be a response to effort or a particular actor, or some sure applause-getting dramatic effect, such as the right kind of cymbal crash or timpani roll" (Fordin 311). The problem with applause is its partiality in related senses: the audience may respond to one of the musical's set pieces in isolation, and it may favor stars. Applauding stars is an audience's way of making direct emotional contact with artifice. Because it is always an interruption, except at the end when it is a preemption, applause is narratively divisive by its nature.

A musical may be, in both ways, all partiality: even in the sort of show Rodgers and Hammerstein claimed as their innovation, a continuity of music, dance, book, and lyrics, the replacement of acting by song or dance is never seamless; the trick is to build a putative whole out of self-contained units, which may be written and rehearsed separately. The star may be another self-contained unit. Thus this dialogue between the veteran lyricist Hammerstein and the neophyte Stephen Sondheim, who at the moment was writing the lyrics for *Gypsy*, starring Ethel Merman. Hammerstein urges Sondheim to write "Rose's Turn" in such a way (with a high note at the climax) that Merman will extort an ovation. Sondheim objects to the dishonesty of it, since the song expresses a nervous breakdown.

> "Yes, it's dishonest," Oscar explained, "and it's the kind of dishonesty that you have to take into account in the theater, particularly the musical theater. Don't forget: there's an audience out there and they want to applaud. The result of your doing it honestly is that they don't listen to the last two minutes of the show, because they feel so frustrated and cheated. And if you want them to listen to those last two pages of dialogue, then you've got to *give them their release* at the end of that song. It's dishonest psychologically, but there's another kind of honesty, and that has to do with theater honesty." (Fordin 331, my emphasis)

If you add that what Tuptim seeks by not returning for applause is release from concubinage, and that what Captain von Trapp seeks by not returning for applause is release from his commission, then what you have is a competition not of two honesties but of two escapes. Or the honesty, Hammerstein implies, is in the competitive escaping. Sondheim's retrospect on Hammerstein's advice is that "he was dead *right*, because the minute we put on the high note for her and gave her applause, there was dead silence instead of the restlessness there had always been" (Fordin 331). The partially dishonest emphasis on the partiality of show-stoppers may serve the honest totality. I do not know how much emphasis to put on the fact that Sondheim's word for two positives is "dead."

Captain von Trapp and Tuptim represent Hammerstein in evoking and escaping popular judgment. His life was a function of it: he could "see no sense in expressing something to a handful of people or to oneself" (Fordin 311). His grandfather quipped, "There's no limit to the number of people who will stay away from a bad show" (O. A. Hammerstein 51), which engages failure as the mathematical sublime. The grandson conceived his audience as "that big black giant who looks and listens with thousands of eyes and ears" whom "every night you fight" (Fordin 311). You don't evade popular judgment by gathering it en masse: the giant Panoptic Argus must be lured to the theater by the Hermetic musical to be fought, performance after performance, though never slain. The updating of the imagery implies that the audience, for example the audience at the festival within *The Sound of Music*, which is in small part Nazis, is always all Nazis, even all Gestapo. The reason Captain von Trapp had never allowed his family on stage is that he had refused to expose his privacy to the surveillance of the monstrous enemy spying from all sightlines in the dark. This comes out almost explicitly when the festival spotlight that is supposed to illuminate the von Trapps for their applause but only reveals their absence is replicated in the next setting by the flashlight that Nazis shine among the tombs of the Abbey where the von Trapps hide in silence.

It is enough to see only an artistic meaning in this escapist competition, though there is an indirect political meaning. Rodgers was a determinedly secular and Americanized Jew; on his father's side, the theatrical side, Hammerstein was Jewish, but he was raised in an amalgam of tepid Protestantisms (Fordin 19). The musical heritage that his Jewish grandfather revered was German opera and operetta; Hammerstein himself performed anti-Nazi political work in the 1930s partly out of Germanophilia.

Are all non-Nordics, who are prominent figures in the Rodgers and Hammerstein canon, secretly Jews? That case has been made for most of them—except for the ones who are covertly Black. When Rodgers and Hammerstein brilliantly create the *Small House of Uncle Thomas* ballet out of disparate incidents in *Anna and the King of Siam* (Landon 182, 213, 246–68), they include the death by drowning of an army of slave-catchers, imposing Exodus on the novel. (Moses had been mentioned at the state dinner just prior [Most, 184].) A famous case is Ali Hakim, the Persian peddler in *Oklahoma!*, a role that was offered to Groucho Marx and was first played by Joseph Buloff, star of the Yiddish theater (Fordin 195). Max Detweiler, in *The Sound of Music*, is the most worrisome case of crypto-Jewishness. He cannot literally be Jewish, or else he would not maintain his position at the top of the post-Anschluss cultural world of Austria. It is unclear whether the fact that he is a cliché of Jewishness—deracinated, worldly, greedy, cheap, conniving, charming or repulsive or both at once, and unscrupulously funny—makes it more or less likely that we are supposed to take him for a Jew; perhaps the universalizing point (as Eve Sedgwick would have put it) is that you don't need to be Jewish to be a Jewish stereotype. In any case, the running gag of the film is recognizably anti-Semitic joking at his expense.

Even if Max is not actually Semitic, he is not the German idea of an Aryan, but he has mastered the technique of escaping persecution by seeming to identify with the persecutors. Though he finds the Nazis repugnant, he claims not to care who is in charge of Austria so long as they believe he is one of them. His camouflage is adapted to fool all predators; he does not resemble the environment, he resembles the predators. We see him working this out in advance with the Baroness: for reasons that the musical does not fully clarify, they are intimate conspirators against Captain von Trapp. Their conspiracy has the qualities of a liaison without romance. Max is regularly identified by critics as homosexual, which would be one explanation for their triangulation of von Trapp in place of a straight connection between them. But since Max is also regularly identified as Jewish, the taboo would be excessive difference rather than excessive similarity. (One critic hedges that Max "*might* be Jewish" [Knapp 231, his emphasis], but another simply refers to him as the "Jewish theater producer" [Most 186]. Can a fictional character who is not Jewish be Jewish in reality?) Finally, Max cannot be in sexual relation with the Baroness because she is glacial; but he wishes to seem to harmonize with the interests of white inhumanity.

So Max stays on stage while the von Trapps escape—the paradox is that Captain von Trapp is a good Austrian with all the requisite qualities to be attractive to the Nazis, while Max might be taken as a homosexual or a Jew. Max nonetheless wishes to stand on stage and receive applause, which he has summoned as impresario, perhaps modeled on the impresario Oscar Hammerstein I, by identifying with the taste of the audience. But Captain von Trapp hates the stage and despises the audience, which represents a threat to his authority and sensibility much like that of the German occupiers.

In the end, Max helps the von Trapps escape, presumably at some risk to his well-being and without remuneration; perhaps the film sees some value in demonstrating that disinterested behavior is possible for a figure of Jewishness. He does not attempt to escape, himself, and the assumption is that we will be as little concerned by his fate as by Earl Johnson's. (Max puts his quasi- or crypto-Jewishness in possibly suicidal devotion to white survival, a reverse Schindler, as if whiteness rather than Jewishness were at risk.) The Jewish question, if it ever flickered in the musical, drops from consciousness altogether. We only care about the escape of the patriotic Austrians, and we know full well what they are escaping from. The question remains, however, where the von Trapps escape *to*. It might be objected that if escapism is the justification and judgment, synthesized in repurposing, of whatever exists, then *The Sound of Music* is not escapist, since the von Trapps make an actual, life-saving escape from Austria to Switzerland. That the musical abhors Nazism and that the von Trapps make a valiant cinematic hairbreadth escape from it (in reality they left on a train) have been the brushed-aside problems of this essay.

Yet what is Switzerland? Switzerland is not neutral in the technical meaning advanced by Louis Marin in *Utopics*, which asserts that a Utopian world stands blindly and emptily within an ideal elsewhere and fallen history here and now, in both at once but neutralizing them both, for the sake of future radical theorization. Switzerland is neutral but does not neutralize anything. As a matter of visual indications, we do not see the von Trapps climbing the last mountain to Switzerland. We see them at the end of hiking up a single undistinguished mountain somewhere, a pretentious hill from the looks of it, green at its summit, resembling the hill on which Maria sings and spins at the beginning of the musical. That's how far the film, as film, travels. There is nothing that marks a change of scenery much less a border, and we only see the von Trapps, at the very last moment of the film, beginning to descend to the other side of what we are meant to take without evidence as the decisive slope. There is no other there over there. A realist might doubt the von Trapp's ability to find such a modest climb as the last barrier to escape, but an escapist might affirm that the appropriately downsized mountain would make possible a minimal rather than a maximal landmark, for the sake of repurposing the landscape rather than traversing it.

Escapism speaks about where we are without recourse to any external system of evaluation. We cannot judge Austria from the perspective of unreached, unimagined Switzerland, and the emptiness of Switzerland is really only an empty transit toward the real native land of the von Trapps, or at least of the Von Trapp Family Singers, Vermont, where they centered their business: records, appearances, tours, hotel, music camp. The summit they reach in their escape is not a snowcapped but a prophetically green mountain. Their singing at the festival is meant to be taken by audiences of *The Sound of Music* as the moment that the von Trapps realize their destiny to be worthy of the musical, their entry into the world market for deracinated culture—not so much the culture industry as the global culture corporation. Arundhati Roy calls *The Sound of Music* a World Hit, and so are the von Trapps. Their new act in the borderless world is rehearsed in annexed Austria; Nazis elicit from them their global identity as national identity in costume. When Oscar Wao's sister Lola dreams of starring in a remake of *The Sound of Music*, she dreams of returning to Austria (Díaz 57), the homeland that has been blessed forever despite its history, capital of globalized, universalized whiteness.

Richard Dyer is the most acute reader of *The Sound of Music* as Utopian. One might think that the disagreement is merely nominal, insofar as Dyer, having listed the deficiencies of capitalism taken up by entertainment (scarcity, exhaustion, dreariness, manipulation, and fragmentation), admits that their "Utopian solutions" (musical forms of abundance, energy, intensity, transparency, and community) are precisely those promised by capitalism itself (Dyer 25). For entertainment, there is no elsewhere. In the example of *The Sound of Music*, Dyer anticipates my view that the von Trapp family has not crossed any visibly crucial border at the end of the film: "although the family has escaped the Germans, where have they really reached? We leave them climbing a mountain, not realizing a dream" (Dyer 58). Dyer salvages this outcome for the Utopian by concluding that though the von Trapps are not seen arriving anywhere, they are seen enduring: "The Endurance of the People is one of the great socialist themes, and I don't see why we should disparage it just because it is in *The Sound of Music*" (Dyer 59). My rejoinder is not merely that socialism is nowhere in the film, nor that the people who endure are not the People; the point of the film is that there is nowhere in the world for anything but the musical's reality, the sound of its music.

In the 1980s, Louis Marin was still barely hopeful that there might exist a late capitalist version of Utopia, descendant of More's proto-capitalist Utopia, which would postpone the triumph of our current condition by suggesting a blind spot on the inside of it. Lauren Berlant, in a book on sentimentalism that includes a full discussion of *The King and I*, maintains a hope that the sentimental project, from Stowe to Siam, insofar as it insinuates in its audience the possibility of novel identifications (as between American whites and the Siamese, or between them and American slaves), makes possible a still-undefined political future, indefinite because the universalism of suffering that is the essence of sentimentality is an unearned apolitical mechanism (Berlant 34–5). Sentimentalism and Utopianism allow a guarded hope for an as-yet untheorized future, starting nowhere in the case of Utopia and anywhere in the case of sentimentalism; but that is not in the wheelhouse of escapism. The burden and fantasy of escapism is that there is no future and no other place. It doesn't get any better than this.

If the explicit psychological point of Adam Phillips's *Houdini's Box* is that we manufacture our own escapism, our repetitious patterns of flight, to keep in contact with what we fear we desire, the implicit historical point is that escapism is the sign of modernity: given the absence of God or gods, we have only our own inventions, the world we have constructed for ourselves out of our own desires, to fear. Modernist Houdini, on the border of criminal and the police, founded a career in devising stronger and more spectacular entrapments from which to stage his escapades. But *The Sound of Music* represents postmodernity insofar as the postmodern shibboleth is inescapability. Derrida: "Il n'y a pas dehors-texte" (Derrida, *Grammatology* 127). Foucault: "The carceral network does not cast the unassimilable into a confused Hell; there is no outside" (Foucault 301). Postmodernism unlike modernism does not manufacture barriers between inside and outside; there is only inside. This is the final shibboleth that admits everyone. While Houdini was the sign of modernity for tours in America, Europe, and Australia, the von Trapps are the sign of postmodernity for the global theater. While escaping death is thus the form of Houdini's art, escaping to death is the final form of Hammerstein's.

The Broadway version of *The Sound of Music* begins in the Abbey; the film version gets there soon. Quickly after that, we are told that one of Maria's shortcomings is that she breaks the Abbey's rule against singing by postulants, though one officious nun ironically sings that complaint as introduction to "[How Do You Solve a Problem Like] Maria?" So much, at least at first pass, for the resistance of the Abbey to the contagious tunefulness of the world musical. The problem is what to make of the relation of religion and the world, and the solution is that there is no longer any place of opposition to it. Max Detweiler and the King of Siam and Oscar Hammerstein try to resemble the unlovely invasive world; Maria just is that world, with a loveable face. You solve a problem like Maria by conceding that she is the solution to all problems—of masculine rigidity, family paralysis, Austrian sovereignty, whiteness, globalization, the death of God—the bride at the end of history. Her syntactic function is to reconcile all disjunctions, starting with the disjunction of the sacred and profane, on behalf of the disjunction of escape and escapism.

Except that religion returns one last time, just after Captain von Trapp sings "Edelweiss," Oscar Hammerstein's swan song. The song has the feeling of closure with respect to not just the musical but also the biography, insofar as closure is defined by the metaphorical connection of beginnings and endings despite the metonymy of history. It is as if, in von Trapp's grudging life-saving decision to sing in public for the first time, we replay Hammerstein's decision to commence a career of pleasing audiences by giving them what they want to hear, of submitting to their honesty instead of insisting on his own. In effect, he has always been bowing before their applause. The escapism he provides audiences concedes to them the sovereignty he authentically wishes to escape; and his own authentic desire to escape gets allegorized by way of an authentically dire historical moment from which his characters *need* to escape. If audiences learn by way of a lesson in dieresis that what borders separate is indistinct, their tutors take that as an affront to their own distinction, to their nonglobalized imagination. Their sin is the desire to be unobserved while seeing all, though their art requires making themselves targets of hidden omniscience and omnipotence.

We might practice that omniscience and omnipotence by noting that the very last song Hammerstein wrote for a musical was turned by the film into a sing-along. This would seem to be the moment of the full immersion of the musical in its audience: the audience is imagined not as glowing or applauding, fully receptive or competitively assertive. The audience is co-performing; it knows Hammerstein's music and makes the music its own upon first hearing. This is the moment at which the musical is already a gay Sing-a-Long and already *The Sound of Mumbai*. Estha is singing along in the movie theater of *The God of*

Small Things; there is no moment in the novel prior to his internalizing of the World Hit. The moment of the sing-along, at its widest logical extent, is the moment of the undoing of alterity, a single world singing in a single language. Popular culture may, on this model, be defined by the immediate unity of performer and audience; the ideal pop song is singable on first hearing by the world.

If we feel intuitively that the essence of musical escapism is the ability of its characters to sing songs in harmony that they are inventing on the spot, this is only to acknowledge that absolute popular music is written to enable it. There is no objective world left by which it may be judged for accuracy, beauty, or justice. Globalization proceeds on its own incorrigibility, which is figured by the audience sing-along, which is prefigured by the spontaneous harmonizing of everyone, in show business or not, within musicals. This is the postmodern verisimilitude of the modern musical. *The Sound of Music* is an apt portrayal of the globe flattened by *The Sound of Music*. Insofar as the musical effortlessly translates the sacred into the profane, it is a self-fulfilling messianism and a performative Utopianism at once. That is what Hammerstein supplies to his sing-along audiences. It is also a staged dystopia posited for the sake of staging Hammerstein's escape from total surveillance.

At the very end of the film, the von Trapps escape the Nazis in escapological fashion—they drive to the Abbey and hide in the cemetery; when they escape from the silent tombs, they drive to the hills that are alive with the sound of music. Their resurrection involves sacred escapological trickery: the nuns remove the batteries from the cars of the Nazis, so that the von Trapps can ascend into eternal screen life.

But prior to their ascent of a hill that resembles the one on which Maria had been gamboling at the film's beginning, the return of the von Trapps to the Abbey feels like alternative closure. (The two forms of closure mirror the alternative beginnings of the musical, the Broadway play in the convent, the film in the hills.) Maria had left the Abbey to save Captain von Trapp and his family from its internal unhappiness; she returns to save them from an external threat. The family needs to hide, for a time, within earshot of the enemy, noiselessly, no sound at all, not even of background music; they need to escape by cloistering in Austria.

It is only in the film that the von Trapps hide among the tombs; in the stage version, they hide in the garden. The change changes everything. For a moment, there is no soundtrack and no spotlight. The von Trapps must escape their pursuers not by running but by standing too perfectly still for all spies and spectators. When the Nazis invade the cemetery shining flashlights that resemble the spotlights of the festival, only family-sized tombs protect the family from exposure. The Mother Abbess has made the dead-right decision in hiding them there, because the cemetery is a place of dead silence. Maria instructs Gretl not to sing "My Favorite Things," though it had been the song that was supposed to conquer fear, like singing about whistling in *The King and I*, at which point the musical repudiates its own livelihood. It cannot whistle past its graveyard; the whistle belongs to the Nazis. There is no music in the cemetery; there is no sound of music in the soundtrack. The musical in general, and this musical in particular, had lived by secularity, the holy sound of profane music, but it would not die for it. For globalizers there is no other place for us. The film knows the only place left to go.

Part II

FAMILY LIKENESSES

Chapter 3

THE ESCAPIST

I began with the admission that upon first reading Michael Chabon's masterpiece, *The Amazing Adventures of Kavalier & Clay*, I was stumped by its Nicene theology of escape, escapism, and escapology, twined over the book's 6 parts, 85 chapters, and over 600 densely worded pages.

Yet the treacherousness of reading Chabon in general is his pose (or, less suspiciously, his posture) of nonsophistication and nonchalance, as if all he ever aspired to do was tell stories. There is enough implicit or explicit self-portraiture of this sort that you begin to doubt it's a pose—or anyway, you begin to doubt that it's possible to comprehend Chabon by disregarding his characteristic mien. (Nathaniel Hawthorne, whom D.H. Lawrence calls "blue-eyed darling Nathaniel," who "knew disagreeable things in his inner soul" but was "careful to send them out in disguise," provides *Kavalier & Clay* with an epigraph from "Wakefield" on escape [Lawrence 81].) Though Chabon worries the encounters of escapology, escape, and escapism throughout the tortuousness of *Kavalier & Clay*, it is also true that in several of his books, his faux-naïf practice is to allude to escapism once and have done with it.

In Chabon's collection of essays *Maps and Legends*, escapism is explicitly contemplated a single time in a chapter appended to the volume as a postscript: a Sunday school teacher of Chabon's youth denounces comic book escapism as a potentially fatal disregarding of reality if you were a child donning a cape to fly out a window. (An anti-Semitic maid restates the teacher's monition in *Kavalier & Clay*.) Chabon advises us that this worry is based on ignorance of the actual source of Superman's ability to fly—Chabon subscribes to the yellow sun theory—and mistakes the function of the cape: "Superheroism is a kind of transvestism, our superdrag serves at once to obscure the exterior self that no longer defines us while betraying, with half-unconscious panache, the truth of the story we carry in our hearts, the story of our transformation, of our rebirth into the world of adventure, of story itself" (Chabon, *Maps*, post script 15).

In his denial of the cape's escapism, in his affirmation of the cape as sign of born-again grace whose works are narrative adventures, Chabon extends Stanley Cavell's argument concerning *It Happened One Night*: "the whole escapade of escape may strike one as a set of games," but the escapade exists to give "*adventurousness . . .* the scope it requires in order to win out" (Cavell 103, 105). But Chabon veers from Cavell's focus on the verbal equality and shared adventures of adult men and women in their remarriages or escapes from bad marriages (though *The Yiddish Policeman's Union* is a perfect Cavellian specimen). When Chabon writes that capes such as Superman's indicate truths carried in our hearts, he is gesturing instead toward juvenile and private truths. Though Chabon's idea of adventure resembles Agamben's—adventures are improvisations and revelations at once—he raises the question of how much its truth can be known even to oneself. The truth is "betray[ed]" with "half-unconscious panache." Chabon's single statement on escapism is less transparent than it pretends; a seemingly ingenuous denial of the dangers of escapism, it disguises its own escape from public view.

Part of the elusiveness of *Maps and Legends* is that it makes two contrary assertions very nearly an equal number of times: what Chabon courts in writing is exposure, and what he seeks in writing is asylum. First ambition: Chabon observes that "telling the truth when the truth matters most is almost always a frightening prospect" (Chabon, *Maps* 155). Second ambition: Chabon admits to carrying out "one search with a sole objective: a home, a world to call my own" (Chabon, *Maps* 158). Both ambitions on one page: "A lonely business, transgressing," but "I guess I was trying to fit in" (Chabon, *Maps* 177). I do not disrespect these interfering intentions as merely self-contradictory, though in fact one feels reading Chabon that he wants to wrong foot or implicate readers as much as he wants to please or appease them. It is possible that Chabon makes us feel at home in his books that he might feel safe from us in his homelessness.

If Chabon is an American, life is easy, though the comfort is discomfiting: "I am an American of course—what else?—but the America in which I feel at home is a kind of planetarium show" (Chabon, *Maps* 158). It's a sentence that takes its home for granted yet slips the rug from under home as such. If America is a planetarium show, being at home in America is to dwell in a lonely projection of home in a void. This is what Baudrillard calls "astral America"—America as an unearthly simulacrum (Baudrillard, *America* 27).

We can make the case for Chabon's consistency by granting that no relation to home can be consistent when home is *unheimlich*, familiar and weird. Finding himself at UC Irvine, Chabon wonders if the prospect of home has been mooted once and for all: "I had no home, and neither, it seemed to me, did anyone—remember that I was living, at the time, in Southern California" (Chabon, *Maps* 178). That is one closed frontier where you can no longer claim an available homestead, a neighborly hometown, an inclusive homeland.

The other is Israel: Chabon recalls the impenetrability for a child at Seder, after 1948, of the phrase "Next year in Jerusalem." "We were happy," he says about his family around the Pesach table, "where we were" (Chabon, *Maps* 161). We can begin to locate Chabon's oeuvre as the superimposition of two closed frontiers, occidental and oriental, which equals the closing of the two alternative, putatively messianic, homelands. *The Yiddish Policeman's Union*, about the failure of a Jewish state in Alaska after a fictionally altered the Second World War, does the critical work of refusing to conceive a plausible Jewish home either as untrammeled frontier or as the Holy Land, either as antitype or type.

In this way, the question of Chabon is the question of all escapism: what to make of a diminished thing, a globalized world, and a world to which you cannot take radical exception because of a twofold failure of national exceptionalism.

A closed geographical frontier, for Chabon, means that any contemporary frontier, as well as any contemporary Zion, must be internal. Chabon characterizes Conan Doyle in an essay as a failed doctor and family man who yearned "for the kind of true adventure that his mother's stories had kindled in him" (Chabon, *Maps* 32). But the empire of adventure was closed to Conan Doyle well before the publication of *The Lost World* in 1912 (not long after the frontier of American civilization seemed closed to Frederick Jackson Turner in 1890), with the upshot, according to Chabon, that Conan Doyle reimagined the metropole of London as if it were a frontier outpost (Chabon, *Maps* 37–9). Chabon has never met an imaginary frontier he did not like, though he does not use the term: in *Maps and Legends* he celebrates the "spaces between genres" (Chabon, *Maps* 12); the "most mysterious border of all" between "wild commercial success and unreserved critical acclaim" (Chabon, *Maps* 13); the "hinterlands" beyond his childhood hometown of Columbia, Maryland, equivalent to the "borders of [his] town and [his] imagination" (Chabon, *Maps* 20); the "borderland of adolescence," in which the wildness of childhood meets the mortal consciousness supplied by one's favorite authors (Chabon, *Maps* 58); the "knife-narrow borderland" between "the Empire of Lies and the Republic of Truth" (Chabon, *Maps* 210). All extant borderlands are internal to Chabon's personal and professional biography. The borders that pertain to writing, especially between "genre" and "serious" fiction or between literature and conventional reality, reduce ultimately to the borderland between childhood and adulthood.

It is structurally reminiscent of what happens to Turner's ideal of perpetual democratic rebirth when the frontier is closed in 1890; Turner seeks a place of regeneration within the occupied civilized world, within, more narrowly, his own profession and biography. No actual frontier, but the free state universities of the Midwest where he began his career, will regenerate American democracy by way of imaginative rejuvenation. Chabon is careful to call his frontiers "borderlands" on the contemporary recognition—also expressible by the notion of "frontier," it seems, until Turner decisively appropriated the term (Turner 239)— that one never stands before an open world of nature happy to be subdued and natives who can be liquidated: there are people dwelling wherever pioneers trek, Arabs in Palestine or Tlingit in Alaska, as *The Yiddish Policeman's Union* observes.

Yet the search inward for a new place once the old places are already fully explored or even settled or even occupied or even colonized or even decimated is the sign of globalization already anticipated by Turner in the 1890s, when the frontier was closed, or by F. Scott Fitzgerald, when he has Nick Carraway define the Midwest as the "returning trains of my youth" (as a direction of motion rather than a region, on Turner's example), but has Gatsby name his Midwestern place of birth, in a hapless improvised lie, as San Francisco. Because civilization advances westward according to eponymous Bishop Berkeley, the globe is circumscribed at the Bay Area.

What is never lacking, what never disappoints, when Chabon turns inward rather than westward for his ideal world is the brave and unadulterated imagination of his youth. The home, which is not one's present physical household, that always beckons is Zion, "where the part of Jerusalem is played by Childhood" (Chabon, *Maps* 175). "Childhood, at its best," Chabon writes, "is a perpetual adventure, in the truest sense of that overtaxed word: a setting-forth into trackless lands that may have come into existence the instant before you first laid eyes on them" (Chabon, *Maps* 21). Childhood is an adventure in messianism, an Agembenian amalgam, an American leaving of home to make possible a Hebraic returning home, though the United States and Israel are no longer its default setting.

This happy synthesis, in which exposure to the world (leaving one's childhood home) is equal to asylum from it (returning to one's home in childhood), is the sort of escapism with which Oscar Hammerstein played, mixing a crowd-pleasing fantasy of escape from a corrupted Austrian homeland with a crowd-pleasing fantasy of perpetual return to the innocence of Austrian edelweiss, both cover-ups for a personal escape from the crowd he was pleasing. As in the case of Oscar Hammerstein, Nazism plays a role in Chabon's distracting his audience from its historical escapism in order to enable his own escape from history, to childhood in Chabon as in death to Hammerstein, after history or before.

Nazism does something like that in *The Final Solution*, which is Chabon's reopening and closing the book on the Sherlock Holmes canon, but it forces the paradoxical assimilation of transgression and restoration, of unsettling and settling, to its maximum intensity. The novel concerns the pilfering of a parrot by way of homicide in 1944; an ancient Holmes is gratifyingly more observant and logical than the modern police and solves the case. The parrot, the only companion of a Jewish German boy rescued by Kindertransport to England, had been parroting a series of numbers, and various murder suspects had variously interpreted their military or financial meaning. Holmes deduces which one committed the crime on the murderer's own erroneous suppositions. So much is a return to the comforts of one's favorite childhood hero and genre. What Holmes never uncovers is the meaning of the numbers. The parrot, according to an ultimate revelation to the reader unnoticed by the characters, turns out to be repeating the boy's recital of the identifying numbers of train cars bound for an extermination camp, one of which carried the boy's parents.

Like *Maps and Legends*, *The Final Solution* takes up escapism, directly, with feigned naivety, once. At a late moment of the book, a Mr. Panicker, Malayalee native of the Indian state of Kerala but currently vicar in the English countryside, is driving in a panic from his vicarage on a stormy day, almost hits Holmes, almost crashes, and swerves to a halt. Before Holmes yanks open the door to demand a ride to London for his investigation of the murder, Panicker questions his own intention: "Where was he going, what was he doing? Had he truly, at long last, escaped? Could one simply roll one's trousers in a grip and walk out?" (Chabon, *Solution* 90). He had been trying to escape, on the undramatic model of Hawthorne's Wakefield, interlocking shames: it is at his vicarage that a boarder has been murdered; his scamp son is a suspect; his wife had once shown a minute attraction to the victim; the vicar himself is therefore a suspect. But having picked up Holmes, and facing a policeman at a military checkpoint who demands to know their business in London,

Panicker seems to forswear his escapist impulse: "Well, we've, er, come to look for a parrot, haven't we?" (Chabon, *Solution* 98). He seems newly intent not on escaping the murder case but on investigating it.

He has not utterly forsworn his escapism, however, because while he stays in England to help Holmes solve the murder, he is as innocent as Holmes of the Final Solution, which is key to the final solution of the case. On the aesthetic level, he does not inhibit *our* escapism, because he chooses to join a fictional detective in a childhood genre rather than realistically face, for our enlightenment, his own condition of exile. He enables our genre for us. Why is Panicker in England? That mainly unasked question needs to be paired with an asked question: What is the parrot doing in England? We are given, elliptically, some of its itinerary from colonized Africa to Germany to England. We do not know how to characterize Panicker's migration from Kerala to a vicarage in England, but the parrot has been plundered. It is not that Holmes can understand British homicide but cannot conceive the Holocaust because he is a remnant of a more rational and civilized era only transiently threatened by crime; it is (as Chabon writes in *Maps and Legends*) that criminal London serves him as a substitute borderland for the one Conan Doyle regrets being too belated to subdue on behalf of empire, which means that Holmes redux is unprepared to follow the clew from German to British imperialism in the Scramble for Africa, as traced by the provenance of the parrot.

We might have worried that when Panicker almost runs over Holmes and almost crashes his car, it is the wrong time for him to wonder, "Had he truly, at long last, escaped?" It is a hypothesis more appropriate to the Wakefield moment he walked out the door, and would have become fully plausible only at a future arrival in Kerala, or wherever he intended to flee. The least appropriate moment, too late and too soon, is when his car is stuck in the driving rain, just after it has almost run into the decisive impediment to his flight. The best theory of his mistimed question is that his local surrendering of escapism to join Holmes in the investigation of a local, exceptional homicide reveals a deeper escapism from European racist history that arrives at the Holocaust. Running from his family and its implication in the world of greed and violence is one escapist act; a more egregious one is conceiving of greed and violence as containable matters susceptible to rationality and justice in a country that has colonized not just parts of Africa but also his homeland.

Does *The Final Solution*, whose title may also make an allusion to the Holmes story called "The Final Problem," share the secret of Auschwitz with readers at the last moment of Holmes's final final problem, when we realize the meaning of the parrot's numbers, as a way of exculpating or condemning escapism, including the adventurous escape from adult moral captivity to the frontier messianism of the juvenile imagination? The Jewish child in the novel does not have that option; he is first glimpsed running away, but not having an adventure.

Readers retain that option. The question is what to make of the imperfect resemblance, the antithesis that resembles a similarity. What is the point of correlating the child's escape and childish escapism? The interest of Chabon's meta-escapism, of his ultrasophisticated ingenuous escapism, is in the impossibility of finding a point from which it can be condemned. Panicker is deputized to play the syntactic role of Maria, the adventurer who makes possible the indistinction of escape and escapism. Escaping Nazism is the paradigm of both escape and escapism: to England for a child, to a childish fantasy of England for adults, even adults from the colonies. Here is the Kafkan way of putting the conceptual predicament: the impossibility of justifying escapism after the Holocaust; the impossibility of anything but escapism after the Holocaust; the impossibility of escape.

Justifying the invocation of Kafka is easy when one of the two protagonists of *The Amazing Adventures of Kavalier & Clay* is Josef Kavalier from Prague, whose name suggests a fusion of the real-world comic book writer and editor Joey Cavalieri and Kafka's Joseph K. Probably Josef Kavalier's attempt to get his brother Thomas out of Prague, funding his berth on a ship purchased by a humanitarian named Hermann Hoffman that is delayed eight months by "reversals, mechanical failures, and governmental tergiversations," is more like K's frustration in *The Castle* than Joseph K's in *The Trial*. *The Ark of Miriam* is finally set to depart Lisbon when Hoffman

> placed a call . . . to the Washington offices of the President's Advisory Committee on Political Refugees, just to make certain that everything was in order. To his astonishment, he had been told by the chairman of the committee that it looked as though all of the children's visas were going to be revoked for reasons of "state security." The head of the State Department's visa section, Breckinridge Long, a man with, as the chairman carefully put it, "certain antipathies," had long since established a clear policy of refusing visas to Jewish refugees. Hoffman knew that perfectly well. But in this instance, he argued, the ship was about to depart, and the "security risks" were three hundred and nineteen children! The chairman sympathized. He apologized.

He expressed profound regret and embarrassment at this unfortunate turn of events. Then he hung up. (Chabon, *Kavalier* 381–2)

The Kafkan involutions end and the *Ark of Miriam* sails from Lisbon. But it does so only by the intervention of Eleanor Roosevelt, which could be read as a tethering of the fiction to history, except that Eleanor Roosevelt is described obliquely as a kind of patrician Super Woman, first glimpsed descending from the sky (i.e., debarking from an airplane), who saves the voyage by the magic of her "invisible hand" (Chabon, *Kavalier* 384). Perhaps this means that only superhero escapism, reliant on the elementary superhero capacities of flight and invisibility, on the vanishing skills of the vanishing mediator, escapes the Kafkan world bureaucracy.

A more purely literary path from Kafka to Chabon is by way of Borges. The essence of Kafka is to consider a particular life as a theorem whose value is to suffer inferences of the system's secreted axioms and definitions; the essence of Borges is to reveal the atrocious elegance of those axioms and definitions. In this sequence, we can think of Chabon as providing axioms, definitions, and a full set of theorems in his often copious novels. The challenge he sets himself in *The Yiddish Policeman's Union*, for example, can be conceived as axioms and definitions: the defeat of the Jews in Palestine after the Second World War, and the granting to them, as a temporary homeland, of US territory in Alaska. Once the dys/Euclidean geometry is posited, Chabon makes deductions.

Borges published "The Garden of Forking Paths" in a collection by that name in 1941. Hugh Everett III submitted his Princeton dissertation with a similar speculation exfoliating from a paradox in quantum physics in 1956, which may mean, if Everett was right in particular, that the philosopher Michel Serres was right in general to argue that even ahistorical truth has its historical conditions, which art may intuit in advance of science. In both the Borges and the Everett multiverses formed by continuously bifurcating histories, two temporal paths may, from time to time, coincide. That is, presumably, Chabon's starting point, so that his Alaskan fantasy state is of interest to the extent that it shares features with our own. In case the objection to identifying Chabon in this way is that that starting point must pertain to all literature—in fact, Chabon considers Philip Pullman's oeuvre by way of Pullman's adaptation of the "many-worlds hypothesis," commenting that "this may or may not be physics, but it is indisputably storytelling" (Chabon, *Maps* 60–1)—then agree that Chabon's distinction is to formalize and materialize his alternative fictional worlds, so that they may seem as axiomatic as Borges's and as granular as Kafka's. If the many worlds-hypothesis is the essence of storytelling, the cape of a superhero is the curtain between adjacent universes.

The donnée (an idea actually floated in the Roosevelt administration) that Alaska rather than Palestine might serve as a homeland for Jews, like an alternative to the parallel postulate, defines the world system of *The Yiddish Policeman's Union* against our own. Like *The Final Solution*, *The Yiddish Policeman's Union* solves a local murder mystery; the two novels only bring into partial view their global meaning, which entails that they only intimate their points of intersection with the globe we inhabit. In the case of the Alaska novel, what is left partly obscured is the place of the murder in a Jewish messianic plot to conquer Palestine tardily, which is subsumed into a Christian and American messianic plot that depends on hijacking the Jewish messianic plot for its fulfillment. This coincides with the path of actual history in which Israeli security relies on an American-Christian fantasy that the Second Coming attends Jewish possession of the Holy Land. On Chabon's view, however, what the two worlds of fiction and history share is the collapse of any possibility of that messianic second coming, which means that both prongs of forking paths testify that there are only forking paths indefinitely: in the Alaskan novel, a plausible and cherished Messiah-candidate submits to his human weakness, withdraws in effect his candidacy, and gets himself killed. The Kafkan phrasing of the prospects of the world according to Chabon can be rewritten in three pronouncements: the impossibility of Jewish messianism; the impossibility of subsuming Jewish into Christian messianism; the impossibility of living without messianism; and one might add a fourth, the impossibility of the Messiah.

Chabon's brimming masterpiece, *The Amazing Adventures of Kavalier & Clay*, begins with his implicit premise that messiahs in America will always be confused with superheroes, which means that messianism will always coincide with escapism. In *The Yiddish Policeman's Union*, the broken false Messiah, reliant on a wheelchair, sarcastically claims that he is "perfectly capable of flying on my own . . . X-ray vision. Bulletproof. The whole bit" (Chabon, *Policeman's Union* 350). The false Messiah's wryness represents one of Chabon's moods. Yet *Kavalier & Clay* is an artistic thought experiment on American messianism; if superheroes fail, so does the imaginary Zion whose Jerusalem is childhood.

We need to recount more of the plot of *Kavalier & Clay*, because Chabon differs from most of his postmodernist peers in locating much of his meaning in his plotting. Josef Kavalier escapes from Prague in 1939 by hiding in a coffin with a deactivated golem, a kind of Jewish

Frankenstein's monster with salvific potential, that is disguised as a merely human corpse on its way to burial in Lithuania. Kavalier can make his escape by way of his mastery of techniques concocted by his escapologist mentor. *Kavalier & Clay* proceeds on the assumption that escape is revocable unless it traverses death, unless it includes escapology as an aspect. The novel refers to this feature of escape as "transformation."

But Kavalier does not consider the escape successful even insofar as he emerges from his coffin and arrives in New York, because he does not get his family out of deadly Prague and reborn in America with him. Like many of the messianic novels of my archive, *Kavalier & Clay* focuses on the salvation of a younger brother, in this case Kavalier's beloved Thomas, left behind in Prague. The world and the world to come overlap at younger brothers. Saving Thomas is one reason Kavalier goes to work for a comic book company and creates his superhero, The Escapist, who is called Tommy Mayflower in his ordinary life, in order to identify the escapist comic book hero with Thomas Kavalier and his antitypical pilgrimage across the Atlantic.

It takes two sections, one third of the book, to get Kavalier and golem to Lithuania, then Kavalier eastward across Asia to California and then New York, into the home of his cousin Sammy Clay, with whom he creates The Escapist, partly an escapologist like himself and partly a golem like his strange deathbed fellow. It takes two more sections of the novel, its middle third, to bring Kavalier and Clay to the brink of good fortune. After two years as a comic book team, Kavalier and Clay are making money. Their success has brought the artist Kavalier into the company of his beloved Rosa, the artistically inclined daughter of a peripheral surrealist, and it has brought Clay into the company of his beloved Tracy Bacon (doubly *treif*, Christian and gay), a radio and briefly a movie actor portraying The Escapist. Clay makes a tentative escape from the closet on the model of Kavalier's emergence from his coffin. It is Rosa who has put Kavalier and his money in contact with her boss Hermann Hoffman, so that Thomas Kavalier has been allowed out of Prague and is on his way across the Atlantic. If his crossing had been the end of the book, it would have completed a perfect, unproblematic union of escape, from Prague or compulsory heterosexuality; and escapology, from the coffin with the golem or from the closet with the actor; and simple escapism, on the power of *The Escapist* comic books, at the intersection of success and love.

Chabon brings the perfection of his story's escapism into contact with all the elements of a nondenominational messianism: a coming, a second coming, a homecoming, a reunion, a resurrection, a revelation, a response to a haunting injustice, a triumph of law over lawlessness or love over law. The nearest typological model may comprise Josef as Moses, who attempts to bring Thomas across the sea; and Sammy as Aaron, priest of the Jewish comic book world, temporary idolater of the golden calf, who speaks to oppressive power on behalf of his cousin; and Rosa as Miriam, who leads Josef to *The Ark of Miriam*. What is the basis of this crypto-sacralization of escape, escapism, and escapology? Money; the golden calf. Add to the picture that Kavalier and Clay work for Empire Comics, whose offices, once the company prospers, are in the Empire State Building, and you can envision the closing of the globe as the infinite opening of the American monetized Promised Land.

In the event, however, capital fails, even as fetishized by Eleanor Roosevelt's invisible hand. On December 6, 1941, *The Ark of Miriam* is torpedoed by a German U-boat, and then hit by a storm; all the children drown. If Thomas ever had a chance, the purchasing of a berth on the Ark of Miriam has destroyed it. Money is the idol of Kavalier's escapology.

That is not the only proof of Kavalier's failure to produce real historical escape by way of redirecting escapology and escapism, though it had worked to remove himself from Prague and to earn a large income. As if to acknowledge that everything is escapist that doesn't contemplate the Holocaust, even in advance, Kavalier confronts the Führer in his art: the sensational cover of the inaugural *Escapist* comic book, two years before America declares war, is a drawing of The Escapist socking Hitler in the face. Kavalier concedes that this is hardly a setback for the historical Hitler, and he goes on to initiate a farcical feud with a real if bedraggled American Nazi, wrecking the pathetic Nazi's disheveled headquarters; but it develops that the Nazi is a fan of The Escapist, from which we infer that escapism is neither a politics nor a theology. Can it discriminate Christs from anti-Christs? (In passing, Chabon records the common observation that the name Superman derives from George Bernard Shaw's translation of *Übermensch*. I wonder if the Man of Steel makes reference to Stalin.) Trying to return from escapism to reality after the death of Thomas, Kavalier undertakes the project of joining the Navy and killing an actual German serving the Reich, which he eventually manages to do. Does an actual duel with an actual participant in the atrocious world mean that Kavalier finally transcends escapism and faces the twentieth century?

It does not: the German, a harmless Antarctic scientist, is targeted because he happens to be the only enemy available to Kavalier, who at the moment of killing the solitary German is himself the only survivor of a more or less pointless Antarctic naval expedition. Kavalier leaves his Gothic Antarctic incarceration with a pilot who dies in the course of their escape; they abandon a station they have been sharing with the frozen corpses of humans and dogs, their late colleagues, dead from carbon monoxide; they had lived at the station for nine months of preparation to fly across Antarctica to kill their German. It is an A. Gordon Pymian allegory of entombment at the bottom of the world, re-enwombment, and rebirth. That is Chabon's very definition of the truth of misidentified escapism, the truth of childhood adventure, the truth of Superman's cape. Yet the mission only accomplishes the death of a mirror German.

Why does Chabon go to exotic lengths to produce escapes that are not escapes, that always devolve to reversible escapism, over and over? Chabon does nothing in *Kavalier & Clay* but describe escapes from tombs and wombs and multiple versions of submarine and subterranean incarceration to other tombs and wombs and versions of reburial by land or sea. Every rebirth by one criterion is re-death by another, requiring another pregnancy and parturition.

There is no mark by which you can determine whether you are on the inside or outside of an imprisonment, as if there were only one prison. We may find ourselves temporarily free, but not by any nonescapist realism about where to seek freedom, and, indeed, after Kavalier kills his polar doppelganger, he wanders out into the crystalline cold seeking his own mirror death, and happens to wander ten miles to an abandoned German station, from which he is eventually rescued, as if an abandoned German. The lesson is the indiscernibility of escapism and escape. The ambiguity entails that everything is escapism, because it is not possible to identify the direction of all mortal dangers and face them, and all one's security in life represents a tomb of its own. Escape if it were possible would be marked by the self-evident distinction of escapism and escape; escapism is identified by the confusion of escapism and escape. No journey escapes that confusion. Escapism succeeds by pretending to be its realistic double, but there is no realistic double.

After being rescued in Antarctica, Kavalier escapes from society in general for a decade or so, unsure on what terms he might reenter the world. When Kavalier had impulsively joined the Navy in 1941, his beloved Rosa was pregnant; after Kavalier's disappearance, Clay had almost immediately married her to assume the fathering of Kavalier's imminent son. Unable to explain, mitigate, or do penance for his family irresponsibility, Kavalier uses his escapist skills, by a chronic irony, to keep himself isolated and unloved and almost immobilized in a single small office of the Empire State Building for half of his missing decade, until 1954, near to Clay's office but unbeknownst to Clay. Escapism and escapology are not modes of escaping death in this case, they enable escaping *to* death, to lonely self-interment in a skyscraper graveyard. At the perpetual borderland of living and dying, characters can only guess which direction, even up or down, is lifeward.

Clay, meanwhile, has been unable to locate the direction from his closet to freedom, which cannot be simply from in it to out of it. On December 6, 1941, Clay is spending an abandoned weekend on the Jersey Shore with his lover Bacon and Bacon's beautifully athletic and sophisticated male friends, when the gay utopian vacation household is raided by police. They are betrayed by a quasi-Nazi American maid, the one who delivers the anti-escapist warning about kids and capes—a token of the real world that Clay flees by not fleeing his real sexuality. Clay hides under a table: a close escape (all the others but one are arrested) that is a kind of submergence or burial; by way of metaphorical death, he escapes literal incarceration and professional destruction. Having momentarily escaped the closet, he climbs under furniture to escape the law. The latter evasion is of course as much escapism as escape. The means of escape is a nightmare version of his half-liberated gayness—he agrees to be sodomized by the policeman who finds him under the table as payment for his freedom—and Clay returns from his sexual dream-turned-nightmare, his sexuality's birth-turned-reburial, to the ordinary, daily prison of pseudo-heterosexual domesticity for the sake of Rosa and Kavalier's son.

When a senatorial investigation into the corruptions of comic books outs Clay at long last, the most knowing character in the book congratulates Clay on his liberation, his freeing by way of his entrapment. In fact, Clay sets out for California at the end of the novel, in search of a society such as the one his lover Bacon had originally invited him to join.

The novel does not tell us how that adventure turns out, which means it does not tell us whether it is an act of escapism or escape. An answer, however, may appear in another of Chabon's fully realized, quasi-realistic, crypto-fantasy novels: *Telegraph Avenue*. Telegraph Avenue, which connects Berkeley and Oakland, attracts Jews by way of the liberal politics and culture of its Berkeley side. Why has Oakland become a privileged destination for African Americans? Here is a bizarre inventing of a Black frontier hypothesis, spoken by a character sufficiently immersed in addled fantasies to inhabit a kind of American comic book truth:

> He described the Pullman porters in terms that conjured up giant sleek-haired warriors of the night, armored in smiles, how they went from place to place, all these little backwoods, boondock towns, seeing the world, carrying like undercover spies, hidden about their persons, all the news of the clandestine world of Black America, the latest records, gossip, magazines, hairstyles, spreading the lore and the styles across the country, to every place where Black people lived, and most of all singing the song of California, to be specific the city of Oakland, where Pullman porters got off the trains to rest on their sunset couches in the houses they bought with the money they wrestled loose from Mr. George Pullman, houses in which they built up families that sent children to college and trade school and eventually to the United States Congress, then getting back onto the trains in the morning to ride south and east, spreading the news of their own prosperity, so that by the time World War II blew up, Oakland was the Hollywood of middle-class black aspiration, except that unlike in Hollywood, once you got to Oakland, you actually stood a chance of making good. (Chabon, *Telegraph* 416)

It almost sounds allegorically plausible, with porters in Pullman cars substituting for students taking trains beyond Chicago in Nick Carraway's version of the Midwest, stretched by Gatsby to San Francisco. But the allegorical linearity disguises a labyrinth of conceptual paths. In case it is not enough that Pullman porters must display the qualities of frontiersmen, giant warriors, unseen spies, armored knights, storytellers, superheroes, the proletariat, and the bourgeoisie at once, the full looniness of this manifestation of American destiny emerges in its Egyptology: the real America is Amenthe-Ra, Land of the West, where souls go to die and be reborn, visited by Pullman porters at night while whites sleep (Chabon, *Telegraph* 415).

Unfortunately, the westward African American escape (to middle-class Oakland), escapism (to Oakland as a counter-Hollywood of warriors, knights, spies, and scouts), and escapology (to Oakland as Amenthe-Ra) has worked out exactly as it has for whites on Turner's hypothesis. The centrifugal, libertarian, violent, democratic spirit of both whites and Blacks, having reached the end of the frontier, turns to the centripetal, exploitative, and hierarchical organizing of enormous wealth by figures who hoard all the available individualism: the most powerful frontiersmen, according to Turner's monomania, become captains of industry. In the instance of West Coast African American life as imagined by *Telegraph Avenue*, a powerful Black football player turns his individual and violent greatness in the direction of monopoly capitalism and chain stores, which threatens the tenuous businesses of Oakland, in one of which a Jew and an African American have worked out a fragile relationship, as have their wives and sons. Meanwhile, in recognition that the frontier has closed, the dreams of several other *Telegraph Avenue* denizens across generations have turned away from Oakland to the world of films, especially to its escapist genres, including blaxploitation. Oakland had supposedly been the bourgeois and practical Californian alternative to Hollywood, but Hollywood regains its role as Jerusalem of African American Zionism when the frontier closes and the only escape is regressive escapism.

Telegraph Avenue makes it hard to sustain much faith in Clay's westward train journey to Hollywood in *Kavalier & Clay* as an escape rather than another phase of the reduction of all escapes to escapism, which equals the reconceiving of all outsides as the insides of something larger, national, and, finally, global, the reorienting of all gestures toward messianic transformation to the direction of eternal repetition. It is at the temptation of death that Hammerstein bids farewell to *The Sound of Music* and to his genius. Once it is proved that the system is corrupt and complete, the only hope is to find a way out of life.

If *Kavalier & Clay* does not end with resurrection, it does not end with death, either: Kavalier's jumping from the roof of the Empire State Building in Tracy Bacon's old Superman costume (stolen from Clay's closet) does not result in his boomeranging up again courtesy of thousands of elastic bands, as intended; when some of the elastic bands snap, he winds up splayed but alive on a lower ledge, his body of course assuming the shape of the letter K. Neither is it triumphantly revealed that Clay makes it as far as California to claim his sexual reorientation and rebirth. He and Kavalier switch positions: Clay not Kavalier disappears in the end; Clay not Kavalier is the book's ultimate escape artist, once Kavalier reappears and domesticates; Clay heads west to California, an adventure against the direction of Kavalier's advent. But if Clay is to find his freedom in imitation of Bacon's prior adventure in California, it seems unpromising that it is enabled by Kavalier's, not Clay's, reappearance wearing Bacon's closeted costume, the drag that indicates a concealed truth. The concealed truth might well be (or might as well be) the desire to have a home, to find a world to call one's own, to fit in. The chiasmic destinies of Kavalier and Clay diagram the contradictory aspects of Chabon's ambition.

We see Clay disappearing; we don't see him reborn in California. The conclusion of the book is as inconclusive as the von Trapp family's arrival at the top of a nondescript peak. More precisely, we can recall the anticlimactic disappearance of Clark Gable and Claudette Colbert into the middle of America, an inland honeymoon silently substituted for their envisaged island paradise, in *It Happened One Night*. For that matter, we can compare Karl Rossmann's arrival at Clayton in *Amerika* (whose actual title would be translated as *The Man Who Disappeared*)—an aptly named, aptly ambiguous waystation for Clay on his adventure to the Nature Theatre of California.

When Kavalier jumps from the observation deck of the Empire State Building, it seems a refutation of Chabon's Sunday school teacher and his novel's quasi-Nazi maid: on the model of comic book superheroes, someone dons a cape, launches himself from a roof, but does not die. He does not ascend, either: it is a peculiarly unmagical escapological feat. Clay takes flight as well, but we don't see where he lands. The best that can be said is that he has not died yet. That bathos seems to be the fate of the comic book aesthetic, as well, which Chabon half-ironically resuscitates and imitates. If Americans have lost their faith in messiahs, they struggle to replace them with fallen superheroes. The empire of Empire Comics in the Empire State Building is not the Kingdom of God. There is no Jerusalem or New Jerusalem; there are only forking paths. History does not have a single liberating direction, no grand narrative, which means that there is no reason that all paths of freedom or salvation should be one path. Every Utopia exists within Dystopia, and every messianic return is a new diaspora. The bathetic comic book performative restoration of childhood by adults is as good as it gets.

Chapter 4

MELLON

Yunior, the narrator of almost all the fiction Junot Díaz has published, may or may not be the only lasting friend of Oscar de León, the actual name of the title character of *The Brief Wondrous Life of Oscar Wao*—not that there is competition from anyone else, only that the limits of Yunior's sincerity cast doubt on the proposition. Through Díaz's three works of fiction, Yunior is increasingly self-aware, self-critical, and literary—but at no point does he safely outgrow his intrinsic self-destructive juvenile selfishness. It may be a display of studied cynicism when he informs us that he moved in with Oscar because it improved his Rutgers housing; it is certain that he roomed with Oscar partly to ingratiate himself with Oscar's sister, Lola, the deepest love of Yunior's superficial life. So it seems merely to mortify Yunior when Oscar provides the inscription for their shared residence:

> Do you know what sign fool put up on our dorm door? *Speak, friend, and enter.* In fucking Elvish! (Please don't ask how I know this. Please.) When I saw that I said: De León, you gotta be kidding. Elvish? Actually, he coughed, it's Sindarin. (Díaz 171–2)

Well, we might want to inquire how Yunior knew the language of the sign, or almost knew it—or even knew there was such a language as Elvish or Sindarin. Yunior begs us not to wonder ostentatiously, so that we cannot fail to be curious. (Actually, by this moment, we easily surmise how he knows. The f-expletive is a token of familiarity.) A short time later, Oscar unsuccessfully attempts suicide by throwing himself off the New Brunswick railroad bridge, and at the end of that phase of Oscar's story, which would seem to entail an end to Yunior's intimacy with Lola's story, Yunior writes: "Not much more to tell. Except this: That spring I moved back in with him. . . . I don't know who was more surprised: Oscar, Lola, or me." "In Oscar's version" of the reunion, Yunior continues, "I raised my hand and said, *Mellon*. Took him a second to recognize the word" (Díaz 199–200). When Oscar does recognize it, he echoes, "Mellon," and perhaps the most moving episode of the novel is complete, an episode that also allows the novel to proceed. What just transpired?

What has happened is that *The Brief Wondrous Life of Oscar Wao* and J.R.R. Tolkien's *Lord of the Rings*, the book that of all the fantasy literature to which Oscar is devoted most determines his imagination, have snapped together. The Tolkien trilogy had been a continuous allusion of the Díaz novel, but this is a literary brotherhood's swapping of blood. In Tolkien's quest story, the nine initial heroes—hobbits, men, an elf, dwarf, and wizard—arrive at immovable doors to a mountain tunnel, inscribed: *The Doors of Durin, Lord of Moria. Speak, friend, and enter.* The dwarf Gimli is confident he knows what the words signify: "If you are a friend, speak the password, and the doors will open, and you can enter" (Tolkien I, 342–3). The wizard Gandalf agrees, but he cannot summon the magic word. At wit's end, it finally occurs to Gandalf that the magic formula is the word "friend"—the sign means, in effect, "Speak 'friend' and enter" (Tolkien I, 346). "Mellon" is Elvish, or Sindarin, for friend.

The promiscuous, muscular, masculinist Yunior wishes we would forget that he was as devoted a reader of *Lord of the Rings* as the nerdy, wordy, fat, virginal Oscar—but at a sacred moment, he is more attuned to the Tolkien books even than Oscar, and it seals their friendship in the act of sealing the fraternity of the two books. The assimilation takes one of the essential points of *Lord of the Rings* and imports it into *Oscar Wao*: that the sufficient advantage of good over evil is its embedding in durable male bonds.

The theme of male friendship is made explicit in both books at a scene of translation. A human and an intertextual alliance can be formed in one gesture because friendship is inspired interpretation; we might begin to wonder at this point what kind of friendship is possible between the novel itself and its interpreters. Here is a difference between the books: *Lord of the Rings* takes care to translate *Mellon*; *Oscar Wao* does not. If readers of *Oscar Wao* have an unfading memory of their middle school obsession with Tolkien, their recognition of the recognition scene may only take a moment longer than Oscar's. For other readers, it will take the length of a trip to Google, if they care to take it. On the understanding that friendship is the potency of male virtue, what are we to make of a book that pays its debt to another book in the species of eternal friendship but does it so obscurely as to threaten its obligation to amicable readers? That is the issue most decisive in categorizing the book as escapism or not.

I, myself, do not know what to make of such a book—if I am right about it, I am meant not to know. One assumption might be that by intersecting *Lord of the Rings*, not to mention scores of other classics of genre fiction, comics, sci-fi films, and video games, *Oscar Wao* is simply a fantasy quest. This would be hasty for at least two reasons. For one thing, the book has a modern, identifiable political setting. Footnotes on Trujillo and Balaguer and lesser Dominican malefactors keep the book anchored both in history and historiography—and when characters from Oscar's family chronicle interact with Trujillo in person or by proxy, narrative and scholarly apparatus flow into one another. This tends to make the history read like metafiction, but it also makes the fiction read occasionally—admittedly—like a remedial text in Caribbean Studies 101.

For a second thing, the book's violence is minutely tabulated (often in terms of injury points on the body) and unglamorous. Oscar's grandfather Abelard is beaten up by thugs of Trujillo, who is enraged to be kept from possessing the more beautiful of Abelard's two daughters. Both of them, Oscar's missing aunts, are assassinated off-stage. A third sister, Beli, eventually Oscar's mother, born after the start of her father's fourteen-year imprisonment and torture, is severely burned as a child by a guardian and beaten up by thugs in the employ of Trujillo's sister, the wife of a Trujillo minion whom Beli loves. The assault on Beli is summed as "167 points of damage," with this stone-faced addendum: "was there time for a rape or two? I suspect there was" (Díaz 147). The victims are usually innocent, but their suffering is not nobly sacrificial, except perhaps Oscar's climactic assassination, and their deaths are not beautifully or excitingly or even pruriently graphic.

Categorizing *Oscar Wao* as a fantasy quest in the manner of *Lord of the Rings* would be definitively wrong. There are hundreds of violent deaths in the Tolkien trilogy, but only one hero, fatally compromised by lust for the Ring, dies before his time. Its characters fight evil with inherited or cultivated nobility of heart, whereas Oscar's family only struggles, with partial success, to survive it. Tolkien's heroes are willing to sacrifice their lives to the cause of the freedom of the West of Middle-earth, whereas the characters in *Oscar Wao* never imagine that they might have an effect on anything grander than one another, and that effect, however well intended on most occasions, is often not a benefit.

There is no point, in short, in trying to demonstrate that *Oscar Wao* is escapism in the simple, nearly unqualified mode of *Lord of the Rings*. But the conjunction at the word "Mellon" means something about the family likenesses of escapism, simple and complex, and to begin to say what, we need to look at both works as analyses of power. It is in this respect that the resemblance, though imperfect, is most uncanny.

For both books, power is miscellaneous at the same time that it is binary. It is true that in *Lord of the Rings*, Sauron the Dark Lord, Saruman, ring wraiths, and orcs are evil and that hobbits, elves, dwarves, the Ents, and Gandalf are nobly, steadfastly, or ingenuously good. There is some fraying at the edges, some tempting of the good and passing from good to evil, but the demarcation generally holds. It is also true that goodness exists in *Oscar Wao*, in pretty much unmitigated form in Oscar and family protector La Inca, in mitigated form in Lola, in embarrassed disguise in Yunior; and Trujillo is explicitly named the novel's Dark Lord, surrounded by henchmen. But the center of goodness in both books is less apparent than the center of evil: there is a Lord, in both works, of Evil, but not a God of Mercy and Justice, at least not conspicuously. Because the center of goodness is absconded, there is no reason to assume, in either work, that the ultimate victory of goodness is assured, except insofar as one guesses the generic inevitabilities. We are told at the outset, or before the outset, that Oscar Wao's life has two primary aspects, brevity and wondrousness. We do not know how to weigh them.

The asymmetry of good and evil in the two books, the capacity of both books to name the summit of evil but not of good, though goodness may have a summit, has this effect: it is impossible to measure the power of Power. I mean: it is impossible to know, in any conflict, who or what force will prevail; there is no teleology or theory of history in either book that would guarantee victory to the righteous. This means, in turn, that it is impossible to know what power, essentially, is—an influx of the creativity of the world, an influx of the destructiveness of the world, or a neutral manifestation of physics and biology. Powers exist, even superpowers. But what is power? That it could be anything (that there might be a superhero or super-villain with any superpower) may be the essence of fantasy fiction.

In *Lord of the Rings*, this sort of passage is frequent: "[T]here is a power in Rivendell to withstand the might of Mordor, for a while: and elsewhere other powers still dwell. There is power, too, of another kind in the Shire. But all such places will soon become islands under siege, if things go on as they are going. The Dark Lord is putting forth all his strength" (Tolkien I, 249). It is hard to see a distinction between power on one side, and might or strength on the other. It is also difficult to discern why power on the side of freedom should come in regional flavors. So does power on the side of slavery: "The power of the Black

Land grows and we are hard beset. . . . We were outnumbered, for Mordor has allied itself with the Easterlings and the cruel Haradrim; but it was not by numbers that we were defeated. A power was there that we have not felt before" (Tolkien I, 275).

Readers can infer several predicates of power: it has unlimited varieties; its source cannot be ascertained; new varieties of it are born into or revealed to the world on occasion; it cannot be measured except in relation to other powers, but the comparison may involve different quantities or different qualities. As much as Tolkien divides the world into impenitent evil and tempted but persevering good, he describes Middle-earth as a field of contending, multiplying, miscellaneous forces, with victory to one or the other side, at least temporarily, dependent on the marshaling of available power or the unveiling of new forms of power rather than on history's arc.

There is the Dark Lord Sauron as centralizer of evil power, but though he is an eminence on the side of evil with no equivalent on the side of good, he is not responsible for the bad faith of Saruman, which results from his own centrifugal ambition, or the mischief of orcs, who are nasty without prompting. The miscellany of kinds of power includes: the power of wisdom possessed by wizards and others; magic powers possessed by wizards and others; the power of observation possessed especially by wizards, humans, elves, and dwarves, in different ways; the power of rhetoric; the power of animate nonhuman or humanoid but intentional actors such as trees and the wind; the power of inanimate but intentional objects such as swords and rings; the power of the temptation of power. It is against the corrupting power of the One Ring that the willpower of humans or hobbits is exercised: "And sometimes [Frodo's] right hand would creep to his breast"—where the Ring usually resides, tied around his neck—"and then slowly, as the will recovered mastery, it would be withdrawn" (Tolkien III, 227).

It is difficult to absorb this miscellany into the binary of the tale: there is magic on both sides; high rhetorical force on both sides; organic and inorganic power on both sides; even impressive displays of will on both sides. Power itself remains impenetrable. It is often only by reiterated regret at defaulting to the concept of luck that characters allude to some superior but unnamable moral tendency of the world. "In the end Bilbo won the game [of riddles], more by luck (as it seemed) than by wits," and thus came to possess the Ring instead of Gollum (Tolkien I, 13). Tom Bombadil says that "just chance brought me" to save the hobbits from malign trees, "if chance you call it" (Tolkien I, 142). Or as Elrond obscurely puts it, addressing a council: "You have come and are here met, in this very nick of time, by chance as it may seem" (Tolkien I, 271). Only these unspecified second thoughts suggest a power behind goodness, an unnamed interested God. Tolkien said that the trilogy was unconsciously religious and Catholic at first drafting, "consciously so in the revision" (Pearce 100). Characters in the book have second thoughts about the relation of luck to providence because, apparently, so does the book. The nature of power floats between conscious and unconscious claims.

The miscellany and lumpy disposition of power in *Oscar Wao* may be even more surprising: more overtly political than its British precursor, its sense of power might have been more overtly partisan. The book does trace the curse of Dominican history and the world to "the arrival of Europeans on Hispaniola" (Díaz 1)—the book's equivalent to "There is no bad luck in the world but whitefolks" in its American precursor, *Beloved* (Morrison, *Beloved* 89). Nor are the two US invasions of the Dominican Republic in the twentieth century neglected. Yet very soon after the account of the European and US sources of Dominican misfortune, Yunior traces the course of the curse back to the United States by way of Trujillo's involvement in the Kennedy assassination and the curse's own power to avenge in the case of Vietnam, payback for LBJ's invasion of the D.R. in 1965. In both cases, the curse is called by its African name, fukú, but instances of it are practically and theoretically various.

All of this is laid out in the first few pages of *Oscar Wao*, a prolegomenon by Yunior as the text's principal narrator and metaphysician, who has doubts about fukú's existence during the narrative but none at all in its frame. The story is preceded by a remarkably nonpartisan description of fukú: the United States like Columbus himself is as much cursed as it is the fount of the curse of others, or, more accurately, it is cursed to the degree that it is the curse of others. As opposed to an asymmetry of imperial powers and their colonies or satellites or unlucky neighbors, or of racists and people of color, or of rich and poor, the book begins by dividing power into fukú and its contrary, zafa, and both powers can be found on both sides of all binaries. Fukú, in particular, is pervasive; the globe is globalized by it. The book registers the racism of whites toward Dominicans, but it is as willing to condemn the racism of Dominicans toward Haitians, and rather more invested in recognizing the bigotry of the attractive toward the repulsive. And all winners in one theater of interpersonal, racial, or national operations turn out to be losers in the next, even the sexually attractive—fukú is inevitably double-edged.

Zafa seems a somewhat weaker explanatory concept and force. As fukú is sometimes represented in the text by a man with no face, zafa makes momentary appearances as a magical mongoose—yet the golden mongoose appearing before Oscar on the train bridge from which he attempts suicide cannot prevent the leap. Power may be as miscellaneously arrayed in *Oscar Wao* as in *Lord of the Rings:* the book is a detailed investigation into the physical and financial power of men over women; the seductive and judgmental power of women over men; the social power of light skin; the cultural prestige that sometimes accrues to dark skin; the economic and military force of the United States; the cultural and aesthetic force of the D.R. Occasionally, the book isn't sure how to assign a narrative event to a conceptual dichotomy: about the pregnancy of Socorro after the incarceration of her husband Abelard, which eventuates in Beli's birth and the continuity of the Cabrals, Yunior writes: "Zafa or Fukú? You tell me" (Díaz 242). Three generalizations survive the complexity: power is everywhere; power is nonpartisan; power has its own purposes, which may be inscrutable.

This may seem charming to white American bourgeois male readers who expected a less symmetrical judgment on their racism, their sexism, their classism, or on US imperialism. Though the book is rather more dubious about zafa than fukú, it names the benign world principle zafa as its own impetus: the theoretical opening concludes, "I wonder if this book ain't a zafa of sorts. My very own counterspell" (Díaz 7). This hope or hypothesis may owe something to Norman Mailer's *Why Are We in Vietnam?*

> We will never know [Mailer writes] if primitive artists painted their caves to show a representation, or whether the moving hand was looking to placate the forces above and the forces below. Sometimes, I think that the novelist fashions a totem just as much as an aesthetic, and his real aim, not even known necessarily to himself, is to create a diversion in the fields of dread, a sanctuary in some of the arenas of magic. . . . By such logic, the book before you is a totem, not empty of amulets for the author against curses, static, and the pervasive malignity of our electronic air. (Mailer 4–5)

A white American bourgeois male may cherish a pathetic hope that the story promises a doubled diversion, a mirror escapism, zafa all around: absolution for the curse he enables; relief from the retributive curse he suffers. But I want to argue that the book is escapist only in the interesting way: that we readers hold the power from which escapism seeks escape, and that Díaz's zafa like Mailer's amulets exists for the protection of the author.

Oscar Wao does not seek to escape us in the way of Utopianism— by way of voyaging to another society in which sovereignty works a different way, where political and economic power is justly distributed. When Oscar ends his travels in Santo Domingo, the capital of Trujillo's machocracy, the scene of three generations of brutal violence against his family and himself, we are reminded that Frodo's epic quest is to Sauron's Mordor, to the place where the One Ring, which can deliver, by merely persisting in the world, the ultimate triumph of evil, was forged.

Both journeys are thus anti-Utopian, still less are their returns home messianic, but the cause of the anti-Utopian and anti-messianic impulse is different. *Lord of the Rings* is nostalgic for the world as it has been, at least for hobbits: mild, benign, traditional, familiar, oral, frank, uncontaminated, unambitious, and preindustrial. There are representations, in *Oscar Wao*, of alluring beauty in Hispaniola, visible in its bodies and beaches, but Oscar, unlike Frodo's simple hobbit companion Sam, cannot return to it as a lifelong dwelling place. The anti-Utopianism of *Oscar Wao* depends instead on the failure, not the undesirability, of Utopia. For a couple of characters, the ideal or oneiric alternative is Cuba, though that means, depending on the character, either pre- or postrevolutionary Cuba. Other characters dream of Mexico or France. Oscar's sister Lola dreams of Ireland: "the plan was that we would go to Dublin . . . . I would become a backup singer for U2 . . . and Oscar would become the Dominican James Joyce" (Díaz 68).

Later, Lola determines to emigrate to Japan—"it's going," she enthuses, "to be *amazing*." Yunior challenges her: "What the hell is a Dominican going out to Japan for?" "You're right," Lola retorts: "Why would *anyone* want to go *anywhere* when they have *New Jersey*" (Díaz 197). It's a convincing rejoinder, except that leaving one place is never, in this book, arriving someplace superior. The Cabral or de León story is a version of slave narratives in which a brutal legal enslavement is fled from south to north, only to engage more subtle and unofficial confinements. It is the Utopian Lola who pronounces the book's final anti-Utopian verdict on foreign travel: "if these years have taught me anything it is this: you can never run away. Not ever. The only way out is in." Yunior adds: "And that's what I guess these stories are all about" (Díaz 209).

"The only way out is in" becomes Oscar's motto when he returns, in what will be the last best hope of his quest for heterosexual sex, for the wondrousness of his brief life, to the Dominican Republic, where he falls in love with a prostitute who has herself returned from unsatisfactory elsewheres. But it is difficult to determine where he winds up, incarcerated or free, even dead or alive, because it is hard to assess where the book ends. For one thing, it keeps ending. Oscar is assassinated—all you can ask for in the way of closure. The chapter that follows, the final chapter with both a number and name, is called "The End of the Story," and its first sentence is "That's pretty much it," as if to agree that a violent premature death, as comeuppance for the book's sexual and narrative consummation, has the ring of finality (Díaz 323). Perhaps we have learned, though, from previous rhetorical shrugs ("that's pretty much it" recalls "not much more to tell") not to be seduced by the apparent guilelessness and, in fact, the final named and numbered chapter is followed by an unnamed, unnumbered chapter that begins, "It's almost done. Almost over. Only some final things to show you" (Díaz 329). This chapter ends with a quotation from Alan Moore and David Gibbons's comic series *Watchmen*: "Nothing ever ends" (Díaz 331). These valedictory anti-valedictory words are followed by a named but unnumbered chapter called "The Final Letter," which contains a posthumous communication from Oscar received in New Jersey and the promise of another package with all of Oscar's writing, though that culmination never arrives.

All of this mirror self-consciousness seems a sufficiently explicit, or overexplicit, demonstration of mise en abyme nonclosure—even statements of closure delay it—that we may subdue our unthinking readerly desire for an ending worthy of the name, comic or tragic or tragicomic. The problem is that once we identify Yunior as a trickster narrator, we concede that we don't know whether his shrugging closure or his labored disclosure is his truer impulse or more transparent pose. His prose may be all pose. Thus we arrive, disarmed, at one of the most effective, affecting, ingenuous or disingenuous final gestures in the history of novels. In Oscar's last, posthumously received letter, he narrates the final overcoming of his virginity. For now, I will quote only the concluding words of the story, bequeathed by Oscar to the story as his last testament: "So this is what everybody's always talking about! Diablo! If only I'd known. The beauty! The beauty!" (Díaz 335).

One grants, grudgingly, all the qualifications one has to make as a responsible critic before accepting these words as the consummation of the story. These are the book's last words only because Yunior put them there—the words were written before the final narrated events of the story (we hear something of the continuing post-Oscar lives of Yunior and Lola and offspring: nothing ever ends). In fact, Oscar's last words are not Oscar's last words. His final word, spoken before his execution to his assassins, is nothing like these words, and perhaps Oscar himself would not have appended these words to his life if he had known he would be murdered shortly after writing them by the enemies of beauty. Because his life's work in literature never arrives, we are reading Yunior's book about Oscar rather than Oscar's own, and it is only an illusion that Oscar's last words as selected by Yunior are his final contribution to literary history. Moreover, if Kurtz's last words from *Heart of Darkness* resonate too loudly, they have the effect of spoiling the experience: Oscar is recording a successful erotic relationship that gets him, for once, outside texts (though he is recording it, though he is in fact making the allusion).

But it is fair to say that if these words are not taken with wholeheartedness as well as guardedness, the stature of the book is diminished. Without these final words, no BBC poll would conclude that *Oscar Wao* was the best novel, through 2015, of the twenty-first century. Does this mean we have to drop our suspiciousness?

The first question to be raised about the book's climactic exultation is what causes Oscar to exclaim, "The beauty! The beauty!" The question is how to get so much from the satisfaction of desire that it becomes joy—a joy of man's desiring. Here are the facts: Oscar, in the Dominican Republic, falls in love with Ybón, once a prostitute and now kept by a Trujillo underling called only the (lowercase) capitán. Ybón treats Oscar unexpectedly like an intimate friend, though not as a lover; the capitán, unconcerned by the nuances of their intimacy, has Oscar beaten to the verge of death, as well as Ybón. Oscar retreats to the United States, then with perfect heroism or foolhardiness returns to the Dominican Republic. He is there for twenty-seven days, during which Ybón mostly resists his protestations and entreaties, but then they have, at long last, sexual intercourse. In retribution, the capitán's thugs take Oscar away to shoot him. They ask him to translate "fuego" into English; Oscar does so, committing suicide as an act of translation. This is the closing correspondent of the opening "Mellon" moment, and it is possible that this male-male bilingual violence undoes the "Mellon" homosocial multilingual concord.

Thus, we must examine the virtue of heterosexual love rather than homosocial triangulation. It is, however, unclear precisely how to get a read on Ybón, Oscar's entire love-making sample. One doesn't hold her profession against her as much as her irresponsibility with respect to the farmed-out children she has reproduced along the way; on the other hand, one feels kindly toward her for suffering Oscar to make a claim on her affection. What it probably all cancels out to is that Ybón exists in the tropics of womanhood, not at the time-honored polar extremes, though she has been universally available to others and purely unavailable to Oscar. As unsatisfying as her mediocrity may be to readers long awaiting Oscar's induction into heterosexual consummation, it does have the corollary that whatever beauty Oscar finds in intercourse, its source is not located uniquely in Ybón.

It might have been located, at least by Oscar, in any girl or woman, because Oscar's attitude toward every female he glimpses is worshipful, which means that its source is Oscar. His sister tries to encourage and coach him from his teenage years onward: "'Oscar,' Lola warned repeatedly, 'you're going to die a virgin unless you start *changing*.'" "Don't you think I know that," Oscar responds, making his finest witticism of the novel: "Another five years of this and I'll bet you somebody tries to name a church after me" (Díaz 25). Lola has two friends in her youth who incite Oscar. One of them tells Oscar he is cute, and the other one says, "Yeah, right. Now he'll probably write a book about you." Yunior observes: "These were Oscar's furies, his personal pantheon, the ones he dreamed about and most beat off to and who eventually found their way into his little stories" (Díaz 27). The females in Oscar's vicinity are always transformed, transmuted, apotheosized: they are turned into onanistic and oneiric images, into icons, and into literature. He doesn't change, so he changes *them*.

The terms "furies" and "pantheon" suggest that Oscar's goddesses are pagan, yet his joke about his virginity means that something of Christianity still flowers in Oscar's hothouse psyche; there is an unassimilated Catholicism in the novel as a whole. Mainly it is embodied by La Inca, protector of generations of the Cabral/de León family, whose organizing of group prayers for Bela's and Oscar's lives, after they are nearly beaten to death, may be what saves them. This would seem to be an example of benevolent force independent of zafa and the mongoose, which perform their miracles well outside Christian theology and iconography. Yet Yunior or Díaz is not sure whether zafa might not be the inclusive term, and answered prayers merely an instance of it. Christian prayer is another example of the multiplicity and indefiniteness of force in the novel, akin to that in *Lord of the Rings*, where Christianity also lurks. We don't know how to put Christian and pagan force into relation.

We should not equate the two books too quickly on the score of residual Christianity. For one thing, there is just about no sex in *Lord of the Rings*, so no Christian or pagan attitudes about its power to compare.

Among its heroes are the Ents, men grown to resemble trees, who have been forgivably abandoned by their Entwives and will never again produce semiarboreal offspring. Other heroic species remain tacitly reproductive, but the entire book seems to prefer the noble sacrificing of the future to participating in its decline. (The book concludes with the two most noble hobbits, along with the book's one wizard, granting the simultaneous completion of their lives and their moral epoch.) Sex reappears in the book almost entirely in the guise of the most genital landscape ever created in fiction: an environment of engulfing trees and spiders and abysses, and forbidding mountains and towers. The sexual world for Dominican men can appear just that ubiquitous, threatening, and provocative—and Trujillo's sister is called a "shelob," after the spider-monster of *Lord of the Rings* (Díaz 139)—yet in the Caribbean, genitalia are not surreally displaced.

Still, there is a connection between the two books: all ladies are objectively dazzling, beautiful, and powerful to the point of divinity in *Lord of the Rings*. And all women are subjectively dazzling, beautiful, and powerful to the point of divinity in Oscar's imagination in *Oscar Wao*. These almost invariant female qualities seem consistent with feminine unapproachability or invincibility in both works. Yet the case I want to make is that Oscar's prolonged saintly virginity, to which he fears the names of churches will testify, is of a piece with his long-standing and finally realized desire to have sex with a woman. The relevant connection is anticipated by Tolkien's precursor G.K. Chesterton in his little biography of St. Francis of Assisi, the troubadour who became a *jongleur*, as he said, *de Dieu*.

> There was a strain in the southern romance that was actually an excess of spirituality . . . . The love [expressed in troubadour poetry] was not always animal, sometimes it was so airy as to be almost allegorical. The reader realizes that the lady is the most beautiful being that can possibly exist, only he has occasional doubts as to whether she does exist. Dante owed something to the Troubadours, and the critical debates about his ideal woman are an excellent example of these doubts. . . . [The] idea of Beatrice as an allegorical figure is, I believe, unsound; it would seem unsound to any man who has read the *Vita Nuova* and has been in love.

> But the very fact that it is possible to suggest it illustrates something abstract and scholastic in these medieval passions. But though they were abstract passions they were very passionate passions. (Chesterton 79)

It is not a large leap from profane to sacred worship; Oscar's "adoration" for one woman is "like the light of a new sun" (Díaz 185). St. Francis and St. Oscar may leap in opposite directions, but the interval is the same.

I am saying that Oscar achieved his sainthood after all, in losing his virginity, even to a woman who does not merit the worshiping. But that is not quite right; there is still a mystery in his final quoted words. These words are quoted but not within quotation marks, and come at the end of Yunior's paraphrasing of Oscar's posthumous letter, with the effect that the final words seem to be from three voices—author, author's representative in the text, and holy ghost—concentered only at this final moment. Again: "So this is what everybody's always been talking about! Diablo! If only I'd known. The beauty! The beauty!"

The puzzle is in the words, "If only I'd known." If only Oscar had known what sex is, the beauty of sex, then what? Readers, perhaps overwhelmed by the tragic ecstasy of this climax, might be excused if they think something like the following: then Oscar would have fought his way to successful consummation earlier. But Oscar had never delayed it intentionally. On the contrary, he had been seeking it actively, passionately, for a lifetime. Nor is there any sense of his learning more accurately where to find it or how to achieve it. What is the object of knowledge at the very end of the ultimate ending of the book?

Here is a full quotation of Yunior's paraphrase of what Oscar learned, with its climax in the directly quoted exclamation that transcends quotation marks:

> [W]hat really got him was not the bam-bam-bam of sex—it was the little intimacies that he'd never in his whole life anticipated, like combing her hair or getting her underwear off a line or watching her walk naked to the bathroom or the way she would suddenly sit on his lap and put her face into his neck. The intimacies like listening to her tell about being a little girl and him telling her that he'd been a virgin all his life. He wrote that he couldn't believe he'd had to wait for this so goddamn long. (Ybón was the one who suggested calling the wait something else. Yeah, like what? Maybe, she said, you could call it life.) He wrote: So this is what everybody's always talking about! Diablo! If only I'd known. The beauty! The beauty! (Díaz 334–5)

From the passage in its entirety, we learn that what everybody has always been talking about is not sex but what sex enables, and what sex enables might be called, in various senses, nakedness. But "The beauty! The beauty!" does not refer precisely even to that: it refers to life, which is how the title of the novel can call Oscar's brief life, viciously truncated, "wondrous." The paradox is that Oscar waited almost too long to find out neither the beauty of sex nor the beauty of intimacy that sex made possible, but the retrospective and retroactive beauty of his life made visible by the intimacy that sex made possible. He was not, it turns out, waiting for something else full stop. He was waiting for something else to assure him that his waiting was not for something else, that it was equally life. One of the benefits that post-virginity confers is redeeming the story of your virginity. Post-virginity is the only condition that makes possible containing virginity and nonvirginity in your vision, reconciling innocence and experience.

At this moment, we seem no longer to inhabit the zone of ambiguity between troubadour poetry and Christian prayer: it is not so much that Oscar continues to worship Ybón as that he has found something sacred in their leveling. "Life" is the term of art for what they share in equal measure. However, rejection and renunciation are preserved even in Oscar's final sexual success, in his long-postponed vita nuova. What he renounces is the Caribbean male conception of sex as colonization; the virtue of friendship can be transferred to heterosexuality.

What Oscar has embraced is powerlessness, as St. Frances embraced poverty: "It is necessary to realize that St. Francis was talking the true language of the troubadour when he said that he . . . had a most glorious and gracious lady and that her name was poverty" (Chesterton 79). This is the point at which we can make one final reference to *Lord of the Rings*, which also counsels the passionate embrace of powerlessness. Each time Frodo needs the Ring and its power of invisibility even for the sake of evading evil, the access of power is itself evil. It is his weakness that has saved him all along from Sauron, the Dark Lord, who cannot bring himself to realize that his enemy in the world is a "halfling," a hobbit, of no great stature, literally or figuratively. Sauron makes the further conceptual blunder of not comprehending that what he needs to combat is not an individual rival for the power of the Ring but a communal intention to destroy that power. This is a failure of recognition that is intrinsic to his evil. It is corollary of his friendlessness, the Achilles heel of heels. He makes the strategic error of concentrating on the apparent Armageddon between good and evil that is taking the form of siege and attack while two hobbits destroy his dream of conquest by walking, riding, and climbing along, escaping attention.

The trick for Frodo and his loyal companion Sam is to avoid attracting notice without invisibility. Invisibility, as Augustine and others know, is a sacrilege. It is the desire to be God in his absconded omnipotence, the mortal sin of authors. But it is possible in *Lord of the Rings* to stay small, to avoid the sight of sin and not the sight of God by pious insignificance rather than presumptuous invisibility. The distinction between invisibility and imperceptibility is the distinction between sin and salvation: "Therefore," Paul tells the Corinthians, "I take power in infirmities, in necessities, in persecution, in distresses for Christ's sake: for when I am weak, then am I strong" (*King James Version* 2 Cor. 12:9).

Is it also possible in *Oscar Wao* to avoid exposure to sin by modesty rather than invisibility? The problem is defined in exactly the same language: Sauron is "the Eye"; Trujillo is "the Eye." *Oscar Wao* instructs us to consider any agency, including Trujillo, Trujillo's entourage, Trujillo's underlings, and ordinary Dominican males who take Trujillo as their model in how to take brutal possession of women, as "the Eye" in its division, multiplication, and dispersal. "Ten million Trujillos is all we are," Lola says (Díaz 324). In that case, the end of Oscar Wao and the end of *Oscar Wao* are skewed. The end of the book suggests that what Oscar learned is how to avoid power even in heterosexual intercourse: he achieves one of the traditional goals of escapism, queer heteronormativity, as in the gender swapping of Maria and Captain von Trapp, a function of the power of weakness. In caring more about the pre- and postorgasmic than the orgasm, Oscar prefers the beauty of the meaningfully uneventful. This is the book's hope for freedom and equality within the heterosexual paradigm of all power.

Yet Oscar's intercourse with Ybón lends him just enough significance in the eyes of the Eye that it entails not the closure of the book but the assassination of the book's title character. This may be the point where the escapism of *Oscar Wao*, its fantasy that power, like the power of the Ring, can be subtracted from the world, that there is no principle in moral physics of the conservation of force, runs into the novel's naturalism, whose premise is the expansion and concentration of power and thus the expanding disparity of victors and victims. Or say that it is the nature of escapism to run escapism into something that needs to be realistically escaped. Oscar's death both denies and enables the novel's escapism. It denies it because Oscar cannot hold onto the life that Ybón advises him to call "life"; it enables it, in the manner of *The Sound of Music*, as the only way of preserving the wondrousness of that life against the return of the desire for significance. If you cannot eliminate the Ring from the world by way of a Utopian state or a messianic kingdom, you have to curtail the desire to snatch at rings. In *Lord of the Rings*, that may take the form of a desire to be the hero of oral epics, a temptation in oral cultures, we learn from the book, even of the lowly. In *Oscar Wao*, it may take the form of a desire to be a great writer, shared by Yunior and Oscar.

This raises the final relationship issue of *Oscar Wao*, which is not the political relationship of the powerful to the weak or the interpersonal relationship of the weak to the weak, but the fluctuating professional relationship of author to readers. Will the temptations of authority, including the temptation to be unseen and all-seeing, be the undoing of the book's escapist vision of the beauty of powerlessness?

The novel is unreadable. The ideal reader would be required to understand Tolkien languages, plus (Dominican demotic?) Spanish, plus English—plus allusions to scores of books, films, comics, and video games, plus some Yiddish and Hindi. Even the outsourced internet gloss omits the majority of important special terms. In their relationship to each other, Oscar and Yunior share all necessary languages and texts, but the basis of their friendship cannot be duplicated by Díaz and readers. At the speaking of "Mellon," the moment of the bonding of Oscar and Yunior, Diaz and readers may feel estranged, even after readers return from their Google search. For a monolingual speaker of English, the book is an exercise in feeling some of the humiliation of nonnative speakers of English in the United States; and for academic readers, the book is an exercise in feeling multidimensional limits to their erudition. There seems less benefit in making nonnative speaking nonacademics feel humbled by references to Yeats, Melville, and Conrad.

And there would be less benefit in including at least one joke in the book that is only for academics. Here is a slightly abbreviated retelling of one of Yunior's jokes, which concerns the pummeling of Oscar for his love of Ybón:

> It's not clear whether they intended to scare him or kill him. . . . All I know is it was the beating to end all beatings. It was the Götterdämmerung of beatdowns, a beatdown so cruel that Camden, the City of the Ultimate Beatdown, would have been proud. (Yes sir, nothing like getting smashed in the face with those patented Pachmayr Presentation Grips.) He *shrieked*, but it didn't stop the beating; he begged, and that didn't stop it, either; he blacked out, but that was no relief. . . . He tried to drag himself into the cane, but they pulled him back! It was like one of those nightmare eight-a.m. MLA panels: *endless*. (Díaz 298–9)

Actually, the setup of the joke is largely Greek to me. I had no advance knowledge that Camden is the capital of beatdowns. I had to look up

"Pachmayr Presentation Grips," from which I seem to understand that these are handgun grips of a particularly prized kind, designed by a Mr. Pachmayr. The joke is a microcosm of the polyvalent unreadability of the novel. But the punchline of the joke is intended to be legible for a very small number of people like me, and that we have been interpellated is attested to by the wild inappropriateness of the joke. The inappropriateness is not merely in the tasteless rhetorical bathos. The inappropriateness is narratological: we had not been given reason to assume that Yunior had ever attended a convention of the Modern Language Association.

The book is written to be available at different moments to different constituencies, egalitarian in its relation to cognoscenti of both Bayreuth and battery. Different readers may be reading different genres: Should the beating of Oscar be read in the terms of Nordic myth or New Jersey naturalism? I miss almost all the references to science fiction literature; I miss half of those portions of the text that are in Spanish; I am specifically addressed by this joke. It is possible that I might read this very paragraph at an MLA panel; the joke is aimed not merely at me but at me as I type this sentence. But as close to me as the joke trespasses, I am still uncertain of my relation to it. I laugh at it; I am even slightly proud to get the meaning of the joke, as Walt Whitman might put it. Yet the joke only reaches me by attacking me—if I am proud to be in on the joke and to invoke Whitman, I am its object. Am I meant to share the humor of it (I might have made something like this very joke to Junot Díaz if I knew him and ran into him at an MLA convention), or am I targeted by it?

I can open the door to the meaning of this joke to the uninitiated, but the secret to doing so is not the word *Mellon*. Perhaps Gandalf's act of interpretation of the elvish door identifies him as a friend of its ancient inscribers, and perhaps Yunior's act of interpretation of Oscar's door reveals his surprisingly authentic friendliness to Oscar, and perhaps the translation of *The Lord of the Rings* by *The Brief Wondrous Life of Oscar Wao* suggests a sympathy between the two works. But my own displays of knowingness seem to me akin to Oscar's inability to repress knowing that "fuego" means "fire"—"Fire, he blurted out, unable to help himself" (Díaz 322)—which gives his non-English-speaking persecutors the order to kill him.

Perhaps not. Reading *Oscar Wao* with imperfect comprehension, I am unsure who is giving pain to whom, or who is bent on appeasing whom, as in the case of Chabon's evasive oeuvre. The most frequent allusions of the self-conscious escapism of *Oscar Wao* are to *Lord of the*

Rings, in which readers can only identify with men and, more easily, with hobbits, but cannot identify with Sauron. Insofar as *Oscar Wao* works as escapism of the simple kind, Sauron is transformed into Trujillo, with whom no reader identifies. The unexpected inference is that political realism is escapist for us—we are not, to our credit, Caribbean tyrants. In the process of not identifying with Trujillo, readers who are white as well as Dominican readers who are male can neglect to consider their own implication in the poverty and hopelessness of the Dominican Republic: call Trujillo their author, call both imperialism and political retribution by the name fukú, and conceive politics as a field of disinterested and reversible force. Accordingly, feel the text's incomprehensibility not as its escape from violence but as disinterested zafa. That is escapism we all can perversely enjoy, a guilty pleasure. But when we observe the novel in its determination to escape its readers, we may catch a glimpse of power in the world genuinely worth subtracting. We have met the enemy, *Pogo* says, and he is us. The linguistic virtuosity of *Oscar Wao*, the strength of its weakness, may be taken as a counter-curse for protecting Díaz from the cultural totalitarianism that threatens to turn every author into a colonial subject, and from which they plot their escapes.

Chapter 5

BATH AND BATHOS

You can conceive minimalism by way of the difference between "The Bath," a story written by Raymond Carver under the Procrustean influence of Gordon Lish, and "A Small, Good Thing," an expansion of "The Bath" that sheds the Lish aesthetic. Both stories concern an accident in which a boy named Scotty, near his eighth birthday, is hit by a car; in both, his parents are tormented by a baker, unaware of the accident, who insistently calls the young couple demanding payment for an uncollected birthday cake. The end of "The Bath" is the beginning either of another hectoring call from the baker or of a call from the hospital, presumably to report Scotty's death; "A Small, Good Thing" makes explicit that it is the baker who not only calls but also reveals that the child nonetheless dies. The latter story goes on to bring the parents and the baker together for a midnight-to-dawn conversation in which the baker serves coffee and hot rolls, and a human connection, with ritual overtones, is achieved.

The second story is, in sum, more forthcoming and less severe. In my minority opinion, it also ruins what is most interesting about "The Bath." Here is how "The Bath" describes the accident. "At an intersection, without looking, the birthday boy stepped off the curb, and was promptly knocked down by a car. . . . The birthday boy did not cry. But neither did he wish to talk anymore. . . . The birthday boy got up and turned back for home, at which time the other boy waved goodbye and headed off for school" (Carver, *Talk About Love* 48).

Here are the corresponding sentences in "A Small, Good Thing." "Without looking, the birthday boy stepped off the curb at an intersection and was immediately knocked down by a car. . . . The birthday boy didn't cry, but he didn't have anything to say about anything either. . . . He walked home, and his friend went on to school" (Carver, *Cathedral* 60–1).

The revised version is sparer than the original—minimalism is not measured by word count. What I call attention to is the estranging language of "The Bath," which Carver mitigates in "A Small, Good Thing." In the former, the child steps off the curb and is "promptly" hit by a car, which is replaced in the latter by the bland "immediately." The adverb "promptly," except when spoken by elementary school teachers, always carries a faint intention of the humorous. "But neither did he wish to talk" is replaced by "but he didn't have anything to say"; the former sounds like a bad translation into English, replaced by a more colloquial phrasing. "At which time," in the third quoted sentence from "The Bath," is replaced by "and"—a seemingly inexplicable turgidity in the original story gives way to the simplest of conjunctions.

Why attribute the inappropriate and ironizing aloofness of diction, as opposed to flat neutrality, to "minimalism"? In the environs of "The Bath," no one can do anything for anyone else: the friend can do nothing for the injured birthday boy; the doctor cannot speak either comfortingly or cogently to his parents. The husband cannot support his wife:

> The husband sat in the chair beside her. He wanted to say something else. But there was no saying what it should be. He took her hand and put it in his lap. This made him feel better. It made him feel he was saying something. . . . From time to time he squeezed her hand until she took it away. (Carver, *Talk About Love*, 52–3)

And when the husband worries that their dog needs feeding while he and his wife remain at the hospital, his wife tells him to "call the neighbors. Someone will feed him if you ask them to." His wife "tried to think who," and concludes, "Maybe I'll do it" (Carver, *Talk About Love* 54).

In contrast, "A Small, Good Thing," by the hedging neutrality of its account, allows the possibility of reconciliation between baker and grieving parents in the final scene of the story. That susceptibility is quietly established in the revised story's version of the dog conversation: Ann suggests that Howard (unnamed in the former story) "call the Morgans" (Carver, *Cathedral* 71). There is that hint of a neighborhood. But pervasively in earlier Carver, America is a country without affective bonds. Human relations, especially between husbands and wives and often between parents and children, are arbitrary and short-lived intersections.

In minimalist America, mortality does not create solidarity, which entails, at least in this textbook case, a technique opposite to free indirect discourse. The narrative voice of "The Bath" does not presume to share a syntax, diction, or style with a child who is hit by a car or with his helpless parents, or even to imply that omniscience is the appropriately objective stance. There is no appropriate stance; the point of the writing is to establish inappropriateness, to preclude both empathy and knowingness, to bear witness to the haplessness of witnessing. We cannot be there for the characters, nor can the author be there for us. As Carver's best student Denis Johnson (insofar as he himself did not seek compensatory communion rituals in unpromising places) puts it to his readership: "And you, you ridiculous people, you expect me to help you?" (Johnson 12). The capacity of authors to help readers is what is minimized in minimalism. What is the implied relationship of writers and readers in capacious novels with such maximalist titles as *The Amazing Adventures of Kavalier & Clay, The Brief Wondrous Life of Oscar Wao, A Heartbreaking Work of Staggering Genius, Everything is Illuminated,* and *Extremely Loud and Incredibly Close*?

All my archive concerns the question of whether x can save y. In each case, the question is asked with respect to equals or near equals: men and women of closely competitive spirit, friends, siblings. In no case is it a question of salvation by gods, surrogates of gods, or representatives of gods. Nor is there a question of the salvation of societies or peoples or humankind. When parenting is at issue, it has to be turned almost horizontal. It remains to be seen whether readers can be saved in the rotation.

*   *   *

Though the seminal moment of my escapism project was the comparison of *Oscar Wao* and *Kavalier & Clay*, this chapter on Dave Eggers and Jonathan Safran Foer might as well have begun with a family tree ramifying from Michael Chabon's corpus. Chabon's *Telegraph Avenue* and Eggers's *Heartbreaking Work* are set in Berkeley, California, and neighboring cities of the Bay Area. Chabon's *The Yiddish Policeman's Union* and Eggers's *Heroes of the Frontier* take place in Alaska. Chabon's *The Yiddish Policeman's Union* and Foer's *Here I Am* are premised on the elimination of the State of Israel. Chabon's *The Final Solution* and Foer's *Extremely Loud and Incredibly Close* track the wanderings of a lost boy, as does Eggers's *What is the What*. Chabon's *The Amazing Adventures of Kavalier & Clay* and Eggers's *Heroes of the Frontier* feature actual escapologists. All these resemblances point to the relationship of escapism to messianism or Utopianism (the Utopian potential of California or Alaska, the messianic calling of Israel, the thwarted messianic hope of restored or preserved innocence, and the faux messianism of cheating death on stage). These are family-crisscrossing, family-demarcating phenotypes.

What is the family likeness of Eggers and Foer? Foer is notably Jewish in his authorial identity. Eggers, in *Heartbreaking Work*, makes a running gag of his lack of ethnic credentials, including the regret that he is "not even Jewish" (Eggers, *Heartbreaking Work* 204–5). Foer's imagination moves from west to east, Eggers's from east to west. Foer's imagination looks backward in time, Eggers's mainly forward. Though both authors stake claims, explicitly or implicitly, to the honorific of genius in early works that made their reputations, Foer goes on enhancing that claim in two more novels, whereas Eggers has anchored his prose to protagonists of modest intelligence, as if doing penance for his inaugural, partly ironic, partly brazen, advertisement for himself.

But there is in fact a family resemblance of Foer and Eggers, and it first reveals itself in family relations. The central question of *Heartbreaking Work* is whether mainly real (fractionally fictional) Dave Eggers can free or save his younger brother, Toph. And unexpectedly, the off-centered question of *Everything is Illuminated* is whether mainly fictional (fractionally real) Jonathan Safran Foer, by a mechanism he sets in motion, can induce his Ukrainian translator Alex to free or save his younger brother, Little Igor.

The answers are not self-evident because there is nothing in either novel like a messiah to play the messianic role: both older brothers are strikingly immature, as much in need of saving as their younger brothers. In both books, there is reason to suspect that the point of saving the younger brother is saving the older brother.

When we consider *Heartbreaking Work* in retrospect, one surprise is that we do not share with Dave Eggers's younger brother Toph anything like the intimacy we feel with, say, Rufus Follett, whose half-orphanhood is twice as heartbreaking, in James Agee's *A Death in the Family*. It is almost fair to say that Toph doesn't make much of an appearance in *Heartbreaking Work*, except as object of Eggers's idealizing and paranoid devotion—Toph is bright, handsome, goofy, great at Frisbee, and what else? (How bright, how handsome? We hear mainly his hyperbolic and hyperventilating brother's praise.) Eggers hardly trespasses on Toph's childhood-to-adolescent privacy. Meanwhile, we hear in vivid detail the vicissitudes of Eggers's sexual and professional lives, along with several stories, one about a failed suicide, one about a woman in and out of a coma, that are moving but do not ascend to the level of heartbreaking, and appear in the book as echoes, audible perhaps only to Eggers, enclosed in referential mania, of his father and mother.

The centrality of Little Igor in Foer's *Everything is Illuminated* is even more paradoxical. Jonathan Safran Foer, or a fictional character by the author's name, visits Ukraine to find a woman, called Augustine, who purportedly saved his grandfather from Nazis in the shtetl of Trachimbrod. The search for that woman seems to be for the Augustinian principle of salvation, itself. Whether the mediator vanishes or not is obscure. The woman he does locate, called Lista P, who may or may not have saved his grandfather, has some relation to Foer's driver, Alexander Perchov, the grandfather of Foer's guide Alex and his little brother Igor, and the tale of the Ukrainian grandfather's *failure* to save his best friend from execution by the Nazis. Whatever inspiration Foer had hoped to derive from the search for someone capable of saving his grandfather seems denied him, and his search arrives instead at a grandfather lengthily deformed by his inability to save someone else (in fact by his sacrificing his friend to Nazi sadists). The complicated plot machinery does, however, manage to impel Alex, who seems to consider his father's brutality a consequence of his grandfather's betrayal, to drive his father from the Perchov household. This has the effect of saving Little Igor, Alex's little brother. From what? For what? From the necessity of leaving a partly demystified Ukraine with Alex to a fantasy America. He is saved to stay at home. The peculiarity of the book is that we never encounter the saved younger brother.

As a first condition, (invisible) Little Igor can only be saved by the deliberate exiling from his home of his one remaining parent. In *Heartbreaking Work*, on the other hand, the independent deaths of both of Toph's parents within five weeks of each other, from different strains of cancer, do not seem to save Toph but to necessitate his being saved from a heartbreakingly devastated home. Still, Toph's father had his drunken and violent side (Eggers, *Heartbreaking Work* 230–5), grudgingly but increasingly revealed as Dave's negative paradigm, and saving Toph is not accomplished by Dave's imitation of parental responsibility, rather by establishing a different principle of salvation based on fun, freedom, and unruly love without discipline or punishment. We need to figure out what saving and freeing mean in these two books, as salvation, on a new fraternal rather than parental or paternal model, becomes a matter of play rather than law, and thus a temporal escapist interim in the present rather than an Utopian or messianic leap into the future and past.

The question for Eggers is always whether any frontier Utopia is still possible in the United States, in the present or future; the question for Foer always concerns the possibility of a mutual messianic redemption of present and past. Foer's third novel, *Here I Am*, threatens a Henry Jamesian chiasmus: one cousin, Tamir, considers emigrating from Israel to the United States to free himself from Jewish history, while the other cousin, Jacob, considers emigrating from the United States to Israel to save it *for* Jewish history. But the direction of Foer's imagination is characteristically one-way across the Atlantic to original familial homelands—Germany, Ukraine, Israel; middle Europe, eastern Europe, the Middle East. And his Jamesian imagination not of symmetry but of disaster takes for its object the impossibility of salvation, not recreation; the failure of the Messiah and the fulfillment of history, not the failure of the political future in redirected history; the failure of homecoming, not the frontier; the failure of divine illumination, not Utopian visibility or frontier invisibility.

In *Everything is Illuminated*, it is close to the truth to say that nothing is illuminated. To the question of whether the character named Lista P is really salvific Augustine, the literal answer of the book seems to be no. Nevertheless, the guide Alex, the most powerfully intuitive of the novel's characters, persists in calling her Augustine. Lista P tells a story about the escape of her sister, which probably is her traumatized way of remembering her own escape. The grandfather Alexander recognizes in Lista P another member of a circle that had included the Jewish friend, Herschel, whom Alexander betrayed; this may or may not mean that the grandfather was Jewish before he was anti-Semitic.

Do these ambiguities of identity—at the center of questions of saving and escaping—matter? They matter as ambiguities: the book makes nonsense of simplicities of identity on which Germans and Ukrainians (and Russians and Poles) justify pogroms. Foer locates his novel on, it seems, every possible fault line of the bloodlands: on territory disputed by Poles and Ukrainians, and coveted by Russians and Germans, with Jews and Christians in proximity. Even the Jewish shtetl is divided in two, in two nonidentical ways: between its Orthodox and Reform Jews (called Upstanders and Slackers) and between its Jewish and secular quarters (in the ratio of one-quarter to three-quarters). American fault lines are exposed in the comic relief of the Perchov family's dog, named Sammy Davis, Jr, Jr. Can a Black be a Jew? What kind of American is a Black Jew? Can a dog be Black or Jewish? In challenging the principles of national, racial, religious, or species identity, the book challenges the value of genealogies. What difference does it make if it is Lista P or her sister who survives? The one we encounter is the surviving sister. And the only person in the story with a direct interest in the woman who saved Jonathan's grandfather is Jonathan. The interest in her is circular: "if it weren't for her, I couldn't be here to find her" (Foer, *Illuminated* 150). The corollary is that millions of the nonexistent cannot be there to research the demise of their ancestors.

Only the surviving theorize the meaning of survival. The circularity entails that there is no messiah, no messianic salvation, no illumination (no revelation) at the Armageddon of world war and holocaust.

It is, however, not quite the whole truth that precisely nothing is illuminated in the book. The open question is how much. It is Alex who claims that everything will be illuminated, but he does so in the hope that Augustine will provide the illumination, and Augustine may no longer live. Alex is also responsible for the emptying of the notion of illumination; in his spotty English ("as I illuminated before"), illumination only means "explained" or "noted" (Foer, *Illuminated* 68). Somewhere between total and specious illumination is Alex's suggestion that, in Jonathan's book, "Brod could be Augustine" (Foer, *Illumination* 143). Brod, a baby in 1791 when she is emitted by the river Brod, hence her name, after an accident in which her father (this is the Trachim B of Trachimbrod) seems to drown, represents the miraculous or accidental origin of the Foer family genealogy as retrofitted by Foer; on Alex's hypothesis, a woman born in the eighteenth century saves Jonathan's grandfather in the middle of the twentieth.

There is evidence that Alex is absurdly correct: Brod had a prophetic dream of the destruction of Trachimbrod in which her namesake and alter ego, the river Brod, saves Jonathan's grandfather (Foer, *Illuminated* 272–3). Brod in this sense is the vanishing but returning mediator of the novel's messianism. But she does not, in her dream, save anyone else; in fact, everyone else who flees the bombing to the river drowns. When Alex proposes that Brod might be Augustine, and adds, "Do you comprehend what I signify?" it is still likely that we do not. It could simply mean that every surviving ancestor has saved every surviving descendant, by definition. Or we could trust Alex's largest illumination, based on the multiplying affinities between Jonathan and himself, each one writing a book with a shared set of characters, that everyone can identify with everyone else (Foer, *Illuminated* 214): in this way, the scandal of survival (no one is entitled to a messiah because no one is entitled to be saved) is the democratic salvation of the world (everyone is equally chosen not to be entitled). In Alex's mind, once he outgrows his illusions about both Ukraine and the

United States, there are no slaves or masters, men or women, Jews or Greeks because there is *no* messiah. It is on the basis of democratic imperfection and nonentitlement that Little Igor is saved where he abides, unilluminated.

Foer plays a similar game of illumination with the titular adverbs of *Extremely Loud and Incredibly Close*, in which the child whose salvation is at stake, Oskar Schell, makes his appearance in full control of the narrative, its hero and narrator. Oskar uses the word "incredibly" as promiscuously as every kid, and it is paired with "extremely" at various half-illuminating, quasi-prophetic moments. When Oskar, letting down his filial protectiveness of his mother after the death of her husband, tells her that he wishes she and not his father had died on 9/11, he feels "extremely depressed" and "incredibly alone" (Foer, *Loud* 171–2). When Oskar, pursuing the lock that will be opened by a key left by his father, which (falsely) promises, for almost the length of the plot, a revelation and a kind of resurrection, returns to the apartment of a newly divorced couple, he is "incredibly close" to the wife when he complains to her that, at his first visit, he had been as close as he had ever been to the correspondent lock; but she had been distracted by her husband's "extremely loud" yelling from the next room (Foer, *Loud* 290–5). In this case, the closeness and loudness are simultaneous but fatally out of synch.

Anticipating the thing that is both extremely loud and incredibly close in one synchronized salvific event is a waiting game the reader might be more or less enthusiastic about playing, but it's not just a matter of clever or annoying adverbial suspense. We might be awaiting bathos or hyperbole, or both. We might be awaiting a revelation and/or a veiling. What, finally, is extremely loud and incredibly close? Oskar, who is perhaps a genius of a child suffering from PTSD, or perhaps an Asperger-ish savant, or perhaps just an uncannily intuitive, ingenious, and curious kid visited by an overwhelming catastrophe, designs imaginary inventions as if an elementary school Leonardo. His research into the Twin Towers had revealed to him that 2,000 birds died every year from smashing into windows. "So I invented a device," he informs adults, "that would detect when a bird is incredibly close to a building, and that would trigger an extremely loud birdcall from another skyscraper, and they'd be drawn to that" (Foer, *Loud* 250). There it is; that's it. One of the advantages of protecting all these birds would be that another of Oskar's inventions, a birdseed shirt that would attract birds to any falling body so that they would fly it to safety, would work more reliably.

The job of salvation has become cyclical: humans manufacture artificial bird calls to save birds to save humans. One building would notify another to save the birds. The son would save birds to save the father to save his son. This is a weaker messianism for ecologists, recyclable and sustainable, the only kind of messianism credible to anti-messianists. The conjunction of the title, which might have referred to the sensuous experience of 9/11 itself (New Yorkers might have experienced the hijacked planes as extremely loud and incredibly close), has been replaced by a choreographed disjunction. A deadly crash is what is prevented (saving the birds *from* the towers); the title of the book might have been *Extremely Loud So Not Too Close.* There is a play of apocalyptic loudness and spatial near missing, as in *Everything is Illuminated* there is a play of messianic luminosity and temporal near missing. The thing to note is the coexistence of hyperbole and bathos. Salvation is a nonevent. It is the outcome of what fails to happen, the postponement of tragedy.

The past is represented in *Everything is Illuminated* by the destroyed shtetl in Poland or Ukraine. The past in *Extremely Loud and Incredibly Close* is represented by fire-bombed Dresden, which is treated by the book as a corollary of Hiroshima and a precedent for 9/11 in the history of universal repetition compulsion, an entailment of the death drive. But *Here I Am* is a conversation between present-day America and present-day Israel: Israel represents what all the European origins fail to represent, the extended promise of the past, which equals the messianic promise of returning home.

The first sentence of *Here I Am* seems to announce the future of a fait accompli: "When the destruction of Israel commenced, Isaac Bloch [grandfather of the book's protagonist, Jacob] was weighing whether to kill himself or move to the Jewish Home" (Foer, *Here I Am* 3). The Jewish Home is an old-age facility, not the Promised Land already in the process of extermination. Toward the end of the book, when Jacob has to move out of his home after the breakup of his marriage, we again confront a sentence distinguishing extinct eternal homeland and extant stopgap domicile: "In the long aftermath of the destruction of Israel, Jacob [AKA, in the Old Testament, Israel] moved into his new house" (Foer, *Here I Am* 537).

Then what does it mean when Foer finally informs us, on the very next page, that "Israel wasn't destroyed" (Foer, *Here I Am* 538)? Israel has been saved, finally, as a military and political outcome, not by the intervention of the Messiah. It no longer survives as a messianic promise, as itself, as Israel: "the Messiah was too distracted or non-existent to awake the living or the dead" (Foer, *Here I Am* 13).

The earthquake has aftershock effects on all the local messianic projects of the book. Why does Sam, the eldest son of the family, destroy a synagogue he had constructed online in the virtual reality of Other Life, as if destroying the Third Temple? Because of an imperfection in the virtual construction. Why does Julia, Jacob's wife, blow up, in effect, her family by divorcing and remarrying? Because of a virtual transgression of perfect spousal fidelity. The imagination of perfection, not as a project but as an expectation, is the imagination not of Utopia but of the Messiah; a local failure of home or synagogue is a microcosmic failure of Jerusalem. If there is an escapist hope of the book that escapes, in particular, this self-destruction by way of local messianism, it is implicit in the title, *Here I Am*, a translation of Hineni, Abraham's response to God and Isaac, repeated term in the biblical story for Abraham's availability to sacrifice his son. But the typical sacrifice is called off, unlike that of the antitypical Messiah. The escapist fantasy of *Here I Am* is that the children of divorce are not quite sacrificed. The nonsacrifice of children and their childhoods is the bathos that measures the devolution of messianism to escapism, of salvation to survival. Not losing your loved ones, that nonevent, is as good as it gets.

The messianic dream is always invoked and jeopardized in Foer's escapism; the Utopian vision is endangered in Eggers's. Perhaps inevitably, Eggers's meta-trope through all stages of his meta-Utopian journey is, as in Foer, the bathos of survival: in his first book, he has already arrived at the Bay Area, where American frontier Utopianism should exist minimally as improvised unconventionality but does not. (And the book's Bay Area is in dialogue with Hollywood to the south, where frontier Utopianism is parodied by reality TV.) We have come half-circle, in both Foer and Eggers, to a kind of bathetic triumphalism. In Foer, the destruction of Israel and the destruction of the Bloch family would be climaxes, even if anti-messianic climaxes. But both survive— even the Bloch family continues to function, though dispersed—by compromising their constitutive dreams of homecoming perfection. Diaspora is as good as it gets.

If *A Hologram for the King* is more than a tedious account of the attenuated life of a salesman, narrated closely enough to his consciousness to stifle Eggers's prose virtuosity, it is a deep investigation into the poetics and politics of bathos. From before the outset of the narration of Thomas Clay's business trip to Saudi Arabia to interest King Abdullah in hologram technology for King Abdullah Economic City, we are forewarned by the epigraph of the novel ("It is not every day that we are needed"—Samuel Beckett) that King Abdullah will never arrive to make the purchase. Despite this warning, which defuses narrative suspense from before the plot, we are jarringly enervated by every mini-anticlimax along the way. Clay, shooting a rifle at an unidentified target for sport, does not accidentally kill an exposed shepherd boy. Though Clay jokingly implies that he works for the CIA to a suspicious Saudi, no mistaken identity thriller ensues. He has a growth on his neck that turns out not to be a tumor. He refuses to pursue an affair to consummation; then he does pursue affairs toward consummation but cannot be aroused. This is a literalization of the structural detumescence of the novel. The principle is first time farce, each time farce.

There is something hyperbolic in the novel's dedication to bathos, and at the end of the novel, when Clay decides to stay in Saudi Arabia for no comprehensible purpose, his intentional homelessness comes as something of an anticlimactic shock. The book neither seeks a new home in the way of Utopias nor secures a return home in the way of messiahs. It moots the issue of home. In fact, the entire book turns out to be premised on the anticlimax of the long American century, which mirrors the anticlimax of Clay's home life. King Abdullah does not make an appearance at Clay's company's hologram presentation to reject the American product on the merits; his hologram deal with China had already occurred out of sight, compensation for China's larger importation of Saudi oil. The book is about globalization, except without American technology and representational magic, the virtual American dream, at its center. Globalization in Stiglitz's rather than Friedman's version is accomplished by the circumnavigation of the globe from one direction by the United States and the other by China, meeting in the Middle East, with the same technology for sale in trivialized physical and conceptual space. Globalization in this novel also entails the importation of professionals from Europe and cheap labor from Malaysia, Pakistan, and the Philippines. It is not merely Clay's xenophobic father who infers that the United States cannot compete without ceasing to be America in any exceptional sense (just as Foer's Israel cannot continue to exist without ceasing to be Israel), and that the homelessness of global capitalism implies the impossibility of an old messianic or new Utopian homeland.

The single most important fact in Eggers's career as a writer is that even when he tries to reimagine the meaningfulness of America, even when he tries to imagine reopening the frontier rather than foreign markets for the purpose, he cannot transcend his commitment to bathos. His prose says, almost in the way of minimalism: I cannot save anyone by my writing; America cannot save the world or even transform it in its own ideal or fantastic image; it is all days of the week that we are not needed. Even so, it is necessary to find a new frontier in the ruins. And not merely hidden in the ruins or by shoring fragments against them, but by means of the ruination—which, translated into rhetoric, means in the bathos, itself, which requires maximalist hyperbole for its force.

Eggers's recent novel, *Heroes of the Frontier*, will sound, at first, much like a repetition of the repetition compulsion of *A Hologram for the King*, though with a hyperbolically promised heroism. The donnée is that Josie, a single parent with two children, needs to escape her life in Ohio. The array of conditions that she considers worth escaping seems designed to muddle the issue of whether it is a good idea to take her two children out of school, with a diminishing sum of money and no plans, for an unspecified length of time in socially and climatically turbulent Alaska. Her ex-husband's family negligence seems to have left Josie feeling justifiably rootless. We may assume that the malpractice law suit that Josie is trying to outrun is opportunistic. But Eggers is not out to justify Josie at every turn, and the fact that she hastened the death in Afghanistan of a young patient named Jeremy by her unthinking enthusiasm for his enlistment keeps alive the possibility that Alaska is Josie's escapist unheroic retreat from guilt, not an authentically heroic escape to a moral frontier. According to the book's binary, she is either "an evader" or "a crusader" (Eggers, *Heroes* 228, 233)—a spiritual adventurer or an escapist. One of those. The confusion itself is escapist.

If Josie's Alaskan adventure with her two children is an escapist evasion of her guilt, it may entail a dark irony for the trip per se: Alaska may be a second Afghanistan where Josie's thoughtlessness (plus occasional drunkenness) endangers children, in this case her own. Is guilt the reason she risks their lives? It seems inevitable at short intervals that she will get them assaulted or killed. Josie leaves the children, Ana and Paul, with a strange man; Josie does not prevent Ana from running toward a moving truck; Josie allows her children unsupervised play at an archery range, even after their family is joined by a man who shoots a rifle randomly; Josie makes an inexplicable mistake and drives her family toward a forest fire; and at the end of the book, she underestimates the distance to a shelter and exposes her children to ground zero of an apocalyptic lightning storm. Here are the results: nothing happens, nothing happens, nothing happens, nothing happens, nothing happens.

The book is bathetic at every crisis, with a climax of bathos at the end. Josie is an aficionado of musicals, the locus classicus of American escapism, but she spends much of the book working out the plot of an imaginary show called *Disappointed: The Musical*. The point of fusing musical comedy with hopelessness, which equals fusing musical comedy with the illness of American life it is meant to cure, is that only bathos can save the Alaskan adventure, can keep it from ending in tragedy. If everything after *A Heartbreaking Work of Staggering Genius* must be bathos almost of necessity, because there is no place else to go after that bipolar grandiosity, this is the way that bathos can reopen the adventure of leaving Ohio, heading northwestward, and saving lives by the technique of disappointment, of missing one's appointment with tragedy.

The novel ends this way: the family survives the fire that they fled, once Josie gets the direction right, in the direction of a lightning storm, and then survives the lightning storm, by soldierly endurance and bravery. They reenact Jeremy's deployment—"they sat side by side like soldiers in a foxhole" (Eggers, *Heroes* 427)—only with savage fulfillment at the end of it.

> Josie found herself smiling, knowing they had done what they could with what they had, and they had found joy and purpose at every footstep. They had . . . faced formidable obstacles in this world and had laughed and triumphed and had bled freely but were now naked together and warm, and the fire before them would not die. Josie looked at the bright flaming faces of her children and knew this was exactly who and where they were supposed to be. (Eggers, *Heroes* 433)

This is a transvaluation of survival, in contradistinction to Foer: the bathos of surviving tragedy, even of surviving Alaskan apocalypse, of staying alive in an imperfect world, is a renunciation of messianism in Foer, a triumph of frontier Utopianism in Eggers. Facing down death in the wilderness lends adult knowingness to Josie's feral daughter Ana, and brings out the independence and physical courage of Josie's pure and self-sacrificial son Paul. By way of Josie's escape, her children have been freed. Yet Josie overestimates her family's heroism and underestimates her moral luck, as Bernard Williams would call it, in not getting her children killed. Eggers is indulging the indirect free discourse version of Josie's hyperbole. Will her moral luck hold indefinitely? The uplifting, unconvincing sentences I've just quoted are the final words of chapter 23, the penultimate chapter of the book. Chapter 24 consists of a single ultimate sentence: "But then there is tomorrow" (Eggers, *Heroes* 434). This may sound like Scarlett O'Haraesque resilience, but as a response to the exultant previous chapter and beginning with a negative conjunction, the midnight sentence means that the next morning may bring desperation, or despair, or, if the characteristic events of the book have done any adumbrating at all, accidental, careless death.

My chapter began with the hyperbole of Eggers's and Foer's maximalist claims, but it has arrived at the inevitability of their post-messianic and post-utopian bathos. This declination is inevitable in a globalized world, where globalization can begin as in *Hologram* with the homelessness of labor or capital or technology, but which specifically means for Foer and Eggers the end of the exceptionality of the United States and Israel, of the perpetual frontier (California, Alaska, the eternally renovated American dream) and the Promised Land (Israel or messianic America), of values that cannot be monetized. How do you escape the global flatland?

The answer is not by way of the illuminating power of a messianic author or by the heroic imaginary trailblazing of a Utopian author. An unnerving similarity of Foer's *Everything is Illuminated* and Eggers's *Heartbreaking Work* is the fury they generate in their last pages, when they contemplate the futility of their expansive books insofar as the books themselves interfere with their messianism or Utopianism.

Foer's rage takes fire from his sense that he has become another contributor to Trachimbrod's *Book of Antecedents*, a Borgesian record of shtetl history that grows to the size of that history.

> Even the most delinquent students read *The Book of Antecedents* without skipping a word, for they knew that they too would one day inhabit its pages, that if they could get hold of a future edition, they would be able to read of their mistakes (and perhaps avoid them), and the mistakes of their children (and ensure that they would never happen), and the outcome of future wars (and prepare for the death of loved ones). (Foer, *Illuminated* 196)

All that *The Book of Antecedents*, a monstrous combination of "On Exactitude in Science" and "The Library of Babel," records in Jewish history is the Jewish history of books like *The Book of Antecedents*. Foer does not escape implication in this self-consuming recursiveness. The chapter of *Everything is Illuminated* that includes chapters from *The Book of Antecedents* ends with the phrase "we are writing" repeated about 200 times, about one time for every page of the book to that point (Foer, *Illuminated* 212–13).

Near the end of the book, when Trachimbrod is about to be destroyed by Nazi bombing, the townspeople are engaged in one of their traditions, the celebration at the Brod River of the death of Trachim that led to the naming of their town—a characteristically past- and origin-directed event. Foer writes parenthetically: "(And here is becoming harder and harder not to yell: GO AWAY! RUN WHILE YOU CAN, FOOLS! RUN FOR YOUR LIVES!)" (Foer, *Illuminated* 269). Foer attempts to extract himself from the future-blind tradition of Trachimbrod historians in order to scream a warning to his ancestors, or rather to those coreligionists of one of his ancestors who fail to have descendants, because they cannot read his retrospective writing, as they had hoped, prophylactically; it is hard for him, he says, not to scream at them, though he cannot scream at them. He cannot transpire from distance to unbelievable closeness, from silence to an extremely loud warning. His capitalization cannot escape his parenthesis. The failure of the Messiah to irrupt in their present to save them includes as a special case the impossibility that Foer in the future might be that Messiah. (Benjamin in *Theses on History* concludes with the Jewish prohibition on futurology.) The constitutive rage of Foer may be the failure of his capacity to warn. On the contrary, Foer plays his part in ensconcing Jews in the past that has left them blind to the near future, about to be the futureless present. Those who write the past are condemned to repeat it, because the blunder is absorption in the past.

The rage of Eggers at the end of *Heartbreaking Work* is more mysterious, more profane, more explosive. It seems to come from contrary directions at once. It begins with a scene of Dave and Toph on the beach throwing a Frisbee, and it seems to begin in perfection.

> It's never too gusty on this beach, it's just balmy, the air waving around, loopy and soft, which makes you wonder why anyone ever goes to Ocean Beach, which is always insanely windy, pointless for anything . . . . To throw and have it be any fun we need some calm, because we need to *wing* that fucker. And of course people stop and watch us, we're so fucking good. People young and old, whole families, gather to ooh and ahh, thousands of people, they've brought picnics, they've brought picnics, binoculars—. . . . We're just good, so good—. We throw it high and far. (Eggers, *Heartbreaking Work* 434)

Or perhaps not perfection. Perfection is what we expect from the passage, because we have encountered it at a previous Frisbee moment: "We are perfection, harmony, young and lithe, fast like Indians" (Eggers, *Heartbreaking Work* 67). They are at the best beach for it, though the insult to an imperfect rival beach seems gratuitous. The hint of violence in the insult is suddenly realized in the winging of the Frisbee, verbally and physically, strangely soon after the word "calm." Something is disturbing the universe along the beach. Perhaps it is the thousands of beachgoers with their binoculars, who seem reminiscent of the "millions of photographers" in *Pale Fire* publicizing the coming to America of a more competent Gradus. The Utopian hope of the Bay Area had been premised on evading Gradus further westward to an unconventional, free, nonjudgmental, undying world; it had been Hollywood, the other California paradigm, that stood for shameless momentary visibility, Eggers's chronic temptation. What Eggers wants in California is what Josie seeks in Alaska: "what could better grant her invisibility than this, a rolling home, no fixed address. . . . No one could ever find her" (Eggers, *Heroes* 4). "I feel like I'm already inside a fishbowl," Eggers writes in *Heartbreaking Work*, "I feel like I'm being watched at all times" (Eggers, *Heartbreaking* 212). Perhaps this Frisbee throwing is a private celebration of fraternal love.

(We might recall Oscar Hammerstein's scorn for the applause of his audience, and fear of its judgment, upon which his livelihood depended: all judgment reminded him of Gestapo surveillance. When Oskar Schell's grandfather hears the beginning of the firebombing of Dresden, the "horrible noise, [the] rapid, approaching explosions" seem to him "like an applauding audience running towards us" [Foer, *Extremely Loud* 210]. The bizarreness of the simile should make readers of *Extremely Loud and Incredibly Close* feel that they themselves are increasingly loud and close.)

And again the beauty of the Frisbee throwing reveals violence. I cannot overstate how unexpected it is, how inappropriate, how crazed— something is making Eggers, who has kept his life and Toph's barely under control with almost unflagging good humor, improvisatory openness, and patience, lose all that:

> We're best at the long high throws. Like when you take four or five steps and rip it—It's almost like a shotput approach, the steps, four or five quick, one over the other, kind of sideways-like—and then you slash away with that fucker, it's such a violent act, throwing that white thing, you're first cradling it to your breast and then you whip that fucker as hard as you possibly can while keeping it level, keeping it straight, but otherwise with everything you can send with it you whip that fucker like it had blades on it and you wanted it to cut straight through that paperblue sky like a screen, rip through it and have it be blood and black space beyond. (Eggers, *Heartbreaking Work* 435)

"What he really wanted to do was to tear a hole in his world and escape," writes Nabokov of Eggers's unnamed precursor in referential mania (Nabokov 69). The passage continues without interruption, addressing John, the failed suicide, amalgam of perhaps several real-life figures and father-symbol, who descends from the ripped, paperblue sky:

> Oh I'm not going to fix you, John, or any of you people. I tried about a million times to fix you, but it was so wrong for me to want to save you because I only wanted to eat you to make me stronger. I only wanted to devour all of you. I was a cancer. (Eggers, *Heartbreaking Work* 435)

Suddenly Eggers is Denis Johnson or Johnson's narrator in *Jesus' Son*: we seem to the author or narrator to be making a claim on him, reading the book to be freed or fixed or saved, and the author or his narrator cannot begin to do anything for us. He has already gone for the millionth time to forge in the smithy of his soul the uncreated conscience of his race, and he's tired of it. Only it is worse: far from failing us out of incompetence or weakness or (as in Foer's case) belatedness and bookishness, Eggers, unable to hide behind a narrator, admits to wanting to destroy us. He is cancer, the disease that killed his parents, or he is the cannibal who nourished his book and reputation on their corpses; this is the precedent of his designs on us. He cannot find in Berkeley and San Francisco the invisibility he craves to relieve him from judgment, from guilt and shame. His genius only publicizes his shame and guilt. And yet (the passage continues without interruption):

> Oh but I did this for you. Don't you see I do this for you? I have done this all for you. I pretend that I do not but I do. I eat you to save you. I drink you to make you new.

He is momentarily Jonathan Safran Foer, who takes up a sliver of the Holocaust because he is a writer or because someone needs to save his people; he is either a cannibal or a messiah. (In the book's terms, Eggers is either avatar of his sacrificial mother, insufficiently adored outside the family, or the priest who sacrificed her.) To be cannibal and Messiah at once requires a reverse communion; the communicants are the wafer and wine. Or Eggers is Whitman in reverse, looking for his dead readership under his own boot soles: "And I am with you there, when you're under that fucking building all centipedey and everything you motherfuckers" (Eggers, *Heartbreaking Work* 456). This enrages Eggers, because he is dying through us and for us and into us, but we cannot see him and the beauty and perfection that he has wrought:

> And when Toph catches his, he flings it with a fury, his muscles just these taut strings, his mouth open, teeth straight and pushing so hard against each other. And when I catch I do it, too, I flex and yell and vibrate—Can you see this? Goddamn, look at that fucking throw did you see Toph throw that goddamn thing, the trajectory on that fucking thing? It's going way past me but I can run under it, I am barefoot and run like an Indian and I can look back and it's still coming, I can see Toph in the distance blond and perfect—It's up there and rising, Jesus fucking Christ it's small but then it stops up there, it slows and stops all the way up there at the very top, for a second blotting out the sun, and then its heart breaks and it falls. (Eggers, *Heartbreaking Work* 436)

The whiteness—even here to the extent of perfect blondness—that has been a running joke of the book, shared by Dave and Toph, the non-Jewish mid-Americanness which has also taken the form of comic non-Blackness and non-Mexicanity, is redeemed in the passage, redeemed by the native Americanness of the scene. How does this work, exactly? The Caucasian brothers are as much a part of nature, as much unified with its elemental force, as Indians, and the divine self-sacrifice that enters the Frisbee scene only through Eggers's prose suggests a white suicidal wish to die into nature as if in tribute to the liquidated native population: this is death-drive beauty, the unity of death and oceanic oneness felt by Whitman on the shore of Paumanok.

Disappearance is Utopian for Eggers: in *The Circle*, the transparency of the world to us, and of us to the world, is the essence of his dystopia; and the transcendentalist hero of the book tries to escape the dystopia by driving northward toward Alaska, the frontier into which he hopes to evade the sight of the universal corporate-governmental panopticon. But he dies in the escape. The only way to shed publicity without shedding shame and guilt is by dying in full view.

> Don't you know I that I am connected to you? Don't you know that I'm trying to pump blood to you, that this is for you, that I hate you people, so many of you motherfuckers—When you sleep I want you never to wake up, so many of you I want you to just fucking sleep it away because I only want you to run under with me on this sand like Indians . . . . I am somewhere on some stupid rickety scaffolding

and I'm trying to get your stupid fucking attention I've been trying
to show you this, just been trying to show you this— . . . . I'll stand
before you and I'll raise my arms and give you my chest and throat
and wait, and I've been so old for so long, for you, for you, I want
it fast and right through me—Oh do it, do it, you motherfuckers,
do it do it you fuckers finally, finally, finally. (Eggers, *Heartbreaking
Work* 436–7)

And the book is over, and I do not know what happened, exactly:
except that I know that maximalism, if it is defined by Foer and Eggers,
needs to save its audience, cannot save its audience, but cannot write
off the audience that it cannot save; and it despises its audience for
being irredeemable, for not even allowing Foer or Eggers to sacrifice
himself, to be, apparently, raped and crucified—crucifixion as rape—
by their readers for their readers; and despises its audience because
we cannot see that the quality he is willing to sacrifice for us is genius.
In the rage of his ending, Foer, who had wished that everything could
be illuminated by a messianic revelation that he might be anointed to
deliver, wishes instead that his people could flee the sight of history, that
they could simply go somewhere else, unchosen but un-persecuted,
a Utopian nowhere beyond the reach of violence; and in the rage of
his ending, Eggers, who had wished that he and Toph and his family
and his America could disappear into the frontier, as far west as he
could go to outrun the civilization that Berkeley tracked westward,
outside the sight of shame and convention toxically combined, wishes
that someone could see him and find salvation in the beauty of his
messianic self-sacrifice.

*   *   *

I need to make one last argument, because I need to say why the failure
of the Utopian and messianic visions, chiasmically exchanged by
Eggers and Foer, is escapist. This is my inevitably mimetic contribution
to bathos.

1. In *Everything is Illuminated*, I have argued, it is the salvation of
    the offstage Little Igor that gives the book its relief, its escape.
    The fact that we never see him means that we never imagine that
    he will inevitably become Bigger Igor. In *Heartbreaking Work*,
    we track Toph to the brink of an adulthood that would be tragic
    to envisage.

2. Valentino Achak Deng, in Eggers's *What is the What*, is not a perfect example of an escapist's child. Like other boys in the novels of Foer and Eggers, he is preternaturally thoughtful, prematurely forced to the precipice of adulthood, full of a goodness that does not reduce to inexperience, because he was never inexperienced. The difference is that Achak Deng comes to full adulthood before our eyes. The United States, like Ethiopia and Kenya before it, is a false Utopian alternative to genocidal southern Sudan: the event that unifies the account of his experience in the United States is the home invasion and beating he suffers at the hands of African Americans. This is post-Utopian bathos with a vengeance. Yet I risk tastelessness to observe that Achak flees his home in Sudan and treks across Africa with boys—because many more boys than girls could outrun the rapine soldiers from the north. They are known as the "lost boys of Sudan." There is nothing the least Peter Pan-ish about their struggle, but I wish to suggest, on no evidence, that their group name is part of what convinced Dave Eggers that he could be the author of Achak Deng's autobiography. Certainly when Mary Williams founds an organization to help Sudanese refugees called The Lost Boys Foundation, she knowingly makes an unwarranted allusion to *Peter Pan*. This is a truly bizarre hint of the confusion of escape and escapism.

3. In *Extremely Loud and Incredibly Close*, Oskar seems stuck in time. At his age, he is almost perfect; we cannot easily imagine him as a successful or attractive adult. Why is he named Oskar? Presumably after Oskar Matzerath of *The Tin Drum*, also stuck in childhood. The oddity of the German spelling might recall Don DeLillo's Heinrich in *White Noise*, another boy-man with premature knowledge and sense of responsibility in the presence of a death-inhabited father and a skyborne disaster; this is perhaps the first of recent major American novels to feature children who must save their parents. The main reference of Oskar Schell is to Oskar Schindler; *Schindler's List* came out almost precisely at the time of Oskar Schell's birth. The question is why salvation and resurrection have been entrusted to the goodness and illumination of a gentile child.

4. There are three children, all boys, in Foer's *Here I Am*, each on the verge of adulthood in his own way. The oldest, Sam, is about to have his Bar Mitzvah, though he is an excruciating mixture of child and man already. He says in a mock-Bar Mitzvah speech,

"I did not ask to be a man, and I do not want to be a man, and I refuse to be a man" (Foer, *Here I Am* 452). The middle child, Max, is precociously philosophical and tortured by his in-betweenness. The youngest child, Benjy, is prematurely preoccupied with death, introduced to his own mortality by Max (Foer, *Here I Am* 72). The book keeps them at one age for most of its length, but unveils their futures in a few sentences toward the end; the ostensible point is to mark the bathos, which is to say their impressive nontragic professional success despite the heartbreak of their family's disintegration. The oddity is that we hear only the futures of Sam and Max. Of the future of Benjy, the little child who knew death, we hear nothing. In our imagination, Benjy stays at one age forever. In that respect, he resembles the idiot Benjy in *The Sound and the Fury*, who, despite his intellectual stuntedness, is the only Compson child to recognize that his grandmother has died. When we hear the cruel remark that Faulkner's Benjy is not thirty-three but three for thirty years, we can trace his idiocy to Damuddy's death.

5. There is, for novelty, a girl child in Eggers's *Heroes of the Frontier*. That there is a girl as well as a boy to be saved—perhaps from the dangers brought to bear on them by the adult who wishes to save them—is a second turn of the screw. But Ana does not resemble the wise-innocent man-children who appear in every other text I've listed here. She is a wild child, raised as if by wolves, though she comes to a more adult wisdom in the course of the novel. On the other hand is the self-sacrificing, totally honest, almost totally pure Paul. In this book, as in *It Happened One Night*, there are unprovoked references to Lincoln: though at one point the reference is to Lincoln in relation to Seward, at another Paul is thought gratuitously to be "already a great man, a tiny Lincoln" (Eggers, *Heroes* 44). Thus do all escapes to northward freedom invoke escaped slave narratives, with the threat of a messianic sacrifice. But Paul survives, because there is some crossing of his qualities with Ana's: he becomes, in the course of the Alaskan adventure, stronger, freer, and tougher. The whole adventure in Alaska is a kind of escape not from south to north but from civilization to wilderness, on the model of *Huck Finn*—that belated freeing of a slave—or *Peter Pan*.

Peter Pan, though taking flight from Bloomsbury, is partly a fantasy of America: if Captain Hook was a boatswain's mate of Blackbeard, he practiced piracy off the North American coast and in the Caribbean; and Tiger Lily is of course an Indian. (There are North American crocodiles.) Peter Pan and Huck Finn have these traits in common: they are orphaned; they attract the interest of substitute mothers; they wish to escape civilization to perpetual adventures; they flout the law; they float between borders. Peter's address is spatiotemporal nonsense—"Second to the right, and straight on till morning" (Barrie 45)—and Huck and Jim float between North and South, East and West, law and lawlessness, civilization and frontier, past and future. Both Huck and Peter are attracted to death. Huck, whose imagination is characteristically morbid, observes his own funeral with Tom Sawyer, and Peter, about to be inundated, proclaims that "to die will be an awfully big adventure" (Barrie 110). These are the relevant allusions shared by *It Happened One Night* and *Heroes of the Frontier*.

Return to Dave and Toph one last time. They are on the shore of the ocean. Their bodies move over the sand with the grace of Indians, like Peter Pan, in accord with the wind. This is how Eggers imagines they have arrived in the Bay Area: "I take [Toph's] hand and we go through the window and fly up and over the quickly sketched trees and then to California" (Eggers, *Heartbreaking Work* 45). But the desire to escape visibility must be seen to be appreciated: "oh, the cleverness of me," Peter crows (Barrie 30); so does Eggers, somewhat more self-consciously. Toph is perfect, Dave writes repeatedly, but what he means and sometimes specifies is: Toph and I are perfect, united in the freedom and skill and beauty and mutual harmony and universal harmony and genius demonstrated in Frisbee.

This is, precisely, as good as it gets: the post-messianic, post-Utopian, secret, crowd-pleasing, death-haunted, death-taunting perfection of lost boys. One brother is older but willing to retain his childishness; one brother is younger but precocious. And there is a third figure moving beside them, the reader, figured by the admirers of Dave and Toph on the beach, who cannot confidently determine whether the comic exaggeration of the titles of the books he or she has purchased is meant to trigger his infantile vulnerability or her adult protectiveness, and this uncertainty is never allowed to lapse in the course of reading. This is what it means for us to be staggered, not so much by the sublimity of genius as by the vibration of the sublime and the ridiculous, or of symbolic hysteria and emancipation from meaning. But something else happens.

In *Heartbreaking Work*, Dave, as if in a whisper, notices that Toph graduates to junior high; that he begins to look less handsome, more like Dave; and Dave takes special note of Toph's first curse, which Dave claims comes as a relief (Eggers, *Heartbreaking Work* 413). In *What is the What*, Achak marks the moment of his own first curse (Eggers, *What* 106). In *Extremely Loud and Incredibly Close*, we are appalled by Oskar's first act of verbal cruelty toward his mother (Foer, *Extremely Loud* 171–2). In *Here I Am*, the dissonant Bloch parents observe in unison Max's first foray into "talking back" to his parents (Foer, *Here I Am* 75), and the book begins with Sam's unwonted written profanities. In *Heroes of the Frontier*, Josie is startled by the moment that "Paul now knew sarcasm" (Eggers, *Heroes* 194). It is not merely that each character is transitioning from child to adolescent; each character does so by weaponizing language.

In this light, we notice one thing in Eggers's livid climax that we had not remarked on first reading. The Frisbee is

> up there and rising. Jesus fucking Christ it's small but then it stops there, it slows and stops all the way up there at the very top, for a second blotting out the sun, and then its heart breaks and it falls.

Finally, we see why *A Heartbreaking Work of Staggering Genius* is not exactly *Peter Pan*, a fantasy that survives so long as children are "gay and innocent and heartless" (Barrie 207). We grant at last the broken heart of *A Heartbreaking Work*, which belongs to the Frisbee, beautiful and free and sufficiently divine to rival the sun, defeat gravity, stop time momentarily, escape the labyrinth of Eggers's convolutions. It is the still point of the turning world. It isn't the broken hearts of dying parents or orphaned children that break our hearts; it is that the length of time, the delta-time as Pynchon might say, that contains both innocence and death is precisely one orphaned moment. That is the moment of the return of the dead Messiah and the rejuvenation of the closed frontier. We mark the infinitesimal by a curse, a profanity with taking the Lord's name in vain surrounding it. The unfallen moment and the fallen moment, Toph in effect and Dave in effect, coincide. After that is pure bathos: the afterlife of Wendy but not of heartless Peter. "I've been old for so long," cries Eggers in his late twenties. "I am old, Peter," Wendy says, "I am ever so much more than twenty" (Barrie 205). The enormous energy of maximalist novels with their hyperbolic bathetic titles and their inflated deflationary plots, epitomized by the white Frisbee that simultaneously eclipses the sun and lapses, grants readers a chance to live on the border of adulthood and childhood only for one first profanation.

Chapter 6

THE BEAUTY! THE HORROR!

I. Maternal Escapism

Room's *Genre*

Suppose you wanted to understand Emma Donoghue's *Room* by way of Dave Eggers's *A Heartbreaking Work of Staggering Genius*. It seems promising: in Donoghue's novel, as in Eggers's partly novelized memoir, an unprepared, college-aged adult (mother, brother), in a harrowing circumstance, is forced to take sole responsibility for a child. In *Room*, the donnée is the mother and boy's incarceration in a small room by the mother's rapist, the boy's father. In *Room* as in *Heartbreaking Work*, the older relative's determination to create a reality from improvised fun—as full-time as possible, even when educational—shields the younger from acknowledgment of the insularity of his life.

Clearly escapism is in play in both works. But any attempt to understand one of them by way of the other comes up against this difficulty from the start: the contrast of titles. Donoghue's novel is not even called *The Room*—the absence of an article, indicating eventually that Room is a proper noun, serves the immediate purpose of contraction, even as Eggers's unrolling title makes its expansive claim.

Why is the claim of Donoghue's title minuscule, equivalent in scope to the room in which her characters, Ma and Jack, dwell? As a title, *Room* is even smaller than "The Bath," but it is not a book about a sliver of life. Donoghue's book is wildly speculative, though the "genius" of the book is distributed among the precocious narrator Jack, inventive Ma, and Donoghue, author of a tour de force of perspective and ventriloquism. This is unlike *A Heartbreaking Work of Staggering Genius*, whose genius is centered on its author, also approximately its narrator and protagonist. Ma explicitly denies her own exceptional creativity, insisting to an interviewer after her escape that she has protected her son only as any mother would, and denies Jack's specialness, arguing that he is a normal boy who endured an abnormal experience. The book depreciates its own metaphysical singularity.

By an unexpected corollary, *Room*, imitating Ma's pragmatism and Jack's playfulness, also understates its pathos. In this light, conversely, we can observe that Eggers's seemingly disjunctive title—are we meant to see the brokenness or the brilliance?—is of a piece: the genius of the book effects its rehabilitation of sentiment. If messianism is about a return home, and Utopianism is about leaving home, and escapism is about the home in Utopian or messianic masquerade, then sentimentalism says that anywhere can be home, because emotions are universal. Eggers's sentimental and escapist book takes up residence in several Bay Area domiciles, but its pathos is continuous in all homes, and the title's addressees are expected to be staggered by Dave's genius across all addresses.

Posit that Donoghue's *Room* fends off the attribution of genius partly in order to fend off sentimentality: as much as Ma loves Jack, she feels the need to separate from him and escort him to the mediated, mediocre world. This equals a refusal to sentimentalize the genius that could create an alternative universe. I will conscript the novel as an example of maternal escapism on the proviso that only its first section, centered on imprisonment in Room, is escapist in the full trinitarian mode. The escape from Room in the middle of the book is an example of escapology, the staging of an escape from death, but only momentarily; at the end of the escapological emergence from Room, what remains in the third phase of the novel is not escapist or escapological at all.

In order to track the book's unsentimental and veiled genius, we need to begin by feeling the resonances of its hermeneutically sealed title.

Room's Theory

Room goes to some trouble to deny its own genius by disinviting theories, or theory. It risks jeopardizing its adherence to Jack's point of view by planting him in front of a television, after his escape from Room, just when his case is being discussed by humanoid academics. One says that Jack, upon escape, "reel[s] from the sensory overload of modernity." Another corrects this with a slogan: "Post-modernity." When Jack parrots this to his grandmother, she opines, "Those guys spent too much time at college" (Donoghue 293–4).

But there are problems with the grandmother's (and the mother's and conceivably the author's) breezy dismissal of theoretical meaning. For one thing, any reader will take the book as an allegory of *something*, a fact whose tribute is Donoghue's disavowal. Many readers, like Donoghue (PhD 1997, University of Cambridge), have spent a long time at college or university; Donoghue's readership may be less cynical about what is learned there than Ma's mother. Even the attempt to normalize the events of the book can only work by expanding them. In order to keep her case from being celebrated and dismissed as a unique horror, Ma herself notes its relation to slavery and solitary confinement still practiced in the world (Donoghue 235). There is a meaning of the book beyond the titular scope of the book, whether or not that meaning takes the form of a postmodern allegory.

We might hear something off-pitch in the jargon of the professors on TV. They think that what Jack, liberated from his cell, has been exposed to is postmodernity. It seems as likely that a postmodern theorist would focus on the time in the cell as a representation of the inescapable postmodern globe than on several weeks of uncomfortable, hectic freedom.

It is inside the cell that we might begin a postmodern theorizing of power in *Room*. We observe that the power of the rapist and kidnapper who is called Old Nick, unlike sovereign power as Foucault describes it, does not function only in violent response to extraordinary threats; it normalizes and individuates, in the way of disciplinary power. This power may threaten death but prefers the biopolitics of keeping alive: Nick expects Ma's gratitude as a subject for her subjectification, with food, heat, and occasional treats provided to her. Granted that Ma does not agree implicitly to this subjection by disciplinary power, unlike prisoners in a panopticon who internalize the expectations of unseen jailers, and she is subject to continuous violence. Jack has less difficulty imbibing the terms of his incarceration; it makes him who he is. Ma is a link in the distribution of subjectivity.

To what extent has Ma's escapism had the effect of attuning Jack's subjectivity to Old Nick's power? It turns out that we are to think of Old Nick and Ma not only as Jack's biological parents but also as coproducers of his confinement. It is Old Nick's raping of Ma in the second year of her imprisonment that leads to Jack's birth into prison; but it is Ma's escapist dedication to insulating her son from the effects of Old Nick's criminal perversion that keeps Jack from dreaming of freedom, until Ma tries to reorient him after his fifth birthday. When he is freed, there are signs that the effects of Ma's disciplining have been the more durable.

So when Ma tries to limit Jack's knowledge of the outside world to what he reads in books such as *Good Night, Moon*, *The Runaway Bunny*, and preeminently *Alice's Adventures in Wonderland*, meanwhile reducing the real outside world to what can be seen on TV and categorized as fiction, we may find in the cell a correlative of Derrida's "il n'ya pas de hors-texte" (Derrida, *Grammatology* 158). "We're like people in a book," Ma tells Jack (Donoghue 90). This causes Jack to wonder, "how do people in a book escape from it?" (Donoghue 105).

Or perhaps Baudrillard is where the two types of incarceration are synthesized. Ma instructs Jack to think of TV as a fictional report from outer space, and all its shows as independent planets; Baudrillard, alone in a hotel room, thinks of TV as "another planet . . . communicating with you . . . a video of another world" (Baudrillard, *America* 52). Because of Ma's protective premise that their room is the entire real world, Jack learns what he learns of the outer world in the guise of fictions, some from TV, some from books, some remembered by Ma: "After dinner Ma tells me *Hansel and Gretel* and *How the Berlin Wall Fell Down* and *Rumpelstiltskin*" (Donoghue 71). This sentence might have provided an epigraph for Baudrillard's *Simulacra and Simulation*, a theory of the recent arrival of the image from reality to simulacrum. Like Baudrillard's, Jack's Gulf War would have taken the form of a fairy tale or a media event (Baudrillard, *Gulf War* 61–87).

"There is nothing outside of the text" (Derrida, *Grammatology* 158). "The carceral network does not cast the unassimilable into a confused hell; there is no outside" (Foucault 301). "Disneyland exists in order to hide that it is the 'real' country, all of 'real' America that is Disneyland (a bit like prisons are there to hide that it is the social in its entirety, that is, in its banal omnipresence, that is carceral)" (Baudrillard, *Simulacra* 12). Lyotard declares postmodernism to be the death of master narratives of emancipation. Postmodernism, in its post-structuralist aspect, substitutes master narratives of enclosure: they are not teleological, and they do not end in freedom. They are composed of total worlds, unexceptionable conceptions. It is possible to think of *Room* as gathering these obsessions with enclosed spaces (textual, carceral, simulacral) that swallow the world—insides engulfing outsides.

Room's *Philosophy*

Alice's Adventures in Wonderland is the inside of *Room* that is bigger than its outside. Alice, in the antechamber of Wonderland, drinks from a bottle that says, "DRINK ME," which has the effect of "shutting [her] up like a telescope" until she is ten inches tall (Carroll 7–8). This is part of an oscillation of debilitating minuteness and hugeness, whose opposite extreme is Alice's expansion in White Rabbit's house: she grows until the room cannot hold her, and she puts one arm out the window and a foot in the chimney (Carroll 27–8). The parallel is with Ma, who sometimes shrivels in her room to the size of her bed and as much further into oblivion as she can shrink, and sometimes seems to fill the room to its ceiling and walls, unable to move or change or breathe.

Room is much different to Jack. We encounter him on his fifth birthday, which is, in part, a festival of determinate measuring.

> Ma shows me to cut a strip [from a cereal box] that's as big as her foot, that's why it's called a foot, then she puts twelve little lines. I measure her nose that's two inches long. My nose is one inch and a quarter, I write it down. Ma makes Ruler flip slo-mo somersaults up Door Wall where my talls [the marks of his height] are, she says I'm three feet three inches. (Donoghue 19)

Three feet three inches is at least half a foot short for a five-year-old. If Ma, like Alice, expands and contracts rapidly, Jack's growth in height is slow and linear.

Conversely, Ma's *time* is slow and linear, but Jack's, until the end of their captivity, is almost infinitely capacious. The opening chapter of *Room* is titled "Presents," which readers will not suspect is a pun until they read its first sentences: "Today I'm five. I was four last night going to sleep in Wardrobe, but when I wake up in Bed in the dark I'm changed to five, abracadabra. Before that I was three, then, two, then one, then zero." Jack wonders if before his birth he was "minus numbers." Prior to his birth, Ma tells him she was so sad that she "cried until I didn't have any tears left. . . . I just lay here counting the seconds." Jack wonders how many. Ma answers, "Millions and millions of them" (Donoghue 3). We are still on the first page, counting time backward and forward, second by second, day by day, year by year, toward Jack's birthday present.

Ma's time is Aristotelean, countable forward by sublunary beings whose existence comes and goes: millions of seconds of sadness before the birth of Jack, more millions after it. When Jack proposes to measure the room for his birthday, his mother's reaction is anticipatory despair: "What, all of it?" Jack's response means something different to him than to his mother: "Do we have something else to do?" Jack reports that Ma, in the face of a question that defines spacious messianic time for him and the bad infinity of Hell for her, "looks at me strange. 'I guess not'" (Donoghue 19).

The preternatural intimacy of Jack and Ma living in diametrically opposed but crisscrossed spaces and times—their radical oneness and twoness at once—becomes a linguistic issue by ways of portmanteaus. In *Through the Looking Glass*, Alice reads, in a mirror within the mirror world, the following words and pseudo-words: "*Twas brillig, and the slithy toves/ Did gyre and gimble in the wabe;/ All mimsy were the borogoves,/ And the mome raths outgrabe*" (Carroll 130). Alice can make almost nothing of it but later runs into Humpty Dumpty, who speaks to the world on what would seem to be the solipsist's principle that words mean what he wants them to mean. Nevertheless, he produces an exegesis sharable by two subjectivities by using a novel interpretive tool: "'*slithy*' means 'lithe and slimy.' 'Lithe' is the same as 'active.' You see it's like a portmanteau—there are two meanings packed up into one word" (Carroll 186). Not two meanings synthesized in a single concept. The number of words is one; the number of meanings is two.

When Alice is dealing with her height of ten inches, Carroll seizes the opportunity for a pun on her name, lamenting, "alas for poor Alice" (Carroll 9). It is a conjunction noticed by Gertrude Stein, who in *Tender Buttons* cannot leave it alone—"Alas a dirty word, alas a dirty third"—in honor of Alice Toklas (Stein 492). The second section of *Tender Buttons*, "Food," which traces the physical itinerary of food from outside the body as object, through the subject's body, and then outside the body as abject, ends with the imperative to "ex-create a no-since" (Stein 496). The nonsense seems to justify Jabberwocky portmanteaus by way of a portmanteau.

Picking up on the alimentary Steinian trope, Jack and Ma love what they call "word sandwiches," which they usually ex-create as jokes, probably why Ma resorts to one at a dangerous moment. As they plot Jack's escape from Old Nick, Ma tells Jack that "Scared is what you're feeling . . . but brave is what you're doing," and summarizes this as "scaredybrave." Jack further telescopes or suitcases or sandwiches this complex concept to "scave," a sonic allusion to "toves" and "wabe" (Donoghue 116).

Later, just before Ma rolls Jack into the rug she hopes Old Nick will take outside the room, having been tricked, they hope, into believing that Jack's corpse is inside it, Ma "leans over, she doesn't even kiss me, she just touches her face to mine till I can't tell whose is whose." She says, "We're scaved, aren't we?" (Donoghue 134). In the process of compromising the distinction of feeling and doing, hence of antithetical subjectivity and objectivity (you can be scared and brave because what you show need not mimic what you feel), she compromises the distinction of herself and Jack.

In the tradition of William James, Stein deprecated the notion that subjects and objects are the comprehensive components of the world. In *Tender Buttons*, she divides the world into thirds, instead. First are "Objects," but objects are redefined from the start: tender buttons are (among more private things) coins, buttons that are legal tender because they are tendered, that is, passed between subjects. The second object of "Objects" is "Glazed Glitter," which begins, "Nickel, what is nickel, it is originally rid of a cover"—a coin that is metallic but penetrable (Stein 461). Insofar as nickels are tender in the first "Object" section, they share a quality with, say, roast beef in the second section, "Food."

The third section of *Tender Buttons* is a tour of a house. Stein is preoccupied with windows: no sooner are we in the house than we are looking outside it. Stein asks, "why is there a difference between one window and another, why is there a difference, because the curtain is shorter" (Stein 503). The windows of a room may be identical in appearance; all Stein may mean is that when their curtains are drawn to different heights, windows are *relatively* unlike. More likely, she means that a shorter curtain reveals more outside: we may infer that all windows as windows, rather than as affairs of glass and wood, are *radically* unlike, defined not by appearances but by views. Jack in *Room*, recovering at the psychiatric clinic, puts it this way: "My favorite bit of Outside is the window. It's different every time" (Donoghue 190).

Looking at the world through different windows raises for Stein the question of perspective: "This cloud does change with the movements of the moon" (Stein 507). The changing cloud foreshadows a change in weather: "A window has another spelling, it has "f" all together, it lacks no more then and this is rain" (Stein 507). The f-word may be *fenêtre*, so that Stein acknowledges the play of linguistic difference on intercourse. She seems to describe the juxtaposing of two languages in two visions at one window, as if on Badiou's account of the eventual epistemology of love: "the encounter between two differences" (Badiou, *Love* 29). Two people, one American and one French, stand at the window and see the rain from two vantages, in two languages. One points at a shared disparate outdoor phenomenon, a falling together of individuals, and perhaps teaches the other English: "This is rain."

The text itself resembles St. Teresa in Stein's opera *Four Saints in Three Acts*, "half in and half out of doors" (Stein 585), an affliction that may be compared to Alice's giant phase. Jack, toward the end of *Room*, in his new apartment, leans precariously out a window: "I was being in and out at the same time" (Donoghue 314). In a room at a window, one is half out of the room. One's subject position becomes a subject exposition. The third and final section of *Tender Buttons*, after "Objects" and "Food," is "Rooms."

Stein creates a trinitarian division of a world made of a single substance: a tenderness of objects and subjects in three phases. "Objects" concerns putative outsides that lose their distant impenetrability, like the proper noun intimate objects of *Room*. "Food" frankly contemplates objects that are ingested, digested, and excreted, as does *Room*. "Rooms" is about insides that define themselves by susceptibility to outsides. Half inside and half outside her house, the ontologically obscure narrative identity of *Tender Buttons* is half inside and half outside herself. Saddened, and wondering about her identity when she is a giant, Alice in Wonderland cries enormous tears, attuned to the world by transforming it. After Alice notices that she is tiny again, her foot slips; she falls into salt water and believes that she has fallen into the sea. It is in fact "the pool of tears which she had wept when she was nine feet high."

Alice worries that she might drown in her own tears. Trying to introduce Jack to reality after the period of her devotion to escapism has ended, Ma tells her son about Old Nick: "'I used to be scared to go to sleep, in case he came back,' Ma tells Jack, 'but when I was asleep was the only time I wasn't crying, so I slept about sixteen hours a day.'" Jack wonders, "Did you make a pool?" (Donoghue 94).

Ma reads children's books to Jack in order to sustain his illusion of the room's self-sufficiency, but she invokes *Alice* to induct Jack into the reality of outside: Alice's story is almost the only window of the novel's first half. The lesson of windows even within an almost windowless room is the semipermeability of subjects and objects, moods and weather. That does not mean that Jack and Ma are consubstantial, because neither their subjectivities nor their objectivities align. Jack floats in the world created by Ma's desperate tears, his time Ma's space, his space Ma's time. The syndrome is reminiscent of what Sethe, in Toni Morrison's *Beloved*, calls rememory: someone's memory so tactile that someone else may physically encounter and inhabit it, temporal elsewhere but spatial present. In *Room*, it is almost impossible to demarcate (Jack's) ecstasy and (Ma's) slavery; they compose a single, dual reality, space-time and time-space, a loving carceral chiasmus.

Room's Political Theology

In its physically carceral phase, *Room* is about white people. American readers will nonetheless compare *Incidents in the Life of a Slave Girl*, in which Harriet Jacobs spends seven years in a crawl space more constricted than Ma and Jack's room, watching her children through a small aperture in her wall, awaiting her chance to escape north and reunite with her family. Ma makes an explicit reference to slavery in her interview, but it is an implicit subject for Jack, twice. Jack tells his therapist Dr. Clay that he "ran on the street."

> "When you were escaping, right."
>   "Because we didn't belong to him." (Donoghue 209)

Later, when Ma and Jack are walking in their new city, they pass a store window.

> "They sell men and women and children in there," I tell her.
>   "What?" She spins around. "Oh, no, see, it's a clothes shop, so when it says *Men, Women, Children*, it just means clothes for all those people." (Donoghue 308)

Why must slavery enter the book as its referent by indirection, only, in its most vivid appearance, as a childish interpretive error, a confusion of indirect and direct objects? It is partly a question of tact: How can the smallest inhabitant of this small-scale book presume to draw an analogy with an historical enormity, a shame bigger than the United States?

Recall these corollaries in Toni Morrison's *Beloved*. First, *Beloved* is an attempt to create a new messianism founded on the liquefaction of the female body. That it is a messianism at all is implied by the epigraph from Romans, which retargets chosenness: "I will call them my people which were not my people; and her beloved, which was not beloved." The author of the epigraph does not require naming, but one of the book's protagonists is named Paul D, and two of his fellow slaves named Paul (A and F) appear as minor characters: Pauls known by their letters. In *Room*, Jack begs to differ when Ma reveals that she has a big brother named Paul: "He's a saint." Ma: "No, a different Paul." Jack: "How can there be two Pauls?" (Donoghue 83).

The Pauls in *Beloved* have letters in place of surnames, but the letters are not abbreviations. The putative rationale for the letters that stand for nothing is that slaves need to be distinguished by something other than family names. An aside in Agamben's book on messianism suggests a secondary theory. Herod Atticus assigned letters as names for his slaves as pedagogical tools for his children learning the alphabet (Agamben, *Time* 11). Being turned into a classroom illustration is, to Sethe, one of the foremost horrors of slavery: she is measured, surveyed, and experimented on by Schoolteacher, treated as a biological specimen. Is the Pauline lesson that in order to exist in God where there are no masters and slaves, you must assume the slaves' nonidentity?

But it is the breathtaking ambition of *Beloved* to provide a female theology of messianism that can rule out slavery by doctrinal axioms. It works by taking the liquefaction of the female body at its margins, the aspect of the female body that makes fascists (as described by Klaus Theweleit) insane with fury, as the divine yet incarnate fact that makes ownership, measurement, objectification, and control impossible.

That mothers share their bodies with their children in nursing is the supreme fact of maternal messianism: Sethe "had milk enough for all" (Morrison, *Beloved* 100). This is the bloody horror of slavery transmuted into the messianic promise of milk and honey on the other side of the Ohio. The embodying of messianic love as specifically maternal milk is also attested to by Ma, who tells Jack about a scientific experiment in the technological raising of monkeys, which produces "weird," as Ma puts it, babies: "See, if their mothers were there, they'd have cuddled the baby monkeys, but because the milk just came from pipes, they—It turns out they needed the love as much as the milk" (Donoghue 221).

It is time to propose a theory of a discomfiting fact of *Room*, repeatedly brought to our attention: that in the midst of their deprivation Ma has milk enough for five-year-old Jack. It is the one source of nutrition that is not reliant on Old Nick's biopower, that escapes his life-support despotism; it may also have the virtue of preceding textuality and evading the simulacra of television. Jack in nursing is a singularity in accord with his mother's singularity, a maternal-filial asymmetrical confluence for as long as it lasts. The project as in *Beloved* is to make slavery impossible by way of a theology that makes it conceptually unthinkable.

There is, however, an evident problem in this maternal messianism. Jack does not force himself on his mother in the way of Schoolteacher's nephews, but he is an expert, empirical appraiser of the milk's qualities; he symbolizes it and asserts possession of it. While readers of *Room* may resent being made to think of this connection, Jack nevertheless does: in Wardrobe, where he retreats whenever Old Nick makes a visit for sex, Jack has "a terrible idea, what if he's having some?"—Jack's term for nursing. "Would Ma let him have some or would she say, *No Way Jose, that's only for Jack.* . . . I want to jump up and scream" (Donoghue 47).

This is where the maternal messianic hope falters. The close approximation of slavery and messianic ecstasy, of self-loss and self-loss—if Sethe has milk enough for all, she has milk enough for

Schoolteacher's nephews—is intractable. The messianic hope, insofar as it depends on an interrelation of humans based on liquids rather than solids, river-crossing rather than property-owning, nurturing rather than exploiting, founders on the fact that liquefaction is no impediment whatever to possession: the suckling of Schoolteacher's nephews is a rape. Jack insists on sole ownership of his mother's milk, and desires it at times when his mother is weary of providing it. They are one and two, united by her objective sacrifice for his subjective joy, and by her subjective sacrifice for his objective joy.

It is not only Old Nick (i.e., the devil) who must be escaped in the experimental messianism of this text; messianism itself needs to be escaped. This is the usual conclusion of escapist texts, but generally escapist texts use escapist techniques to cover up and compensate for the death of Utopianism or messianism. *Room* floats a trial messianism in its first third, but the verdict is devastating. It is unclear how much is left: it is even doubtful that x can save y, which, for escapism as a local, temporary, personal, performative sub-messianism, is as good as it gets. In *Beloved*, responsibility at the end is to oneself: Paul D tells Sethe, as if human ownership and human thinginess were unproblematic, that "you your best thing" (Morrison, *Beloved* 273). The dialogue between Jack and Dr. Clay on slavery continues this way:

> "I ran on the street."
> "When you were escaping, right."
> "Because we didn't belong to him."
> "That's right." Dr. Clay's smiling. "You know who you belong to, Jack."
> "Yeah."
> "Yourself."

But Jack refuses Dr. Clay's reprising of Paul D:

> He's wrong, actually, I belong to Ma. (Donoghue 209)

Selflessness demands possession. Maternal messianism is a form of escapism, a sacralization of carceral reality, and needs to be escaped.

II. Filial Escapology

Room *and Life*

There would seem to be no reason for *The Great Escape*, John Sturges's Second World War film (1963) starring Steve McQueen, James Garner,

Richard Attenborough, Charles Bronson, James Coburn, and everybody else, to be given so much credit in the escape of Jack and then Ma from their cell. Tunneling is the method of escaping in the film; it failed in *Room* when Ma had attempted it before Jack was born. Ma uses the fact that the prisoners of Stalag Luft III proceed through their tunnel one at a time to persuade Jack to go out alone. But going out one at a time is different from going out alone. Some of the prisoners of *The Great Escape* come to each other's aid, whereas in *Room* Jack, once outside, does all the escaping for himself and Ma.

It is possible that *The Great Escape* is invoked only for its title. Even so, what does the title mean? The title and the jaunty film score seem to assure us that all will be well; so does the imperturbability of Attenborough and the insouciance of McQueen, epitomizing their nations; so does the implicit moral of the film that there should always be a Plan B and C, a lesson picked up by Ma, who first has Jack fake sickness, which does not work, then death, which does. Yet almost everyone we care about dies in *The Great Escape* (Ma's reference to the film cannot be good for Jack's morale). Is the title meretricious on purpose, like *The Great Gatsby*?

I only note that bringing up Nazism, even this obliquely, represents a considerable expansion of the scope of Donoghue's seemingly modest book. The expansiveness of bringing Nazism into the novel resembles its alluding to slavery, thus to the two historical settings of ahistorical escapist escapes. The book also alludes to Franco via "Guernica," Ma's idea of a realistic painting, which means that we cannot presumptively ridicule any politicization of the book's intentions.

If you are writing a book on escapism and you mention *Room*, someone will inevitably do you the favor of mentioning *Life is Beautiful* (1997). There is a shared setup: the parent, locked up with her or his child, tries to turn the incarceration into a game—both works literalize the situation of *A Heartbreaking Work of Staggering Genius*. Yet in Benigni's film the father is revered, by son and audiences, for keeping this up until his death; Ma decides that the real world must, in the end, be restored. That is the point at which the comparison is useful.

Start with the fact that *Life is Beautiful* is a general meditation on the relation of rules and laws. Their relationship is taken up explicitly at the first moment of incarceration in the work and death camp. A Nazi officer shouts the laws of camp obedience and the capital penalty for not obeying them, which Guido pretends to translate into Italian as the rules of a game in which he and his son Joshua will compete against all the other inmates.

What does it mean to say that the relation of laws and rules is a matter of translation? It might intimate that laws are merely inflated, deflatable rules. This correspondence might be metaphorized in the film by the relation of stylized fascist marching and Guido's parody of it, which on key occasions keeps alive Joshua's belief that he is having fun at the concentration camp. Does the parody reveal the silliness of such things as goose-stepping, its origin in play rather than in mechanized military order? This hypothesis would be passionately denied by Johan Huizinga in *Homo Ludens*, who found the play element at the origin of nearly everything produced by civilization, including war but excepting Nazism. Huizinga did not see even hypertrophied playfulness in Nazism, in what he thought of as Europe "rapidly goose stepping into helotry," a metaphor of nonplay precisely where Nazism seems most like playing. Huizinga saves the hypothesis by considering Nazism as the apotheosis of puerilism, which equals playing at play (Huizinga 206).

It is not the case, however, that *Life is Beautiful* makes the claim that laws can be reduced, by way of insight into their ludic origin, to rules of the game. Guido, ignorant of German, simply makes up rules that contradict the letter and spirit of the German laws shouted by a Nazi. Instead, the rules of the game are necessary to *escaping* the law (which includes the commandment not to escape): when Guido makes Joshua hide from the Germans, he translates hiding from authority (disobeying the law) to playing hide-and-seek (obeying the rules of the game). Obedience of rules is to obedience of laws as life to death.

Rule-bound playing begins in *Room* after the child's birth into prison but begins in *Life is Beautiful* in advance of not only the parents' incarceration but also the child's existence, and the film takes almost half its length to arrive at the concentration camp. At the opening of the film, Guido is on a vacation drive with his friend when the brakes of his car fail; the car careers down a hill and through a wedding party, coming to a stop near a country house. Guido approaches a girl there and begins calling himself the prince. Out of the window drops a beautiful young woman (stung while burning a wasp nest), and Guido, kissing Dora's stings, calls her the princess. Playing at existence within a fairy tale is underway: Guido will rescue and marry his *principessa*. There is no fascism yet for playing to escape. Or more precisely: there is no fascism yet that Guido takes as a threat. His arm gesture to wave the wedding party out of the way is misconstrued as the *saluto romano*, which bewilders Guido. The opposition of fun and fascism is already in progress before Guido sees the deadliness of the conflict.

How are we to understand this appearance and institution of escapism prior to the felt necessity of escaping something? After Dora's defenestration to greet Guido, Guido accidentally knocks a pot of flowers through a window; it lands on the head of a fascist bureaucrat who is engaged to Dora. When Guido first takes Dora away from her fascist, she speaks of herself as a treasure chest requiring a key. Guido had previously noticed that a woman named Maria, at the precise spot he and Dora have luckily reached on their walk, had thrown a key to a man when he called for it; Guido pretends to pray to the Virgin Mary for the key, and Maria tosses it down. This seems to take care of the unspoken difference in Guido and Dora's religions along with, apparently, the difference between sex and virginity, as in *Oscar Wao*.

Escapism in *Life if Beautiful* always depends on consent to accidental falling, or coincidental falling together. In that preliminary sense, we can discern the way that its escapism precedes and transcends a purposeful and historical standing up to fascist Italy. But we must wait until nearly the end of *Life is Beautiful* for the final clue to the film's apolitical, atemporal metaphysics. The time seems to arrive for attempting escape from the concentration camp. Actually, the time is not right: disorder in the camp is caused by the approach of the American army, and it appears that all Guido has to do is wait a few days for liberation. But Guido fears that the Germans are killing prisoners in anticipation of surrender or evacuation. Life-and-death approach at the same rate. Hoping to lead his family to safety, Guido hides Joshua in a storage container for safekeeping while he looks for Dora. When a search light passes by, he climbs a wall, with the effortlessness of Harpo Marx climbing a drop curtain in *A Night at the Opera*, to perch somehow above the historical glare.

A few minutes later, another search light passes, and Guido glides up another wall with just as much supernal grace. The search light almost passes underneath again, but it catches a bit of Guido in its publicity; it passes by for a moment, thinks better of it, and returns to the spot, then moves upward to expose Guido splayed on the wall. There is something comical in the humanly uncertain double-take of the light, past and back and up; and Guido's position on the wall when the spotlight finds him is comically sideways. When I first saw the film, some of the audience laughed: it's a circus moment. The audience has every right to anticipate what comes next: Guido jumps into a coincidentally passing truck; or Guido finds a rope for swinging away to a convenient roof. Neither happens.

Instead, Guido drops to the ground, exhausted. He makes only a half-hearted attempt to run away. His capacity for improvisation has come to an end. He doesn't look around for escape routes, and he doesn't seem terrified. He is done playing. He waits limply for the guards to arrive. It is the loveliest moment of the film, and its meaning is the meaning of the film. The film hadn't put escapism in relation to Nazism; from the first, it had put escapism in relation to gravity. The fairy tale (Guido's flying down a hill, Dora's flying out a window, a pot falling on the head of fascism, Maria's ascension by way of a descending key) had never said that one could escape gravity; it had said that there is happiness only in gravity, by a helpless joyous submission to it, by taking off the brakes, and by making play of the submitting. It is a question of finding the laws that make you free, the Newtonian laws of slapstick free fall. These are the laws that are consistent with, and in fact model, the rules of play. That is why Guido cannot climb his way to freedom from Nazis and their spotlight, unlike the von Trapps.

For the sake of the film's popularity (it was for a time the largest-grossing film in Italian film history), Guido gets up again, stays alive long enough to walk by his son in the storage container; he exchanges a wink with the boy and resumes his parodic *passo romano* routine, *pace* Huizinga, to evoke a last laugh, a minute before being machine-gunned out of sight. We know the boy survives because he is the film's salutatorian and valedictorian, assuring us in advance that his tale, "like a fable, [will include] sorrow, and like a fable, [will include] wonder and happiness." He tells the story of the brief wondrous life of Guido Orefice, drawn from the escapist martyrology.

On the other hand, Ma does not believe in her own escapist heroism, or in her own messianic purity, any more than she believes in her own sentimental genius in the manner of Guido/Benigni or Eggers/Eggers. Insofar as there is a messianic idea behind her escapism, it is that she and Jack can save each other by way of a paradisal chiasmic intimacy that excludes Old Nick's subjectification. But that subjectification is the basis of the intimacy. Guido doesn't save himself, but he saves his child for adulthood by way of his metaphysics; Ma knows that her practice cannot save anyone but a child, and only his stunted incarcerated childhood could save her.

Room *and Death*

Unlike Guido's, Ma's escapism is not a metaphysics; it is (or poses as) a practice geared to a special case. It has, however, provided an ersatz world and worldview to Jack who, for the sake of escaping Ma's escapism, needs to be lifted from unreality to reality, from text to outside the text, as if by the locks of a canal. Thus, Ma paradoxically invokes *The Great Escape* and *The Count of Monte Cristo*, as well as *Dora the Explorer* and *Alice in Wonderland*, to arrive at the realism phase of Plan A: Jack needs to be introduced to reality outside Room, and he needs to help devise a realistic plan to arrive at it. The plan is that Jack feign sickness so that Old Nick will bring him to a hospital, where Jack will deliver the message of their entrapment.

After Plan A fails, Ma proceeds to Plan B: Jack will feign death. The idea is to roll Jack up in Rug, then convince Old Nick to load Rug onto the back of his truck and find somewhere to bury him. Jack must extract himself from Rug and jump from the truck at a stoplight. At this point in the planning, neither reader nor Ma is sure that that the scenario is realistic, or that it serves as a reentry checkpoint from unreality to reality. Ma admonishes her son, "Jack, this is not a game" to keep him focused, yet she invokes Dora the Explorer and urges Jack to be "my superhero" a few seconds later (Donoghue 110, 113). Moments after she encourages him to identify with Jack the Giant Killer, which does not prevent Jack from wishing to call off the plan, Ma stays firm: "We're not playing, we can't stop" (Donoghue 118, 119).

How can any novel resolve the question of whether it is possible to use escapology, an artificial, ludic, simulacral version of escape, to effect an actual escape from actual death? The question returns from *The Amazing Adventures of Kavalier & Clay*. For a while, fiction and reality work in concert. After delays in Jack's emerging from Rug, Jack makes his leap from the truck into ordinary reality. But he cries out in pain, which alerts Old Nick—and for a moment ordinary reality takes the form of a chase, a Great Escape cliffhanger, or a flight from an ogre. As in *Kavalier & Clay*, there is no assurance that one is inside a prison or an escapist fiction.

External reality has its own happy surprise: it is multiethnic. A man named Ajeet, whose daughter is Naisha and whose dog is Raja, presumably an Indian in national origin, prevents Old Nick from recapturing Jack. A policewoman named Officer Oh, presumably Korean in ancestry, arrives on the scene and proves to be as patient and acute as Dora the Explorer, making remarkable inferences from what Jack tells her (she realizes that his reports on the motion of the truck can identify stops and turns) in order to run time backward and locate the cell of a garden shed, carceral Eden, and free Ma.

Dora the Explorer, herself Latina, has been the presiding spirit of the entire escape. When Jack has to memorize his plans of action, Ma tells him: "Look, it's like on *Dora.* . . . when she goes to one place and then a second place to get to the third place." Plan B is "*Dead, Truck, Wriggle Out, Jump, Run, Somebody, Note, Police, Blowtorch*" (Donoghue 132). When Plan B, with death at its inception, actually works and she and Jack are reunited safely outside the cell, Ma exults, "We did it," which is the plural exultation of every Dora episode (Donoghue 154). Who, however, occupies the role of savior? At first glance, Ma and Jack mutually. At second glance, Jack alone: "Well, *you* did it, really," Ma amends. "You saved me" (Donoghue 154). At third glance, the team of Jack, Ajeet, and Officer Oh. At the moment of a Caucasian crossing from incarceration to freedom, as in *It Happened One Night*, *Heroes of the Frontier*, and *Heartbreaking Work*, ethnicity and race make their oblique appearance.

This invokes political freedom for the sake of personal salvation. What had threatened Jack's selfhood was eternal sameness, or chiasmic crossing, with his mother; what saves it is sorting out. Jack's rebirth has to take the form of re-death and re-parturition into the plural world. The moment of escapological escape equals the crisis at which Jack escapes a certain kind of Houdini-esque drowning—his subjective drowning in his mother's liquid objectivity. Jack's traversal of death has been the book's great theme ever since Old Nick had punished mother and son, just after Jack's fifth birthday, by cutting off their heat and food. This had convinced Ma that it was time to devise an escape, and she tried to convince Jack by stressing Old Nick's cruelty. Jack reports: "My tummy creaks really loud and I figure it out, why Ma's been telling me the terrible story. She's telling me we're going—" (Donoghue 97). The final infinitive is unspoken, but the next section of the book, called "Dying," begins with the death of Plant from the cold. Jack has not yet internalized the threat: "Make her alive again," he instructs Ma (Donoghue 101). Yet Ma knows that it is from her death that Jack must be reborn.

This is why *The Count of Monte Cristo* becomes the source of their escapology, and why the one-by-one underground tunneling of *The Great Escape* remains a paradigm, though tunneling had long been impossible. Escapology is always playing the game of resurrection, as in *The Amazing Adventures of Kavalier & Clay*. The two festivals of *Room* are Jack's birthday and Easter, just after the fake death and harrowing of Hell to rescue Ma from Old Nick.

The Christology is not hard to assemble; what makes it worth noticing is the age of the Christ. Divine temporality meets mortal time in the life of a five-year-old, alone with his ritual death. This is the precocious confrontation with finitude characteristic of escapist literature: of Paul in *Heroes of the Frontier*, of Toph in *Heartbreaking Work*, of Valentino

Achak Deng in *What is the What*, of Oskar in *Extremely Loud*, of Jacob Bloch's three sons in *Here I Am*, of Oscar Wao, of Kavalier. Of Huck and Tom attending their own funerals; of Peter Pan greeting death on a submerging island as the "great adventure." Even of Alice, who is allowed not to internalize what she has glimpsed. The Gnat, introducing Alice to entomology, discusses a relative of the butterfly, the bread-and-butterfly, which lives on weak tea with cream. Alice wonders, "supposing it couldn't find any?" The Gnat answers, "Then it would die, of course." Alice worries, "But that must happen very often." The Gnat replies, "It always happens" (Carroll 149–50). If childhood continued forever, the mediators of these books would not vanish, and their genre would be messianism rather than escapism.

The defining escapist claim on escapology is not its messianic hopefulness; it is messianic hopefulness homing on a child. More precisely, the escapist claim is not so much that messianic hopefulness can be focused on a child; it is that time can be stopped at the moment when innocence meets experience, when childhood prematurely learns death. (This is one of Chabon's borderlands.) Escapist escapology is not, like messianism, the eruption of eternity into history; it is the artificial manufacturing of an interval when escapologist children can save the lives of aging escapist adults who escort childhood to mortality for the exchange.

III. The Reality of Escape

Room's Bathos

The escapist phase of *Room*'s escapism seems eternal but is not meant to be; its escapological phase promises immortality but only lasts from the moment that Jack agrees to Ma's plan to imitate death and resurrection until the moment that Ma exclaims, "we did it." This is escapist time, devolved from Agamben's Paul's "time of the end," which splits the difference between resurrection and return: death-informed but life-informed; the time when Ma's heroism turns to Jack for fulfillment, and Jack's reliance on Ma for fulfillment turns to heroism, cosmic and chiasmic optimism.

If *Heartbreaking Work* is escapist insofar as Dave and Toph can stand together in chiasmic harmony against the world, Dave child-adult and Toph adult-child, epitomized at the moment it is lost playing Frisbee on the beach, then the escapology of *Room* likewise culminates at the moment it is lost, at "we did it." This moment is followed by Ma's confusion and ours as to who did it, who saved whom. The book continues, at that point, as *Heartbreaking Work* does not, into the world in which no one can save anyone. This is bathos from escapism, not the bathos of escapism. In its length and detail, this aftermath may feel anticlimactic even to readers (who will remember the first half of the book more vividly in ten years), but it is the book's most original aspect.

The bathos of the second half of the book can be quickly summarized. The outside world is a place of disunity rather than consubstantiality: Ma and Jack can be separated; Ma puts an end to nursing. It is a place of multiplicity rather than singularity: "Outsiders are not like us, they've got a million of things and different kinds of each thing, like all different chocolate bars and machines and shoes" (Donoghue 264). There is time enough for everything in the quasi-eternity of Room; in the outside, Jack "notice[s] persons are nearly always stressed and have no time" (Donoghue 286). Though Officer Oh does her job brilliantly, and doctors are dedicated and acute, the regular people of the regular world almost uniformly fail to rise to the occasion of Jack's first and Ma's second coming. They cannot remove themselves from their trivia, despite good intentions all around. Ma's mother tries hard to help but slips back into her pettiness. Dr. Clay, an African American follow-up addition to the salvific team (his sympathy vouches for the right of white readers, or the inclination of readers of color, to sympathize with an all-white enslavement and participate in its escape nostalgia, as in *It Happened One Night* and *The Sound of Music*), asks Ma if she ever desired "to slap [your mother] before you were kidnapped." Ma answers casually, "oh sure," but adds sardonically, "Great, I've got my life back" (Donoghue 219).

Jack tells Dr. Clay what he doesn't like about the outside world. Dr. Clay, a poetry buff, comments, "World is suddener than we fancy it" (Donoghue 194). Louis MacNeice's poem continues: "World is crazier and more of it than we think,/ Incorrigibly plural." That summarizes Jack's view. But what had Ma fancied? In bringing Jack home, had she forgotten that home is what fictional characters like herself, for example Eggers's Josie in *Heroes of the Frontier*, run away from?

It is at this question that the dual symbolic setting of *Room* returns to haunt Ma and the book itself. If Room is the opposite of the world, as it seems to be for Jack, then the reality of the world (its disunity, multiplicity, mediocrity, stupidity, publicity, busyness, pettiness, selfishness, infection, repetition, and mediation) is deplorable. The virtue of its faults is diversity, but diversity exists in the book as substitute for lost maternal unity, a melancholy recompense. We can regret that the only escape from it had been a prison. From the beginning, however, we have not been sure that the room isn't, in some way, the embryonic postmodern world itself, Ma's prison emblematizing the world prison, a simulacrum of freedom. There is no direction or place of salvation.

Room's *Rage*

It is Baudrillard who seems most to preside over the image-saturated outside world. Already reporters and cameras are present at the reunion of Jack and Ma on the street. Of course, they get everything wrong, and we congratulate ourselves as readers on our capacity for sorting truth from fiction: "The despot's victims have an eerie pallor and appear to be in a borderline catatonic state after the long nightmare of their incarceration. . . . The malnourished boy, unable to walk, is seen here lashing out convulsively at one of his rescuers." The boy isn't catatonic, immobile, or lashing out convulsively.

But when the language of the media begins to inflate the story, we lose track of how to tell it is wrong. When a newspaper titles an article "HOPE FOR BONSAI BOY," it calls attention to what Ma has not acknowledged: Jack is very small. The article goes on: "He is 'Miracle Jack' to the staff at the exclusive Cumberland Clinic who have already lost their hearts to the pint-sized hero who awakened Saturday night to a brave new world. The haunting, long-haired Little Prince is the product of his beautiful young mother's serial abuse at the hands of the Garden-shed Ogre" (Donoghue 215). This is a jumble, but so is *Room*. The article calls Old Nick an ogre, but Ma and Jack think of him as a fairytale giant. The reference to Shakespeare or Aldous Huxley (probably the reporter doesn't care which) captures the Utopian/dystopian ambiguity of inside and outside the shed. *The Little Prince*, devoted to the innocence of singularity and the despair of multiplicity, is an accurate, if fortuitous, allusion, and Ma calls Jack "Prince Jackerjack."

Because the jumble of allusions to texts of all sorts by the vulgar media is not very different from the novel's jumble of references to suggest the verbal and media enclosure of the cell experience, the media has already won the competition to describe: it takes over the book from within the book. "Whereas representation attempts to absorb simulation by interpreting it as a false representation," Baudrillard writes, "simulation envelops the whole edifice of representation itself as a simulacrum" (Baudrillard, *Simulacra* 6). The world that Ma and Jack have escaped to is simulacral before they arrive; the media describe a mediated world. They cannot help their verisimilitude, just as *The Sound of Music* couldn't help its global realism.

The reality that had already entered into the room by way of TV may look and sound this way: "It's Rihanna and T.I. and Lady Gaga and Kanye West." Jack ponders why rappers wear sunglasses at night. Ma answers that they "just want to look cool. And not have fans staring into their faces all the time because they're so famous." Jack infers that the stars must not enjoy their fame. "Well, I guess they do," says Ma, "but they want to stay a bit private as well" (Donoghue 45–6). This sounds like a dialogue about the hypocrisy or self-contradictions of stardom; we are quick to believe that Jack and Ma, unlike the stars, really crave privacy. Jack is emphatic about this: when Dr. Clay asks him what he dislikes about the outside, he is succinct, "Persons looking" (Donoghue 194). "Paparazzi" becomes his newest word. Dr. Clay tells Ma that "celebrity is a secondary trauma" (Donoghue 306).

If Jack and Ma now equally detest the world that has become more or less equal to the fictive world that entered their room, if they rejoin only a simulacrum of freedom, if the world is an all-seeing dystopia, it is surprising that Ma consents to give an interview to the talk show celebrity Jack had already been deprecating as "the woman with the puffy hair" when he had seen her on *Room*'s television. Ma's explanations for her going on TV are somewhat weak and contradictory. But no strong and consistent position on privacy exists in light of Ma and Jack's incarceration. When Ma and Jack return with Officer Oh to the scene of the crime, the policewoman points out to them the "fifteen-foot hedge all the way around. . . . [N]eighbors thought nothing of it." "A man's entitled to his privacy," she quotes neighbors as saying (Donoghue 318). Can privacy be a value if it protects Old Nick? Without principles that do not lead to slavery, to the sanctity of near-solitary confinement with, as a consequence, only TV for context, no wonder Ma's interview goes poorly.

First, Ma denies to the interviewer that the world must seem utterly different to her: they've watched the news on television. The interviewer keeps probing for something sensational. Did Ma suffer from Stockholm syndrome and come to feel a bond with Old Nick? What was her reaction to her prior pregnancy and stillbirth? Ma's answer to the first question is no, she hated him; Ma refuses to answer the second. She resists any prurient fascination that the interviewer or the world might have in her case: things were normal or normalized; though her situation was horrific, her psychology remained proportionate to it. Yet when the interviewer, picking up on her hatred for her captor, infers that Ma might have resented her second pregnancy, Ma herself ups the ante: "Actually, I felt saved" (Donoghue 233).

The interviewer is delighted by this maternal piety, but she mistakes how seriously Ma means "saved." When Ma describes giving birth, on her second try, to a healthy baby "under medieval conditions," she calls it "the best thing" she's ever done. The interviewer decides to make this a relatable moment: "Every mother says—." But Ma interrupts her: "Yeah, but for me, see, Jack was everything. I was alive again, I mattered" (233).

Their positions have reversed. Now the interviewer stresses the ordinary, Ma the exceptional. The interviewer wants horror and perversion justified by uplift, but she doesn't want religion, or not much, nothing enthusiastic. Ma's self-contradictions all have their fifteen minutes of fame: her sense of the horror of her life in the cell and her sense that what is relevant was its normality for Jack; her sense that what she had done was normalize the cell and her sense that she had sacralized it; her belief that she had sacralized the private cell and her certainty that she was compelled to escape it to the profane world.

That Ma and the interviewer agree on nothing is not the result of their taking intransigent positions; it's the result of Ma's hating TV and the TV interviewer and the interview, no matter what turn it takes, on behalf of one aspect or another of her self-contradictions. When the interviewer inquires whether it ever occurred to Ma to ask Old Nick to take Jack to the outside world and leave him somewhere to be adopted, the crisis of the interview arrives. She is picking up on Ma's emphasis that what she wanted for Jack was normality—wouldn't a life outside with a loving family have been more normal? "He had me," says Ma. "He had a childhood with me, whether you'd call it *normal* or not." But he'd be free? "Free away from me?" He'd have "friends, school, grass, swimming, rides at the fair." Ma begins to lose control of her voice: "Why does everyone go on about fairs? . . . When I was a kid I hated fairs."

The interviewer laughs at the comeback, but Ma begins to sob, causing Jack to rush onto the set, causing their lawyer to shout, "The boy is not to be shown." The interview blows up in this hysterical chain reaction (Donoghue 237–8).

Recall the rage of Dave Eggers at the end of *Heartbreaking Work*, when he recognizes that his moment of perfect harmony with Toph must end for Toph's sake, when the question becomes whether or not to publish a book publicizing their harmony, which had been a private perfection. For whose sake would he commit their lives to a book? For the despised audience, the "persons looking," as Jack puts it. Eggers calls them "the watchers" (*Heartbreaking Work* 215). The problem with escapist texts, from *The Sound of Music* on, is that they compromise with audiences: they play to audiences that do not respect their privacy. These texts have contempt for readers and audiences who represent the desire for public escapism from real problems, but what is exposed, Augustinian fashion, is their own private escapism. They cannot imagine anything but escapism from audiences that are the actual Hitlers and Trujillos of their stories. The spotlight that becomes the flashlight of *The Sound of Music* reappears as the spotlight of *Life is Beautiful*; Ma and Jack exit their prison into it. Self-conscious escapist texts, appealing to their jailers with stories of jailbreaks, on the model of *Small House of Uncle Thomas*, have climactic moments of illuminated self-loathing.

Room's *Homelessness*

Heartbreaking Work ends at the summit of Eggers's rage; *Room* does not end at the summit of Ma's. After the interview, Ma tries to kill herself. Her freedom has been almost an absolute failure: instead of allowing Jack to join the free self-possessing world at the expense of their consubstantiality, they sacrifice their unity to a world that is mediocre and mediated. The book might have ended with her despair at maximum pitch, but it is narrated by Jack, not Ma.

When Ma, having failed to commit suicide, regains enough strength, she participates in Jack's return to Room. It is no longer exactly Room (for one thing, it allows entrances and exits), so Jack's reaction is not to demand returning to live in the place where Jack was everything to Ma, and Ma was all in all to Jack, and time was spacious, and rewards seemed to Jack to exceed deserts, to their private, fictive messianism, their Agambenian garden. But it is still Room enough that Jack needs a rite for his passage from it, which he borrows from another fiction, *Goodnight, Moon*. The novel's final farewell does not open into pure impure reality. Nor do they exit Room on the way toward a permanent place to relocate.

If *Room* at times seems like a compendium, a book of books that includes all escapist books, on the order of *Oscar Wao*, it seems to evade escapism at the end in not indulging either a redemptive fantasy or the rage that it cannot be prolonged; or the rage, like that of *Everything is Illuminated*, that texts cannot remove us from texts to freedom; or the rage, like that of *Heartbreaking Work*, that private beauty cannot be published. But it does not say "The beauty! The beauty!" or "Life is Beautiful." *Room* cannot point in the direction of beauty, freedom, or salvation, an incapacity that is usually the motive rather than the conclusion of escapism. As an escapist text, it tries to furnish a home that disguises that incapacity, a semiprivate dwelling for two as good as it gets, maternal salvation within solitary confinement. But it ends, like *Heroes of the Frontier* or *Here I Am*, in homelessness and bathos, which means that diasporic survival scatters the hope of a Utopian departure from home or a messianic return.

Chapter 7

ET IN NOBIS ARCADIA

It is easy to imagine that Emma Donoghue's *Room* and Lauren Groff's *Arcadia* were written in one workshop. This is despite the fact that the two books are antithetical. *Room* is messianist: the question of the escapist aspect of the book is whether life is sacred for Jack in an isolated pretend Heaven, where Ma is all in all. *Arcadia* is Utopianist: the question is whether a new idea of community, on the margins of corrupt society, can be built and sustained or whether an imperfect world can be improved on its model. (In fact, only a short period of *Room* takes place in the aftermath of the escapist incarceration; most of *Arcadia* concerns the aftermath of the escapist Utopia, though the protagonist of the book, Bit Stone, never outgrows it.) The escapism of *Room* takes place in a cell, where salvation, if it is possible, must be imagined by Ma *against the obscenity of Ma and Jack's Inside*. But the first part of *Arcadia* takes place in an expanding, inclusive commune in upstate New York, and its escapism is imperfectly manifest in the real lives of the Arcadians, among whom Bit lives with his mother and father, *as against Outside* (capitalized in both books).

Yet the artificial world produced by Ma and the quasi-natural world produced by Bit's parents, Hannah and Abe, fail to prevent similar incursions of division, domination, and death. Thus, both books require escapes from escapist insides. We follow Jack and Bit, who come to consciousness within their escapist habitats, starting about age five, the age at which both are weaned; yet their first lessons in desperation are also imbibed from their otherwise nurturing mothers. Ma has days when she is "gone" (Donoghue 60): when she cannot force herself out of bed. Hannah has longer periods of the same prostration: days when she'd "just go away" (Groff 250). Both Ma and Hannah have these interludes of debilitating depression while on the Inside; both attempt suicide unsuccessfully on the Outside. Both mothers expand and contract accordingly in the imaginations of their children. When Hannah is dying, Groff writes of her (in mature Bit's voice, in childish

Jack's spirit): "Hannah had once been vaster than Arcadia itself, her body so big it enveloped him"; but "dwindling, she is a burlap sack and bundle of sticks" (Groff 276). That the investment of son in mother is escapist is testified to by the reference of growing and shrinking to *Alice in Wonderland* in *Room*, and by repeated references to the Brothers Grimm, and the sleeping princess who needs a prince to awaken her, in *Arcadia*.

There is no firm diagnosis in *Arcadia* for the maternal acedia, but the general speculation is that it began with Hannah's loss of a baby, probably in childbirth, who we learn in passing was a girl. The beginning of the end of Bit's belief in Arcadia is the psychic distance between his parents, "the size of his sister he'll never see" (Groff 77). We recall Jack's lost sister in *Room*, who haunts Ma, who seems to inhabit Jack.

I have used Donoghue's novel to epitomize an escapist derivative of maternal messianism, in conversation with, among others, Gertrude Stein and Toni Morrison. Despite the matrilineal pedigree, the success or failure of messianism in *Room* is staked on the continuing life of a boy, as is the success or failure of Utopianism in *Arcadia*. Is my own study, from Chabon on, exclusively about boyhood?

It is nearly true. Yet the copresence of Donoghue and Groff at the center of the study swerves the account. The narrative detail that allows this refocusing is the death in childbirth of the two girls in relation to the surviving boys. A repeated fact about both Jack and Bit is that they are very small. Bit weighs three ounces at birth, and is 5'3" as an adult. He is not mistaken, like Jack with his uncut hair, for a girl; but on occasion we hear about the pitch of his voice—Bit remembers "his own young voice, urgent and high" (Groff 264). Later, when his wife leaves him, he must be son and daughter taking care of his mother, and father and mother raising his daughter. Ma explicitly thinks of Jack as the second coming of a female child; Bit comes before his dead sister, but perhaps he keeps himself small and nurturing to absorb the loss.

It is fair to say that both books, insofar as their escapism blossoms from the failure of messianism or Utopianism, maintain their escapist hope in the bond between a mother and an androgynous male child. That this is the gendering of their maternal escapism seems to be based on the hope of a new and viable access of receptive innocence on the part of men, not on the hope of a new access of worldly and aggressive experience on the part of women. It is not that boys are more likely candidates than girls for saving (subjective and objective gerund); on the contrary, it takes the re-gendering of boys to explore Utopian space or summon messianic time. The death of two girls in the two book is the fate of the messianic or Utopian mediator, who more or less returns in the quasi-Messianic *Room* and more or less vanishes in the quasi-Utopian *Arcadia*. I should add, however, that the longer afterlife of *Arcadia* permits us to know that Bit has a daughter, a long-distance runner, who seems predestined to take her place among the powerful women who have always surrounded Bit; it is their power that has protected the inexhaustibility of his innocence.

The escapist hope for a new viable innocence does not survive in Colson Whitehead, who is the subject of the next chapter. Nor does it ever exist for the two global authors, David Grossman and Arundhati Roy, who follow in a rubric of their own: for all three, there was no moment of innocence prior to the moment of experience, hence no innocence that, on an escapist wish, might outlast its allotted time. (We might also compare JoJo in Jasmyn Ward's *Sing, Unburied, Sing*, whose nurturing of his sister is innocent and experienced at once, insofar as his own childhood has been protected by grandparents but has never included a moment unhaunted by absence and death.) Grossman tests his thought experiments in mingled innocence and experience on boys; it is left to Arundhati Roy, at the very end of this study proper, answering the suggestions of Donoghue and Groff, to stake her hopes first on the adulthood of a hermaphrodite and, second, on the birth of a girl on a messianic or Utopian conception.

Chapter 8

THE ETHICS OF IMMORTALITY

At almost the last second of Colson Whitehead's first novel, *The Intuitionist*, the omniscient, if withholding, narrator reveals how the name of the book's heroine, Lila Mae Watson, became known to the book's putative messiah, James Fulton. Fulton, whose salvific claims are primarily based on a missing manuscript of prophetic elevator theory and the design plans for a perfect elevator that will usher in "the second elevation," runs into the Dean of the Institute for Vertical Transport, "nattering on about his dinner date with some other yahoo they got around here" (Whitehead, *Intuitionist* 253). "Yahoo" is Fulton's term, and Whitehead's own diction comes from everywhere, so perhaps the passing epithet is not noteworthy, table setting for Fulton's casual but consequential inquiry about Lila Mae.

It seems more crucial when, in Whitehead's *The Underground Railroad*, the Underground Railroad operator Fletcher warns the escaping slave Caesar that reading *Travels into Several Remote Nations* "will get him killed." Caesar disagrees: "Now a page here and there, in the golden afternoon light, sustained him. Guile and pluck, guile and pluck. The white man in the book, Gulliver, roved from peril to peril, each new island a new predicament to solve before he could return home." Caesar himself would like a home, if only there were a home to welcome his return; in the meantime, he imitates Gulliver, quintessential white man who would "make a home then keep straying" (Whitehead, *Railroad* 235). It is a paradoxical correspondence, which does perhaps get Caesar killed.

I would like to propose the existence of a subcategory of escapist novels, epitomized by Whitehead's *The Underground Railroad*, anticipated by Octavia E. Butler's *Kindred*. In the *Kindred* paradigm, the modern African American woman Dana, who is transported intermittently, unintentionally, and inexplicably to antebellum Maryland to preserve the life of her underbred slave-owning white ancestor Rufus, tutors him in literacy by first reading to him from *Robinson Crusoe*, with its personal relevance. "Crusoe had, after all, been on a slave-trading voyage when he was shipwrecked"; yet, "as a kind of castaway myself, I was happy to escape into the fictional world of someone else's trouble" (Butler 87). The meta-escapist paradox of the remark is that readerly identification with the sorrows of a fictional character is precisely the precondition of readerly escapism. Butler will take up the critique of identification—call it "kinship"—throughout *Kindred*.

The second book on Rufus and Dana's improvised syllabus is *Pilgrim's Progress*, about which we learn nothing. Their third and final pedagogical project is *Gulliver's Travels*. For two pages, we hear about Dana's reading of it to Rufus, yet we never hear Swift's words, themselves. Rufus's hyper-indulgent mother disturbs the tutorial to offer Rufus cake with ruthless insistence and to complain about Dana's reading. After Rufus wordlessly commands his mother to leave, Dana "plunged back into *Gulliver's Travels*" (Butler 104), but the narrative has wearied of its attempt to get that story on record, and we are privy to nothing of its reading or reception. One way to foreshadow the topic of this chapter is to wonder what we would have made of the cameo appearance of *Gulliver's Travels* in *Kindred*, if the former had been quoted in the latter.

It is impossible to ignore the interjection of adventure or fantasy stories into *Oscar Wao* or *Room*. The significance of *Gulliver's Travels* in Butler and Whitehead might be harder to specify, so laconic are the references. Yet something will come of the effort, whose usefulness will consist in isolating what might be called the "ethics of immortality" branch of the escapist contemporary novel. I take that phrase from Borges's commentary on his story "The Immortal," whose temporarily immortal hero is a Gulliveresque Roman soldier named, as it happens, Rufus (Borges 287).

Once we recognize the influence of *Gulliver's Travels* in novels such as *Kindred*, *The Intuitionist*, and *The Underground Railroad*, we can register the significance of an unanticipated yet unmistakable connection between them and a global novel such as Mohsin Hamid's *Exit West*. These are all works in which travel through time and space is discrete. "Each new island" is "a new predicament to solve": saving yourself is both a continual and a discontinuous project. In each of these books, you are always saved somewhere and you are always endangered again somewhere else entirely. *Exit West*, *Kindred*, *The Intuitionist*, and *The Underground Railroad* are allegories of an updated genre, postmodern allegory—featuring pilgrims who do not progress and a kaleidoscopic immortality.

Whitehead is a virtuoso of allegory, capable of structuring *The Intuitionist* as a messianic allegory, mocking it, mocking allegory in general, yet insinuating a contradictory allegory in the process. For most of the novel, we are not sure what to make of the ludicrousness of the only allegorical interpretation that the book spells out. The novel treats the Vertical Transport Industry as a Church that has split like western Christianity in two: the Empiricists and Intuitionists. The bifurcated Church has its denominational colleges and its compromised alliances in secular politics. Its newest claimant to messianic status is James Fulton, who has written mystical transport doctrine in two books; there are fragments and rumors of a chiliastic third book. He has promised the world a perfect elevator that will usher in the second elevation, with unlimited skyscraping potential and absolute safety, which equals, for the purposes of the allegory, salvation. That elevators, without this divine guarantee, are coffins suspended above Hell—we "ride in a box on a rope in a pit" (Whitehead, *Intuitionist* 5)—is a specifically American and Puritan conception, Jonathan Edwards by way of Edgar Allan Poe, with an American messianic counter-vision: the new "shining city" of the elevated future is John Winthrop by way of Ronald Reagan by way of Elisha Otis (Whitehead, *Intuitionist* 198).

Lila Mae Watson is an Intuitionist elevator inspector, which means she tests the safety of elevators by feelings rather than observation, and she takes Fulton as her Intuitionist savior. Mixed up in the politics of religion because her name appears in the marginalia of a Fulton fragment after his casual inquiry about her, Lila is blamed for elevator sabotage and spends much of the book on the lam. Yet she is as much interested in salvation as safety and so, as a result, are readers. The second elevation, a second era of elevator technological innovation, will "grant us the sky" (Whitehead, *Intuitionist* 61). The perfect elevator is "something we cannot imagine, like the shape of angels' teeth" (Whitehead, *Intuitionist* 61). This oxymoronic anti-simile tethers the posthumous solidity of bone to the immortal weightlessness of spirit: a masculine synthesis of mechanics and ideality, in contrast with Morrison's or Donoghue's fluid messianism, a division of intellectual labor Luce Irigaray would have recognized.

Beloved and *Room* are serious experiments in female messianism, while *The Intuitionist*, largely the story of the disabusing of a woman of a form of paternal messianism, never takes it seriously. There is nonetheless a reason for Whitehead's devoting almost all his book to a laughable creed: at the beginning of his career, he establishes his post-messianic premises. That much seems obligatory, but where does he go next? In the taxonomy I have tried to establish, the answer is almost always to the local and familial, and to the chance of saving one proximate innocent rather than the world, by illusion and performance such as a novelist might conjure rather than the truth and illumination of a prophet. But *The Intuitionist* has no Toph, no Little Igor, no Paul, no Jack—it has, startlingly, no children at all, hence no children to save and be saved by. There is no interim between innocence and experience for adults and children to cohabit, an escapist communal moment as good as it will ever get. *The Intuitionist* has all the bathos of the post-messianic, post-Utopian escapist novel, but does not take seriously the complementary hyperbole.

I have not mentioned that Lila Mae Watson and James Fulton are African American. Lila's race is known all along to readers: the book takes place somewhere in the middle third of the twentieth century, and Lila is one of very few Black elevator inspectors, the first inspector who is both Black and female. Fulton's race is veiled for much of the book, and the delayed revelation itself implies a mystery: how has a Black American man become the prophet of techno-eschatological fervor?

To penetrate the mystery requires learning to read differently. Politicians or corporate executives have sent a Black man, an apparent rube named Natchez, to entangle Lila in their machinations, and his method is to insinuate himself into Lila's affections by claiming to be Fulton's nephew, which is the first indication that Fulton was himself a Black man. When Lila discovers Natchez's duplicity, it seems momentarily possible that Fulton was white, after all. But "no, Fulton was colored. She understands this luminous truth." If the book offers compensation for its bathos of post-messianism, here it is. Not everything is illuminated, but one truth is luminous. "She had seen it in the man's books, made plain by her new literacy. In the last few days she has learned how to read, like a slave does, one forbidden word at a time" (Whitehead, *Intuitionist* 230).

At this sentence, *The Intuitionist* transforms itself into a quasi-neo-slave narrative, with literacy its saving virtue, as in many paleo-slave narratives. We know from the acknowledgments to Whitehead's more overt neo-slave narrative, *The Underground Railroad*, that Frederick Douglass is one of his sources; we could have presumed it. Douglass's story of learning to be literate, one forbidden *letter* at a time, is famous. We are, however, discussing literacy in the esoteric sense, the sense in which readers of the book may be illiterate, and Douglass's story about *that*, just as famous, is, at the same time, subtle and elusive. At stake is our compensation for reading a book of disillusion: once we give up on the Christianoid messianic allegory, we are enticed by an African American allegory, readable only by the transmuted consciousness of a special literacy. This means at a minimum that meta-allegory has replaced allegory as the book's access to a new luminous truth.

How does one read the songs of slaves? "I did not, when a slave," Douglass writes, "understand the deep meaning of those rude and apparently incoherent songs." The question is why the songs seemed incoherent even to him. The answer is puzzling: "I was myself within the circle; so that I neither saw nor heard as those without might see or hear" (Douglass 14).

Yet northern whites are not the ideal readers whom Douglas identifies as "those without": "I have often been utterly astonished, since I came to the north, to find persons who could speak of the singing, among slaves, as evidence of their contentment and happiness. . . . The songs of the slave represent the sorrows of his heart" (Douglass 15). That seems a clear enough understanding; it leaves unexplained where the obscurity lies even for slaves, themselves. Douglass specifies exactly who might comprehend the despair and longing of slave singing: "If any one wishes to be impressed with the soul-killing effects of slavery, let him go to Colonel Lloyd's plantation, and, on allowance-day, place himself in the deep pine woods, and there let him, in silence, analyze the sounds that shall pass through the chambers of his soul" (Douglass 14).

The preferred precondition for understanding the allegory of the slave's song is not singing it: Douglass insists on the necessity of silence. The preferred methodology of those not singing is not empathy but analysis, not of the sounds themselves as sensuous vibrations in the air and ears, but of the sounds translated for the soul. The preferred position is not in the circle or outside it but on the circumference of it, in the deep pinewoods surrounding the plantation. The preferred position is on the border of slavery because the incoherence of the slaves' songs cannot be mended: they must be understood by the soul; they sing the murder of the soul.

Lila is told that Fulton is a Black man; then she realizes its luminous truth. She was never on the inside of his circle; in fact, he is the single inhabitant of his circle. They had observed each other tangentially, when he was reduced to an anonymous isolated presence on the elevator institute's campus and Lila was an equally isolated student. She wondered who the old man was; he wondered who the colored female student was. But at a distance, and by analysis, she knows, it turns out, the secret meaning of his prophesying.

In Douglass's formulation, reading slave art requires loneliness. It is not merely that neither northern whites nor Douglass himself as a slave reads songs with full comprehension; it is not merely that Douglass imagines a location neither on nor distant from the plantation for proper reading. He requires simultaneously a (near) witnessing and a (removed) analysis from within the deep pinewoods by a soul not in a community but in self-communion. Accordingly, Whitehead never imagines a hero or heroine of hermeneutics with passionate enacted romantic interests, or with any family to speak of, or even with many friends. There are almost no children for his heroes or heroines to feel responsible for. There are a few prospects of intimacy but nothing intimate is ever achieved. A typical Whitehead adult protagonist is on the run, a solitary female or a man in a world bereft of appropriate women. They make a choice of their loneliness, before or after the fact, loners one way or the other. "Natal alienation," Orlando Patterson's term for the condition of slaves who cannot rely on their place in a community, beginning with their place in a family, is a way of life for Whitehead's characters. Lila is isolated in her role as the only Black female elevator inspector, a life she left home to pursue, devotee of its airborne aspirations. She chooses to live at the intersection of dimensions.

It is therefore from Lila that we learn how to read both the Blackness of Fulton and the significance of his messianism. This means that natal alienation is required of Whitehead's readers. The significance of Fulton's messianism, readers infer, is at least doubly allegorical: if the second elevation stands for the second coming, if the perfected New York of surmountable skyscrapers is the New Jerusalem, it is nonetheless the case that the second coming equals passing, and Zion is a world made safe for passing upward. Reading Fulton as a Black man must take into account that he seems to be a white man. Rebirth as a white man is the preeminent realization of what Fulton calls the "dream of uplift" (Whitehead, *Intuitionist* 186), of social ascension. Inventing the perfect elevator entails perfect safety on the inside of white upward mobility.

The Christian prophetic allegory is a case of narrative misdirection. But the set of racial allegorical equivalents, according to which Fulton is not a messiah but a Black man passing, may also be an allegorical feint as well, or subsumed into a larger allegory. We had been wondering who persecutes Lila for the length of the story—both the Empiricists and the Intuitionists have their strategic reasons, in an election season, for controlling, charming, intimidating, or hurting her. The answer in the end is Arbo, the elevator manufacturer, whose motive is not to save passengers by mystical doctrine but to distract them from the mundane truth of their ascending precariousness.

Lila is incredulous that the company has put its faith in a Black man's invention. A Black Arbo executive explains that "his color doesn't matter when it gets to that level. The level of commerce" (Whitehead, *Intuitionist* 250). The executive keeps the chameleon allegory alive: the penthouse floor that the elevator attains is the level not of spiritual farsightedness or of racial privilege but of race-blind material wealth. Ignoring rather than policing the racial borders is good for commerce. It *is* commerce: fungibility at the level of producer or consumer identity. In greed there are no Jews nor Greeks, men nor women, masters nor slaves. Its world, except for skyscrapers, is flat. That is the disgrace of Pauline messianism in *The Intuitionist*, which leaves Whitehead free to write the post-messianic escape novel of his choosing.

I want to begin by posing a naïve question about Whitehead's neo-slave escape narrative, *The Underground Railroad*: What is the point of the central trope or antitrope, the converting of the conceit of the Underground Railroad, with its metaphorical agents and conductors, into a literal underground railroad, with real trains, tracks, and tunnels? It seems at first glance the unremitting literal-mindedness of a mad allegorist. A micro-example of the same syndrome: early in the book, during a slave's birthday carnival in Georgia, a young slave accidentally spills a single drop of wine on the white shirt of a slave-owner, who regards it as an "eternal stain" and brutally beats the offender (Whitehead, *Railroad* 33). It is a blatant allegory of the violation of the "one drop rule" and its perpetual imaginary ramifications. But who is reading the spilled wine as an allegory—the master or readers? Are we reading the master's own tacit allegorization of the spilled wine? Is the one drop rule itself an allegory of pollution and abjection? Is the substitution of wine for blood a switching point to a different allegorical track?

The mechanical connection of an allegorical embodiment to its conceptual referent (as opposed, in Coleridge's terms, to the consubstantiality of embodiment and concept in the symbol) is the problem of allegory for race theory: Africans and African Americans can be wrenched into identity with any sin or evil in the Bible whatever. But the ontological disconnect of embodiment and concept may be its benefit. Octavia E. Butler's final novel, *Fledgling*, is testimony to the benefit, insofar as vampirism alternately suggests bigoted whiteness, persecuted Blackness, or the deconstructing of the black-white binary. Her book is an allegory of the disruptive potential of allegory.

So is *The Underground Railroad*, which is not a slave's progress but begins as one. Every other chapter is named after a station in the incomplete escape of its heroine, Cora; the railroad stop chapters are Georgia, South Carolina, North Carolina, Tennessee, Indiana, and The North. The itinerary is unsurprisingly northward except that it turns west, and in the final chapter, entitled "The North," heads further west toward California. Whenever Cora enters the underground system on the run, she has no idea where she will surface, with the result that the journey appears formless and discontinuous. Each stop is a new island with a new predicament separated from the last by nullity. In Georgia, where Cora's journey begins, two brothers own adjoining plantations, the northern one less vicious than the southern; yet it is not the case, for the remainder of the journey, that the northern direction indicates a gradual improvement in conditions, let alone an approach to freedom. There is no gradation to Cora's travels. South Carolina seems at first tolerable, compared to Georgia, but its science and medicine disguise genteel genocide; North Carolina, next northward stop, pursues genocide by insatiable lynching.

The reason that *The Underground Railroad*'s most important precursor in the genealogy of the neo-slave narrative is *Kindred* is Butler's analysis of existential and political discontinuity: Dana, a modern African-Californian woman, ricochets between the early nineteenth century and the late twentieth century, and between Maryland and California, with no increments. The best hypothesis for her unwilling backward eastward transpositions is the necessity (if Dana is to exist a century and a half later) of saving the life of her accident-prone white ancestor, the slaver, Rufus. The best hypothesis for her forward returns to California seems to be her fear, or the logical impossibility, of the prenatal annihilation of her adult avatar in the antebellum South.

There are mutually contradictory ways to conceive this inexplicable time travel. The first is that there can be no metaphysical reason why anyone should exist in one century rather than another, yet the arbitrariness of temporality, in tandem with the arbitrariness of geography, makes all the difference. Randomness is the grounds of political significance. In Edward Bellamy's *Looking Backward*, the time traveler Julian West finds himself embarrassed by his departed nineteenth-century generation, but he is set at ease by Edith Leete at the end of the twentieth: "This is your generation, Mr. West," Edith says, "It is the one in which you are living, and it is only because we are alive now that we call it ours" (Bellamy 109). In antebellum Maryland, Dana, though not legally owned, is treated like a slave. Her freedom in modern California includes the right she has exercised to marry a white man; the right to dress in clothing that, when she lands back in the South, makes people think she is male; the right to earn a living, including paid temporary work that supports her budding career as a professional writer.

But even if we take as Butler's truth the arbitrariness of one's dispositive placement in space and time, we must concede that she goes out of her way to stress the correspondence of Dana's discrete worlds, with the result that the journey between them seems as fated as it is capricious, as minimal as it is radical, as immediate as it is absolute, as short as it is long. Either Dana travels instantaneously between centuries because there is no compelling metaphysical explanation for being in one rather than the other, or because there is no real social distance between them. What has been omitted in either case is the possibility of progress from one state or century to the next. Dana meets her white husband Kevin while both are working at temporary jobs to support their careers as fiction writers; Kevin is judged by Dana to be "handling it better. But then he was about to escape," by virtue of his burgeoning career as a novelist. Dana's last word is not accidental: "I was working out of a casual labor agency—we regularly called it a slave market." When Dana adds, "actually, it was just the opposite of slavery. The people who ran it couldn't have cared less whether or not you showed up for the work they offered," readers may be perplexed (Butler 52). The distinction, which would seem to go without saying, is too nonchalant. Even if Dana's temporary work is the opposite of slavery insofar as employers don't insist on her presence, it would not seem to be the *only* way it is essentially unlike slavery.

Similarly, links between Dana's protective, devoted, self-sacrificing husband Kevin, who accompanies Dana back to the antebellum South at risk to his own life, and her ancestor Tom Weylin, Rufus's father, seem tenuous. Yet Butler, through Dana, is determined to forge them. Dana writes Tom's letters for him because his literacy is rudimentary, but (and?) she types Kevin's manuscripts out of some concession to the prerogatives of his professional success as a writer. This is a family likeness (Dana does secretarial work for two men) that requires an unlikeness (Kevin is as literate as Tom is illiterate). At one point, Kevin, one of whose sojourns in the old South lasts far longer than any of Dana's, is back in the present trying to relearn how to use the television; when Dana turns it on, Kevin orders her to turn it off. Dana writes simply, "I obeyed" (Butler 191). Again, the term is pointed. Shortly thereafter, Dana notices an expression on Kevin's face "like something

I was used to seeing on Tom Weylin. Something closed and ugly"
(Butler 194).

At first and second glance, this is unfair. We may decide that the title
of Butler's book, *Kindred*, enables too many quick and guilty verdicts
by association: to propose that men in the past are akin to men in the
present, that whites in the past are akin to whites in the present, is
only to state an approximate truth, qualified by the novel in which it
is proposed.

But there is an incident that unsettles this dismissiveness. Though
Kevin hates the antebellum South wholeheartedly, he wonders whether
that historical period was a horror in all dimensions. "This could be
a great time to live in," he muses from within his exile in nineteenth-
century US history. "I keep thinking what an experience it would be
to stay in it—go West and watch the building of the country, see how
much of the Old West mythology is true." Dana responds, as she says,
"bitterly": "West . . . that's where they're doing it to the Indians instead
of the blacks!" (Butler 97).

Kevin's failure to distinguish himself fully from slave-owners, this
means, is not from cruelty, or clueless masculinity, or peremptory
financial superiority: it results from the blindness of even a novelist's
white imagination. This failure goes part of the way toward undermining
the unlikeness of semiliterate Tom and highly literate Kevin. *The
Intuitionist* has taught us to read like a person of color, and Douglass has
supplied its theory. It is not to read from an exclusive position within
the world of unadulterated Blackness; the first purpose of the word
"kindred" in *Kindred* is to associate Dana and Kevin as writers, and
they stay kindred throughout, despite tensions. Dana is adamant about
dressing in the South in ways that Southerners consider manly; and
her protectiveness with respect to her white ancestor Rufus (and the
existential necessity that he rape her Black ancestor Alice) has made not
just slaves but also Dana herself suspect her own racial identification.
She is neither a white man nor the binary opposite of a white man.
Reading like a person of color means reading at the tangent of circles,
outside all homes, lonely in all societies. Neither Dana nor Kevin is a
Native American, but reading by race means reading not by exclusive
racial solidarity but by dissociation from all that is solid. It means
reading from the position of natal alienation. Though Kevin identifies
his interests with Dana's in the South, he becomes a white man again
in his historical imagination when he fails to recognize the priority of
Native Americans in the West. That is the race he has forgotten not to
identify with.

The neo-slave novel careens between the fatality and the capriciousness of any historical position. One way to put the bind would be to replace the John Rawls question from the "original position"—what society would you choose if you had no knowledge of your place in it?—or Octavia E. Butler's question—what world would you create if you were obliged to take one of the "lowliest" positions in it? (Butler, *Bloodchild* 193)—with: what history would you institute if your future consisted of playing every available role in it? This would remove the spirit of gambling from the imaginary predicament. You might begin to imagine your answer by way of Borges's "The Immortal," his contribution to the "ethics of immortality," whose hero learns the truth of the epigraph, Francis Bacon's quoting of Solomon, "There is no new thing upon the earth" (Borges 183). If the sun shines only on the nothing new, having no alternative, no messianic kingdom, no western Utopia, then the ethics of immortality would require an infinite imagination not of liberated homeland or plantation enslavement but of serial homelessness, of nonidentification with any chosenness, to feel as your future not just a position in a place and time but the sum of all positions in the history of your history.

You could begin to imagine your answer by way of *Gulliver's Travels*: the symmetry of Gulliver's four voyages suggests he has reached the conceptual limit of the world. Gulliver has seen everything and its opposite, scientific complexity and stoic simplicity, disgusting hugeness and ridiculous minuteness, killing and the return of ghosts, courtly duplicity and natural honesty. The point of his exploring is to complete the age of exploration, having visited the world's four corners, a conceptual squaring of the circle. Yet he has arrived nowhere. It is in fact impossible to say why, as a rule, Gulliver continually leaves home, which makes it impossible to say if he has ever arrived satisfactorily. His motive is financial hardship in the first instance, but after that it is his "thirst . . . of seeing the world" (Swift 65). His sailing does not seem to distinguish economic necessity from freedom; there is no known direction of freedom, even as to whether it is toward or away from home. His world is preglobalized. History in its totality is a capricious undirected alternation of slavery and flights from slavery.

Mohsin Hamid's *Exit West* is uniquely positioned to show the bearing of the Swiftian global imagination on the neo-slave narrative. In *Exit West*, characters move between distant spots on earth by way of black doors. The first time we are witness to this immediate transportation, a man "with dark skin and dark, wooly hair" wriggles "with great effort, his hands gripping either side of the doorway as though pulling himself up against gravity, or against the rush of a monstrous tide" (Hamid 8). He is escaping from somewhere to Australia; the process, though planetary, is not far distant from how Dana in *Kindred* escapes the antebellum South back to contemporary California, an effort that costs her, in her last escape, her arm.

A conspicuous distinction between the two books is that travel in *Exit West* is voluntary: for the most part, but not always, black doors make possible escapes from troubled geographies to luckier ones. On the other hand, there is no evidence that refugees get to pick their place of exile. They know what they are escaping from, but not what they are escaping to. The young couple of the book, Nadia and Saeed, flee their decimated Muslim homeland (unspecified) and arrive in Mykonos, London, and Marin. Escape, finally to California, is never ultimate: they are serial strangers in incommensurable strange lands. Contributing to the arbitrariness is that when they land in Mykonos, and when other exiles wind up in Dubai, globalization means the juxtaposition of refugees and tourists. Every place is as discrete as prehistoric tribes in surrounding darkness; every place exists in its own time within one historical condition; destinations are more peaceful or more violent, more or less free; yet in every place, there are winners and losers, those who pick their destinations and those who do not. Everything, as *Gulliver's Travels* has already demonstrated, may be different but that.

In *Exit West* as in *Kindred*, there is a loving couple whose life as a couple is marred by the strains of homelessness; in neither book do they have children. But it is not that these books, plus *The Underground Railroad* and *The Intuitionist* (and for that matter *Zone One*, Whitehead's zombie novel), are futureless, though all of them are childless. Recall the approximate identifying truth that escapist books seek local or temporary or even fictional opportunities for the salvation of children, in momentary conjunction with protective adults; consider in contrast the possibility that the globalized narrative, neo-slave narrative or not, is the literature of childless unprotected immortality. Instead of featuring offspring born into improvised worlds for a limited sacred time, these novels feature adults borne into arbitrary profane worlds indefinitely. Eventually, Saeed and Nadia, together or apart, will live in all countries—there seems to be no closure to their uprooting, though they have reached, by the end of the book, the end of their marriage, which seems to be a moment in the history of their displacements, one of the infinity of things that might have occurred or may still occur. And *The Underground Railroad* never reaches the North and freedom,

Canada and freedom, Africa and freedom, or even death and freedom. It heads north, then west, and never finishes.

The Underground Railroad resembles *Exit West* to the extent that its protagonist repeatedly enters a black space and exits in an unchosen, distinct reality: not London, Mykonos, and California, but South Carolina, North Carolina, Tennessee, Indiana, and somewhere on the way to California. The meaning of the a-structural similarity does not concern the commonality of runaway slaves and refugees, which would conventionally include movement across painfully, minutely measurable space. The meaning concerns the shared fictional trope of the black hole and its corollary, discontinuous transportation. One pops into a black hole and pops out somewhere else in space-time.

"Every state is different," the Underground Railroad agent Lumbly tells escaping slaves Cora and Caesar, "each one a state of possibility, with its own customs and ways of doing things." Caesar no doubt recognizes this as Gulliver's condition, "each island a new predicament to solve." Lumbly adds that "moving through them, you'll see the breadth of the country before you reach your final stop" (Whitehead, *Railroad* 68–9). Later, Cora realizes that the addendum adds a shaggy dog joke to the pun on "state," because moving through states on the Underground Railroad lines, one sees nothing at all, and there is no final stop. The distinction of realities is, however, real: South Carolina's practice of a humane, semi-voluntary, and liberal form of medical genocide; North Carolina's plot to lynch whatever remains unsold of its Black population to prevent a future rebellion; Tennessee's ravagement by fire and yellow fever. You could tie this all together and call it, in the manner of Junot Díaz, fukú. It is the horror of slavery as it devastates three races, if you agree with Cora that "Tennessee was cursed. . . . The whites got what they deserved. For enslaving her people, for massacring another race, for stealing the very land itself" (Whitehead, *Railroad* 215).

The problem is that Cora cannot understand, in these terms, why she has been punished like Tennessee farmers, now on the run for their sins. And on one side of that capricious similarity of whites and Blacks is a capricious distinction of whites and whites: "why had this field escaped while another burned five miles back?" (Whitehead, *Railroad* 215–16). The answer to the question, which might have seemed to be without interest to an escaping slave, is the arbitrariness of human history. The writing, on behalf of Cora's consciousness, can resemble Beckett: "There was only the darkness of the tunnel, and something ahead, an exit. Or a dead end, if that's what fate decreed" (Whitehead, *Railroad* 304). You might be reborn or you might die. There might be an exit west or no exit. Those are the two possibilities. Here is what Cora hears from the slave-hunter Ridgeway about the death of her friend, Lovey, who had tried to escape with her and Caesar: "The young girl was installed in [her gallows], hooked through her ribs by a large metal spike and dangling. The dirt below dark with her blood. The other two gallows stood waiting" (Whitehead, *Railroad* 208). They stand waiting, perhaps on either side of Lovey, for Caesar and Cora. Do not despair; one of the thieves was saved. Do not presume; one of the thieves was damned. In fact, Caesar dies and Cora lives.

The Underground Railroad speaks two opposite truths as one. In the face of Tennessee arbitrariness, Cora infers that "plantation justice was mean and constant, but the world was indiscriminate" (Whitehead, *Railroad* 216). This is the antinomy of all globalized novels; the cognitive distinction of the slave narrative and the neo-slave narrative is that the latter is written in the era of globalization, whose aesthetic is the marathon dance of indiscriminateness and discrimination, a global synchronization with the tribal. Similarly, in *Kindred*, the relation of past and present is arbitrary and consistent.

According to *The Underground Railroad*, the reason that every state is a new state of being is not federalism and states' rights. It is not that every Southern state insists on its own prerogatives or prolongs its own traditions. Nor does Whitehead make any effort to justify his fictional distinction of the methods of genocide in North Carolina and South Carolina by any real historical distinction of the two states. Twentieth-century to twenty-first-century globalization accounts more fully than nineteenth-century history for the discontinuity of states of being in neo-slave novels in general and *The Underground Railroad* in particular. We grasp the mechanism by which globalization is brought to bear on the neo-slave narrative through one of *The Underground Railroad*'s most persistent themes, the theatricality of slavery. There are the actual performances: minstrel shows on plantations for the entertainment of slavers; a coon show that precedes a lynching bee in North Carolina. There is the theatricality of punishment: the "gory exhibition[s]" and "grotesque pageants" (Whitehead, *Railroad* 171, 176) that entertain and reassure whites while terrifying their slaves. Performance has a performative rationale: it enacts slavery by displaying it.

Having escaped to seemingly humane South Carolina, Cora is hired to perform the idealized life of a slave in a museum exhibition. At the moment, Cora is legally still enslaved (though faking her identity to escape), simultaneously a real slave and a representation of one. In *Kindred*, supporting in advance Whitehead's historical license, Dana tries to explain to Kevin that, while in Maryland, they "were observers watching a show. We were watching history happen around us. And we were actors" (Butler 98). It's a difficult feat, being actors and audience at the same time and, beyond that, being actors and audience in the theater of actual history.

The sensation of being history, the representation of history, and the audience of the representation of history seems distinctly postmodern. Nadia has the sensation in *Exit West* when she is looking at her cell phone and thinks that she sees

> a photograph of herself sitting on the steps of a building reading the news on her phone across the street from a detachment of troops and a tank . . . and she had the bizarre feeling of time bending all around her, as though she was from the past reading about the future, or from the future reading about the past. (Hamid 157)

The bizarre Ben Lerneresque feeling is experienced again in *Zone One*, Whitehead's apocalyptic zombie book, when its protagonist is fleeing zombies while "for a second he pictured himself underneath the news copter as folks in more fortunate weather watched from home" (Whitehead, *Zone* 228). Also, a temporary survivor of the zombie apocalypse is developing a video game that will duplicate his experiences while creating it (Whitehead, *Zone* 222). The context seems to be the virtualizing of history by smartphone, television, and computer.

If so, why does the same meta-historicization of history keep occurring in the neo-slave narrative? Part of the answer is that the neo-slave narrative is postmodern. That means many nebulous things, but in this case it means that the neo-slave narrative's author has the feeling of warping time, in which the experience of the present resembles the experience of the past, not so much because the effects of slavery persist as because time has lost its purpose, its relation to revolutionary Utopianism or messianism, on behalf of endless permutations of spectacles of novelty. Globalization means: history is capricious; history is unchanging. Cora, having been employed as an advertisement for slavery in seductively consumerist South Carolina, concludes that "truth was a changing display in a shop window, manipulated by hands when you weren't looking, alluring and ever out of reach" (Whitehead, *Railroad* 116).

This is globalized postmodern truth, not the truth of slavery but the truth of the simulacrum of it. The postmodern question for Whitehead is not whether he can portray African American history accurately but whether he can simulate it differently. Near the end of the novel, Whitehead floats an alternative imaginary past. Cora has been liberated from slave-catchers and brought to a Black-owned, communally governed farm in Indiana, open to escaping slaves from the Underground Railroad. Cora, who was almost ruined for sex by a rape, begins to rejoin the world of passionate relations. The prospect of children had been ruined, too: because children are born into slavery on one or the other side of it, Cora encounters childhood in a variety of wrecked forms concluding with her decisive run-in with a Black boy, Homer, who acts precociously the part of an old servile sycophant, like Stephen in *Django Unchained*, in some sort of intimacy, possibly pederastic, with the most detestable slave-catcher of the novel. Homer seems a summation of all children in the novel, on both sides of racial debasement at once. He is also a nightmare summation of all the children in escapist books, isolated with an adult protector, intimate with him in an improvised adventure. But at the Valentine farm in Indiana, Cora begins to fantasize having her own children, inhabiting a meaningful secular temporality, Utopia for ex-slaves in an ex-slave state.

The Utopian project does not survive the book's catastrophe. The Valentine farm is destroyed by its white neighbors; many of its leaders are shot and killed in a raid. Whether it was betrayed by one of its own Black communards, who seeks to ensure the farm's respectability by informing whites that the place harbored fugitives, or whether the whites are mainly out to assassinate its most charismatic supporter, is uncertain. The catastrophe is not a particular historical outcome but the restoration of history as the book conceives it, in its immortal kaleidoscopic fatality. Cora manages to escape farther north through a tunnel, but she has no idea where she comes out—she resumes that aimless alternation of death and rebirth—and almost immediately, in the chapter called "The North," heads west. We can hope she finds a better world in California than in the East or Midwest, but if *Exit West* or *Kindred*, or for that matter *Telegraph Avenue* or *The Circle* or *A Heartbreaking Work of Staggering Genius*, define or border on the genre, she will discover that she has been revived but not reborn. This is the failure of escapism on its messianic frontier.

Is there nothing in the future besides an endless succession of shop window displays? If an immortality of pointless, will-less resurrections is the problem, it may follow that willing mortality is the solution. I have not discussed how the disappearance, which turns out to be the death, of Cora's mother, Mabel, has fueled *The Underground Railroad*. First, Mabel's character has contributed the most of any ancestor to

Cora's—both possess the loner courage necessary to flee slavery. Second, by a strange complement, Mabel's apparent escape seems to her daughter a betrayal, since Mabel left her behind, which makes it psychologically possible for Cora to cut all ties whenever flight makes it necessary, and conceivably to live with the deaths she causes along the way. Third, the slave-catcher Ridgeway's failure to capture Mabel has created the fury with which he pursues Cora until his own death and her final flight.

This means that the plot of the book has largely been founded on a mistake, because Mabel did not abandon Cora her daughter. She does make a run for it, but decides to return to Cora. At the beginning of her return, in the swamp, she is fatally bitten by a cottonmouth snake.

It means, at least, that the relationship of mothers and daughters has been misunderstood. Cora's new interest in motherhood on the Indiana farm has been a correction, not on Cora's part (she cannot come to know her mother's attempted return) but on the book's. Readers of the novel know what Cora does not, that in the swamp, Mabel, though she has not fully escaped, enjoys a moment of freedom: "No patrollers, no bosses, no cries of anguish to induct her into another's despair. No cabin walls shuttling her through the night seas like the hold of a slave ship. Sandhill cranes and warblers, otters splashing. On the bed of damp earth, her breathing slowed and that which separated herself from the swamp disappeared. She was free. This moment" (Whitehead, *Railroad* 294). It is after this momentary escape, and as a result of it, that Mabel decides to go back. She wishes to share the oceanic experience with her daughter, an interim of escapism in lieu of escape: allowing her daughter to join her not in freedom but in the imagination of it, conceived as oneness with the damp earth.

When she is bitten by the snake, however, Mabel consents to stop moving in any direction: "she stumbled into a bed of soft moss and it felt right. She said, Here, and the swamp swallowed her up" (Whitehead, *Railroad* 295). It is the only moment of the book in which a resting spot has been found by anyone. It is the only moment that does not involve transportation, which entails that the underground railroad allegory makes an unsettling reappearance in concert with the Middle Passage to express the existential homelessness of slavery: "cabin walls shuttling her through the night seas like the hold of a slave ship."

Mabel's euthanasia represents consent not to finding the state of each state, in hopes that one state of being is superior to another, though all in the event are failures and no pattern of perfection, either human-experimental or divine-figural, is ever apparent. It represents consent to the darkness of subterranean sameness rather than to surface change. In the end, the enticing fact about the Underground Railroad is not that it is a railroad but that it is underground. It is the kind of coffin an elevator would be if the elevator did not safely ascend. If the referent of the allegory of *The Underground Railroad* is allegories, its meaning is the impossibility of the allegorical or anagogical, or finding the higher meaning of a mundane event, or the revealed meaning of a veiled event, or the spiritual metaphor of a physical fact, or the ascension of a traveling coffin, or the bare possibility of transcending reality as given. The masculine anti-allegory of *The Intuitionist* arrives at materialism; the maternal anti-allegory of *The Underground Railroad* arrives at materiality.

If, in short, *The Underground Railroad* is finally an anti-allegorical consent to oceanic death rather than an allegory of territorial rebirth, how shall we understand (by what technique, in terms of which genre) Whitehead's zombie novel, *Zone One*? Butler's vampire novel exploits the disunity of allegorical figures and worlds; but if I am right about Mabel's euthanasia in *The Underground Railroad*, Whitehead in his zombie novel is in search of a post-allegorical unity of figures and the world. *Zone One* is a book explicitly about how to read, therefore about how to read itself: one of the anti-zombie highway clearers arranges the cars of the lost on the side of I-95 in Connecticut, green world converted to Black world, as a Rosetta Stone for the future. Knowing how to read *The Intuitionist* means knowing how to read prophecy of that sort as the sign of passing, and in *Zone One* we read almost all of the book unaware—unless we have retained our education in the "new literacy"—that the protagonist is a Black man. He has been called Mark Spitz for all of the book because at a crucial confrontation with zombies on a bridge, he could not bring himself to jump into the water. Nine-tenths of the way through the book, when the question of where he got his nickname finally is faced, the explanation evokes what one character calls the "black-people-can't-swim thing" (Whitehead, *Zone* 287). That's how slower readers, like myself, find out. The character is not passing in the story, but he passes in the novel. Mark Spitz is described as a mediocrity, and I suppose I would have been open to a Black protagonist having any attribute but that. We have been informed that mediocrity has been his method of escape and evasion, but we had not known from what.

If I had been quicker on the uptake, I might have observed that the function of the wall separating zombie fighters from zombies in New York City (the wall of Fort Wonton on the edge of Chinatown) is described this way: "We are safe inside from what is outside" (Whitehead, *Zone* 122). Since what is outside is generally troped as a fusion of AIDS and climate change, I might have doubted that partitioning was an effective or just solution. A few pages later, a dimension is added: "Mark Spitz looked out into a solemn nigrescence that was interrupted only by a white dome of light leeching out of Fort Wonton. The light climbed up a few stories on the Canal buildings like mold. He visualized the hard-core military lamps bleaching the concrete wall to sun-beaten bone white" (Whitehead, *Zone* 124). "Nigrescence" might have detained me, along with the white mold and white bones, associated with leeching and bleaching.

For most of the book, Mark Spitz is glad to be safe inside the walls, only venturing out to fight the undead. Who could blame him? The wounds of the dead are "mushy and livid. They leaked, leaked constantly from sores, eyes, ears, bites" (Whitehead, *Zone* 131). The leakage spreads and becomes the environment, a fetid version of Alice's tears in Wonderland: "Yesterday's pools of blood and gore had expanded into lakes fed by the mass of leaking corpses" (Whitehead, *Zone* 299). From leakage to pools to lakes to tsunami: "the ocean had overtaken the streets, as if the news programs' global warming simulations had finally come to pass and the computer-generated swells mounted to drown the great metropolis. Except it was not water that flooded the grid but the dead" (Whitehead, *Zone* 302). It's not that corpses leak; they are the leakage.

The "black tide," as the book calls it, flows down Broadway: "The damned bubbled and frothed on the most famous street in the world, the dead things still proudly indicating, despite their grime and wounds and panoply of leaking orifices, the tribes to which they had belonged." Tribes are defined by consumer styles—"gray pinstriped suits, classic rock T-shirts, cowboy boots, dashikis, striped cashmere cardigans, fringed suede vests, plush jogging suits" (Whitehead, *Zone* 302)—but not by received identity: "Every race, color, and creed was represented in this congregation that funneled down the a avenue. . . . No matter the hue of their skins, dark or light, no matter the names of their gods or the absences they countenanced" (Whitehead, *Zone* 302–3). Egalitarian death makes nonsense of consumer distinctions, the only truth that is not a changing display in a shop window. The "black tide" may be descended from Klaus Theweleit's "red tide," the *Freikorps* image that merges the horrors of female menstruation and communist egalitarianism, two ways of imaging the failure of borders and hierarchies, by way of Ishmael Reed's "black tide" in *Mumbo Jumbo*, an epidemic that ascends from New Orleans infecting even whites with its joy and jazz.

In this case, the black tide is decay and death, as if an allegory of Lothrop Stoddard's *The Rising Tide of Color*, but Mark Spitz, at the last moment, finds himself revived by it: "He was smiling because he hadn't felt this alive in months. . . . [T]he black tide had rolled in everywhere, no place was spared this deluge, everyone was drowning. Of course he was smiling. This was where he belonged" (Whitehead, *Zone* 311–12). Surrounded by the dead on the island of Manhattan, he decides to "swim for it." In which ocean? The novel ends with his final thought: "You have to learn how to swim sometime. He opened the door and walked into the sea of the dead" (Whitehead, *Zone* 322).

This consent to miasmal death resembles the sui-euthanasia of Mabel in *The Underground Railroad*, except with none of the peace of the inorganic. We might instead think of the muck in which Paul D fights for his communal democratic freedom in *Beloved* by plunging in—masculine liquefied salvation unsanctified by female messianism.

> It rained. . . . In the boxes men heard the water rise in the trench and looked out for cottonmouths. They squatted in muddy water, slept above it, peed in it. Paul D thought he was screaming; his mouth was open and there was this loud throat-splitting sound—but it may have been somebody else. Then he thought he was crying. . . . He lifted his hands to wipe away the tears and saw dark brown slime. Above him rivulets of mud slid through the boards of his roof. . . . The water was above his ankles, flowing over the wooden plank he slept on. And then it wasn't water anymore. The ditch was caving in and mud oozed under and through the bars. . . . One by one, from Hi Man back on down the line, they dove. Down through the mud under the bars, blind, groping. Some had sense enough to wrap their heads in their shirts, cover their faces with rags, put on their shoes. Others just plunged, simply ducked down and pushed out, fighting up, reaching for air. Some lost their direction and their neighbors, feeling the confused pull of the chain, snatched them around. For one lost, all lost. . . . All Georgia seemed to be sliding, melting away. (Morrison, *Beloved* 110–11)

Liberty, on this conception, is a masculine nightmare, a sliminess that muddles dreams of freedom from the possessed body with anxieties about shedding the self-possessed body. But more than masculinity is at risk in *Zone One*: Mark Spitz, in the end, chooses against not just masculine individualism but also human individuality itself. He opts for "the great black hole" where, Aimé Césaire writes, "I wanted to drown," though Fanon values in Césaire the capacity to rise again (Fanon 173). The theoretical equivalent is the argument of Frank B. Wilderson III in *Afropessimism* that the end of the worldwide equivalence of Blackness and slavery "would mean the end of the world," the end of humanity as such, whose basis is an ideal of freedom at the expense of Black "social death," in Patterson's phrase adapted and radicalized by Wilderson. "The Human need to be liberated *in* the world is not the same as the Black need to be liberated *from* the world; which is why even their most radical cognitive maps draw borders between the living and the dead" (Wilderson 252).

On this reading, *Zone One* is the anti-messianic allegory where all proper allegories come to die: "There is no interracial redemption," Wilderson writes. "There is no Afrocentric redemption. Redemption is the narrative inheritance of Humans" (Wilderson 325). Globalization as the telos of neoliberalism promises a continual discontinuity, an eternal shuffling of discrete states, no telos at all. In every strange and arbitrary future, you'll find your familiar world. The commodities change so you don't have to. Against meaningless futurity, *Zone One* does not imagine a messianic redemption from commodification, as contemplated in Lerner's *10:04*, because it does not imagine globalization as finally a matter of economics. Mark Spitz's plunge into anarchy, egalitarianism, borderlessness, leakage, pollution, and decay—into Césaire's "obscene and savage torrents swollen with chaotic streams, rotted seas, convulsive oceans" (Fanon 171)—implies that escape from the gated whiteness of future time is not the salvation of human history but its dissolution.

Zone One does not accompany Mark Spitz on his oceanic plunge any farther than *The Underground Railroad* follows Cora on her overland trek west, with its hint of a new community. These incompletions are antitheses—an immersed undeath, a resurfaced proto-life. Readers cannot say whether Whitehead's characteristic escapes are primarily from or to the human, because his characters flee somewhere but do not arrive somewhere else. Whether social death is once and for all, as in Wilderson, or the condition of rebirth, as in Patterson (Patterson xiii, xxi), is still in question at the open endings of Whitehead novels. Sylvia Wynter would have found in this oeuvre a brilliant reimagining of double consciousness, in the tradition of Du Bois and Fanon: Blackness looking at itself both inside and outside white definitions of the human (Wynter 47–9). But it is precisely this self-disjunction, according to Wynter, that allows the enslaved or colonized to diagnose the limitations of white secular humanism and possibly to invent a different kind, a hybrid humanism that interfuses the materialism of white folk with the souls of Black folk. This may be the only way of imagining a tangential subject, neither a Northerner nor a Southern slave, nor a descendant of Southern slaves, capable of understanding in its soul the songs of murdered souls. (What Patterson calls social death, Wynter calls symbolic death.) If I am right about his project, Whitehead performs a continuous *reductio* on allegorical reduction to arrive at his recent novel, *The Nickel Boys*, in which he confronts the meaning of Black childhood in order to half-twist a fully anti-allegorical Mobius strip of experience and innocence, cynicism and idealism, body and soul, social death and the possibility of renewed life in society, his own escape from the unbending ideology of allegorizing readers.

Chapter 9

THE SONGS OF MURDERED SOULS

Possibly escapist messianism, in its contemporary American form, expired in 2017, the year of Jesmyn Ward's *Sing, Unburied, Sing* and George Saunders's *Lincoln in the Bardo*. The books are uncannily similar, despite enormous differences in style and tone.

1. Both concern the non-Christian afterlives of dead humans unreconciled to death because of unfinished business in life.
2. Both include the afterlives of Blacks whose lives were destroyed by American racism, in the form of slavery or its carceral prolongation.
3. Both center on dead children. Ward's Richie seeks recognition by Pop, his grandfatherly protector, who knows the story of Richie's killing and was by tragic circumstance its agent. Ignorance of this story keeps Richie from ascending to some form of celestial city. Saunders's Willie Lincoln continues to cherish the timeless love of his father the president, which keeps Willie from ascending to some sort of celestial kingdom.
4. Both cases involve a multiplicity of scenes of potential mundane salvation. In *Sing, Unburied, Sing*, thirteen-year-old JoJo tries to shield his three-year-old sister, Kayla, from the absence (one incarcerated, one neglectful) of her parents, a younger version of Dave and Toph, except that Jojo, in racist Mississippi, cannot pretend to buffer Kayla against nearly continuous intrusions of sickness, pain, and death. (That their mother had not nursed Jojo or Kayla is in pointed contrast to the escapist maternal Utopianism of *Arcadia* and the escapist maternal messianism of *Room*; a surprise toward the end of the novel is that Richie seeks maternal nurturing as much as paternal understanding in his posthumous return.) Saunders's Bardo protagonists, Roger Bevins III and Hans Vollman, try to dislodge Willie from faith in his father's unprecedented, seemingly eternal love, somewhat in the

tradition of *Room*'s Ma, who needs to free Jack from entombed escapism, product of faith in her loving omniscience. Jojo attempts to save Kayla, and Bevins and Vollman attempt to save Willie, on opposite sides of the grave; but both cases of saving, one from a too-attentive father and one from a neglectful mother, are experiments in nonparental re-parenting beyond any hope of a shared moment of innocence.

5. Both books imagine an interim between life and death as a way of reconceiving life proper: the impossibility of finding redemption in an afterlife on earth means the impossibility of locating messianic time within life and death on earth. Lincoln should not attempt to save Willie to save himself while required to focus his attention on the fratricidal Civil War; Pop cannot save Richie to save himself insofar as Pop has been unwillingly implicated in the state's murderous power.

6. Both books give over their narration to interior narrators, three in *Sing, Unburied, Sing* and dozens in *Lincoln in the Bardo*. The meaning of the technique is the impossibility of a single consciousness encompassing all subjectivities: the impossibility of limitless messianic sympathy across generations. Ward's characters, on two sides of death, form crisscrossing patterns of spotty awareness and ragged communication. (The book itself does not seem to know what Stag, Pop's brother, is doing in the book; from within life, he haunts the book briefly, then disappears.) Saunders floats the possibility that all consciousness can exist within Lincoln's, which stands for the claim that they all may coexist within a novel's; but there are only occasional, ambiguous signs of communication across mortality. Split narration implies civil wars indefinitely in every dimension, though the literary postwar hope is charity for all.

7. The escapist project of redeeming the past and present by individual acts of reciprocal salvation founders in identical ways in Saunders and Ward. In Saunders, a friend speaks for mute Litzie Wright:

What was done to her was done to her many times, by many. What was done to her could not be resisted, was not resisted, sometimes was resisted, which resulted, sometimes, in her being sent away to some far worse place, other times in that resistance simply being overcome (by fist, knee, board-strike, etc.). What was done to her was done and done. Or just done once. What was done to her affected her not at all, affected her very much, drove her to the nervous shakes, drove her to hateful speech, drove her to leap off the Cedar Creek Bridge, drove her to this obstinate silence. What was done to her was done by big men, small men, boss men, men who happened to be passing the field in which she worked, the teen sons of the boss man or of the men who happened to be passing, a trio of men on a bender who spilled out of the house and, just before departing, saw her there chopping wood. . . . what was done to her was: whatever anyone wished to do, and even if someone wished only slightly to do something to her, well, one could do it, it could be done, one did it, it was done, it was done and done and—. (Saunders 222)

In Ward, the mute dead perched in a tree sing only with their eyes:

He raped me and suffocated me until I died I put my hands up and he shot me eight times she locked me in the shed and starved me to death while I listened to my babies playing with her in the yard they came in my cell in the middle of the night and they hung me they found I could read and they dragged me out to the barn and gouged out my eyes before they beat me still I was sick and he said I was an abomination and Jesus say suffer little children so let her go and he put me under the water and I couldn't breathe. (Ward 282–3)

These passages are partial, heaped transcriptions; they are indications of a collective voice, invented out of silence, which is neither personal nor impersonal. Individual voices flicker almost into life, fade into choruses, fluctuate between singular and plural, thus between presence and oblivion. The shared ambition is to renounce and transcend the escapist project of saving an exceptional child; in the process, both books demonstrate that no childhood exists for a chiasmic death-defying moment with adulthood. The failure jointly announced by Saunders and Ward is that even fiction's capacity to reveal the dead and living to one another reaches its limit before long, somewhere between the one and the many, between what can and cannot be spoken or narrated, between shared life and social undeath.

Part III

FOREIGN CORRESPONDENTS

Chapter 10

CHOICE AND THE CHOSEN

Aron Kleinfeld, the child protagonist of *The Book of Intimate Grammar*, refuses to grow up. He glimpses in adolescence the onset of adulthood, a hateful condition of mediocrity, conventionality, hopelessness, cruelty, disloyalty, and lust. He refuses all that, but his corollary inability to grow physically beginning at the age of eleven-and-a-half is a torment to him. He is reminiscent of David Schearl in *Call It Sleep* and Oskar Matzerath in *The Tin Drum*, but for my purposes the relevant genealogy includes Jack in *Room* and Bit in *Arcadia*, who are also unable to grow normally, and Oskar Schell in *Extremely Loud and Unbelievably Close*: children whose *alter kopf* sensibility and intelligence are mixed with something resembling autism or obsessive-compulsive disorder or perhaps just a desperately thoroughgoing resistance to the surrounding grotesque. The question of David Grossman's novel is: Can Aron be saved?

Who should save him? Aron hopes that his older sister can guide his passage into an adulthood that she equally views as a prison, but Yochi has her own problems; Aron hopes that his friend Gideon will accept Aron's invitation of perpetual childhood, but Gideon joins the world of teenage sentiment and sexuality when it appeals to his egotism. Aron also looks to his mother to save, in effect, his whole life from the start, but she abhors Aron's specialness as an affront to her control and social status.

Aron does not look to his father to save him: his father is a brawny presence in the family but possesses a severely limited spiritual and intellectual range. Aron's ignoring him is odd, however, insofar as his father had saved himself during the Second World War from a Russian prison by way of an almost superhuman endurance and courage (abetted by a ruthless will to live): he passed as close to death on his way to life in Israel as conceivable. It is understandable that Aron does not look for a model of salvation to his father's mother, the other member of the Kleinfeld household—she is mentally, emotionally ruined by the time of the story—yet her own war experience in Poland was a close confrontation with death, and she triumphs over death again, during the time of the story, in an Israeli hospital.

Teaching himself to be Houdini, an auto-didactic version of Josef Kavalier, Aron never considers that he has two nearby models for barely escaping death in actual life. The reason is Aron's hope that he might preserve his innocence—his adventurousness, guilelessness, imagination, originality, and capacity for friendship—into adulthood; and if that is a self-contradiction, his more radical aspiration is immortal authentic childhood, like Peter Pan's. "He would stay as he was, himself, forever" (Grossman, *Grammar* 108). Our normal inclination as readers is of course to root for the survival of innocence, one way or the other, in time or against it.

What puts even our indefinite partisanship in jeopardy, in an Israeli book as opposed to an American escapist book, is the ordinal of innocence. It is not merely that innocence is an American cultural value of the dominant class, preserved against actual American history. It is also that white America assumes the usual chronology: first, innocence; second, experience. Whether or not innocence is privileged over experience, it comes before it. But in the case of *Intimate Grammar* and other books by Grossman, childhood in Israel is preceded by the Holocaust, no matter at what distance. Survival as represented by Aron's father and grandmother cannot model, but in fact threatens, the survival of Aron's innocence. In *Writing in the Dark*, Grossman recounts listening to the Eichmann trial at dinner when he was seven, and to the questions of his son, aged three, following his school's Holocaust Memorial Day (Grossman, *Dark*, 71, 72). This is the first complication of an Israeli book explicitly on the topic of escape, escapology, and escapism, in contrast to American books in which adults join children in a momentary escapist interregnum between innocence and experience, approached from each side.

Two novels by Grossman, *A Horse Walks into a Bar* and *To the End of the Land*, raise the subject of Jewish-Israeli escapism mutually. In *Horse*, a middling Israeli stand-up comedian named Dov Greenstein is performing his act in an undistinguished Israeli city—the single night's performance, as observed by a retired judge and hitherto lost childhood friend of the comedian, provides the structure of the novel. The performance, at least at the beginning, makes reference to Jewish-Palestinian politics, asking in the process whether joking about a tragedy constitutes avoiding it or confronting it.

It may be an unanswerable question in general, but the difficulty of treating it by way of this particular stand-up routine comes out in a review by Stephen Greenblatt, who states at the outset that the book "might be one of the least funny novels I have ever read" (Greenblatt 46), and goes on, as if by a non sequitur, to a meditation on the historical significance of Jewish humor. He is not implying that Jewish humor is unfunny, nor is he saying that Grossman tried to make the book funny and failed. Then what is Dov's comedy doing in the novel? Though the book would not exist without the comedy performance, the answer is not obvious, for reasons that the book, by way of the judge, begins to clarify.

For one thing, Dov is measurably to the political left of his audience, which means that the normal condition of successful joke-telling—teller and listener leaping cognitive and ethical gaps in unison—is never fulfilled. If there are a few moments that the joking is successful, it works by a more insidious coordination. Dov tries to build artificial group solidarity with his audience by naming places they reside. "We're gonna have such a crazy night here! You've come from all over the country, I see guys from Jerusalem, from Be'er Sheva, from Rosh Ha'ayin." Some men in the crowd shout back: "From Ariel! From Efrat!" This prompts Dov to retort: "Wait, you're from the settlements? But then who's left to beat up the Arabs?" He has gone too far, so he adds: "Just kidding! You know I'm kidding, right?" (Grossman, *Horse* 51). He is joking, but he is not kidding.

At this point, Dov begins some ironic bits about the humorlessness of the left, but the rightist audience doesn't grasp the irony. Nor do they detect the more brutal irony of Dov's impersonation of Arabs at checkpoints singing the Israeli national anthem, and then singing, "Soldiers here, soldiers there, soldiers, fuck me everywhere!" A few irony-deficient members of the audience sing along with "their own imitation of a sharp Arab accent" (Grossman, *Horse* 53). The judge's summary of this engagement of comedian and crowd is that "the performer is mocking his audience, playing with them." Yet he is playing with them on their own playground; on second thought, the judge posits that "it's the audience that is slyly pulling him into his own trap, and the interplay makes them both partners in some sort of evasive, fluid transgression" (Grossman, *Horse* 53). The oxymoron "evasive . . . transgression" can be understood if the transgression is against not power but responsibility. The result is escapist in the usual sense, but the escapism has brought out the inescapable resentment of the culture. This is what Grossman recognizes, in *The Yellow Wind*, in Gush Emunim humor: humor "of the old Diaspora type, of sarcasm and contrariety, and reflexive, nervous contrivances, of mocking one's real and imagined enemies" (Grossman *Wind* 46).

The question of joking is more complicated even than this muddle of half-censured, half-uncensored ugliness. The title of the book, *A Horse Walks into a Bar*, is coy, and its coyness hides a turn in the argument. Here is the eponymous joke in its halfwit entirety: *A horse walks into a bar. The bartender says, "Why the long face?"* But the dead joke has an afterlife, because it has been absorbed into the most famous example of an "anti-joke," in which the horse, able to speak but missing the punchline, shares the causes of his depression. Dov's version of the anti-joke goes this way: "A horse walks into a bar and asks the barman for a Goldstar on tap. The barman pours him a pint, the horse downs it and asks for a whiskey. He drinks that, asks for a tequila. Drinks it. Gets a vodka shot and another beer" (Grossman, *Horse* 138). The original punchline has been repressed in this version of the anti-joke, but it returns later in the act, when Dov directs his attention to a waitress and asks, "Why the long face? Did someone die? It's only stand-up comedy!" (Grossman, *Horse* 152).

In fact, someone has died, and Dov's monologue is not only stand-up comedy. We remember this interaction with the waitress when we learn that Dov had begun his life as a joke-teller trying to amuse his mother when he was a child and she was descending into a lonely peculiarity; when Dov's entire performance turns into a reminiscence of the day of her funeral; when Dov recalls that on his way to her funeral from a proto-military youth camp, his driver allows him a final respite from the approach to mortality by pretending to rehearse for a comedy competition. In these contexts, jokes are not a release from political or ethical responsibility. They are a reprieve, even a just or merciful reprieve, from the knowledge of death ("a reprieve by reason of insanity" like *His Girl Friday*, another intersection of comedy and death). That may also be escapist in the usual sense, but it's a more sympathetic kind. It is possible to believe that joking about death is only a partial way of facing it but the only way of facing it at all without pious or wishful extenuations.

But this discussion is misleading, because *A Horse Walks into a Bar* is not about a stand-up routine for its entire second half, and the only reason for analyzing the equivocations of joking in the novel is that, like *To the End of the Land*, it has its reasons for raising the issue of evasion evasively. *A Horse Walks into a Bar* is about storytelling rather than joke-telling. Part way through his act, Dov Greenstein stops trying to amuse his audience, even sporadically and antagonistically, to tell them the joke-free story of his journey to his mother's funeral. In haste to get him on the road, camp officers put Dov, ignorant of whose death he is driving toward, into a truck with a driver who doesn't know, either. Dov alternates between thinking of his mother—sweet, withdrawn, loving, half-cracked child of the Holocaust—and his father, who had escaped to Palestine before the Holocaust and who tried to toughen Dov by hitting him. Because he does not know which of them died, Dov cannot help considering at length which of them he prefers to be dead. Obviously, it would be the father.

Yet he chooses against his mother. (Many readers of the book refuse to notice this, though a few paragraphs are incomprehensible otherwise.) Whatever else we take the book to be about, it must be about that choice. We know that Dov has chosen his father's survival because, for one thing, on stage still trying to amuse his audience, he punches himself in the face several times. His masochism is his father's sadism alive and internalized. Israel has, in effect, likewise chosen the father, which means that its attitude toward Arabs is a masochistic entailment of sadism and vice versa, a demonstration of allegiance to power by turning it against oneself; violence against Arabs is the smallest possible displacement of Jewish-Israeli self-violence, an assault on Jewish history by proxy. "You deserve everything you are; you are an exact punishment for yourself," writes one of the protagonists of *Be My Knife* (Grossman, *Knife* 136). That much is arguable; the point I insist on is that the book's subject turns from comedy to storytelling, and the story of the storytelling centers on a choice.

A parallel misdirection structures *To the End of the Land*. The form of the almost-inverse story is a mother's journey away from her home at the time of her son's reenlistment in the army during the Second Intifada of 2000 and after. It is inviting to make a project of determining whether that act is escapist or anti-escapist. On the one hand, the mother, Ora, seems to be doing nothing to prevent her son Ofer's death; she runs away from the potential knowledge of it. Her action is not at all humorous, but it has something of the structure of a joke, even an especially evasive joke, that gestures toward the ugliness it conceals. You can begin to put into joke format the one about the mother who runs away from the announcement of her son's death to keep him alive.

The first complication in trying to appraise the escapism of Ora's escape is that her motives are uncertain. The most obvious is that Ora's thinking has become "magical": "if they can't find her, he won't get hurt" (Grossman, *Land* 90). That seems escapological in the most primitive way, but one of Ora's alternative motives is symbolically, and perhaps even practically, clear-eyed. She wants to interfere with the smoothness of the Israeli military operation, whose needs, including a fraction of killed soldiers, penetrate most Israeli families, and which discharges its obligation to grieving families by a formal announcement at their homes. On this view, Ora is not running from the possible death of her son. She is obstructing its routinization.

The truth is that at any moment during her journey in Galilee, Ora's rationale for what she is doing must pass through all her other emotions in relation to Ofer: she feels she has suffocated him with her protectiveness, and wants him to be free of her anxious awaiting (Grossman, *Land* 349); or she wants Ofer to know, as a kind of retribution, that if he really craves freedom from her emotions and attitudes at home, she can refuse to be there for him (Grossman, *Land* 87, 89–90); or she feels that she has lost him to Israel already, acknowledging his demise in that sense by not expecting his unscathed return to domestic family life (Grossman, *Land* 605). It is possible that all these motives are operative; it is also possible that some are merely speculative on Ora's part. Grossman is patient about mapping the vagaries of Ora's thoughts and affects as she obsesses over her relationship with her son, husband, family, friend, and nation, but the evanescence of her ideas and moods means that we may need to look elsewhere for the single most important rationale, hers or Grossman's, for her wandering.

The key is that she uses her journey to tell Ofer's story, and the occasion for her telling the story is that Ora has determined to go on her hike with Avram, her nearly lost friend and former lover, and the best friend of her husband, Ilan. Avram has tried to protect himself from the knowledge of Ofer, who happens to be his own biological son in Ora and Ilan's family, for most of his son's existence. Despite what we remember about the book or know about it from reviews, the book concerns a journey of two distinct characters, the mother and father of Ofer, both of them chronic storytellers. "You people," Ora's Arab driver Sami "hisses" at Ora, "you're always looking for a story in everything" (Grossman, *Land* 111). The storytelling urge does not, however, in itself clarify Ora's motive: "I thought that if we both talked about him, if we kept talking about him, we'd protect him," she tells Avram. But she adds, "maybe it's the exact opposite" (Grossman, *Land* 650). Avram professes not to know what Ora means, but she had earlier had that same thought privately (if more regretfully): "Perhaps the more stories she tells Avram about Ofer, the less will remain of Ofer's life" (Grossman, *Land* 589).

We might wonder why Sami's charge that Israeli Jews are storytellers is caustic, why he does not distinguish Jewish stories, Ora's from Ofer's, or Ora's from each other. But the contemporary national Israeli narrative, which Ora perhaps hopes to evade by her own, and which Grossman perhaps hopes to evade by the multiplicity of his characters' stories, including Sami's, has in effect only one character and plot, though incidents vary. I mean that the contemporary Israeli story, which Sami may have in mind, begins with what Ora calls the nationalization of Ofer, of Israeli childhood and family life, of herself in turn (Grossman, *Land* 600, 605). It is a story of interchangeable citizens whose plot is unified by messianic assurance. Every citizen must act his scripted supporting role on every level, psychological, familial, political, historical, and eschatological, at once. The chapters of Israeli narrative life are stacked rather than linked. There is one protagonist, one action, one climax, one setting.

This simplification has the effect of complicating the question of escape: within Israel, there is no place to go. There is no real or metaphorical ocean to cross, in the manner of American typological messianism, though its type is the Red Sea or the Jordan. There is no West of the sort that entices American Utopianism, though the West Bank is meant to serve. There is no northwardness as the direction of freedom from enslavement, though Ora and Avram flee in that direction.

In this light, we can revisit Ora's wandering to notice that in fact it is not simply in the direction away from her home in Jerusalem, away from any potential reception of the news of her son's death. She (along with Avram) walks with much purpose and stamina both away from Jerusalem and back toward it; she sometimes wanders aimlessly; she sometimes retraces her steps; she sometimes walks backward, facing away from her direction; sometimes, she is on the so-called Israel path, and sometimes she is off it, and sometimes she is unsure. That there is an official Israel path entails the difficulty of knowing which direction is toward reality and which away from it, or in which direction lies freedom or redemption.

The book is therefore obliged to imagine fleeing the nation altogether. Surprisingly, only the two indoctrinated children of the family seriously contemplate getting out (Grossman, *Land* 252–3, 270–1, 414–15), which may mean that facing the grimmest aspects of Israeli reality, willingly or even enthusiastically, has liberated them from the divine comedy of Israel; the older generation has begun a narrative that it feels obliged to bring to a conclusion. When Ora floats the idea that "the whole time I'm walking, I'm also saying good-bye to the country," Avram replies, "You won't leave . . . . You can't" (Grossman, *Land* 415). The convoluted form of the book mimics the labyrinth of Ora's consciousness and itinerary: where, we always fail to know, is the book itself headed, toward what escapist or real freedom or salvation, within Israel? Israeli escape may be inevitably escapist, in the sense that a real deviation, toward a Utopian ideal, is foreclosed by the delusion of a messianic status quo.

Perhaps the most significant event in the wandering of Ora and Avram is one that does not occur. They are wandering in the Galilee— approximately as far north as they can go within Israel's borders, in the direction away from Ofer's deployment. But it is impossible to think of the Galilee as a contingent setting. When Ora had been planning her hike there, originally as a mother-son outing with Ofer on the occasion of his discharge from the army, foiled by his reenlistment, "she'd had the feeling that there would be a turning point in the Galilee. The start of a real, full recovery for her and Ofer" (Grossman, *Land* 78). Ora's hope of a rebirth is not surrendered: what she seeks in the event is a real, full recovery and turning point for herself and not Ofer but his father Avram, who had been physically and psychologically devastated by Egyptian torturers in the 1973 war, and whose recovery depends on Ora's love and his own imaginative repossessing of their son's biography. Mount Tabor, for unstated reasons, seems to have a special purpose in that recovery. At "Ein Petel they enjoyed a feast fit for kings in the shade of eucalyptus and oleander trees. They could see Mount Tabor and knew without a doubt that they would reach it" (Grossman, *Land* 490).

Yet when they arrive, the value of Mount Tabor for Ora and Avram seems to be primarily "the clear view of Jezreel Valley's brown-yellow-and-green-checkered fields and the expanses that roll into the horizon— the Gilead mountains, the Menasheh hills, and the Carmel range." The value of Tabor is registered only as the fact that you can see other heights from it. Just before the peak, they had stopped at Shibli, a Bedouin village, for breakfast and coffee, which "revived them" (Grossman, *Land* 584). The peak itself is nondescript: "They get up and walk around the nipple of the mountain, avoiding the churches and monastery, then start walking back down toward Shibli" (Grossman, *Land* 586). It is a peculiar anticlimax, a nadir of narrative energy at the apex of the anticipated mountain. It is a rare example of Ora and Avram's lack of interest in something they encounter; they take in Jewish mystical communities and Palestinian villages and abandoned Palestinian villages and Druze groups and nature and memorials on their journey, but they avoid, at this moment, Christianity. The maternal metaphor is shockingly enervated. There is pointless narrative redoubling in their ascent from Shibli and their descent toward Shibli. Ora and Avram do not wonder why there is a church and monastery in between.

Christianity has made a claim to the summit of Tabor because, according to tradition, that is where the transfiguration took place, when Jesus in radiant white light appears alongside Elijah and Moses, representing the prophets and the law, that is, the Old Testament. It is the moment when Christianity absorbs Judaism in the transfiguration of Jesus, while still alive, from his human to his divine aspect. We can dismiss Ora and Avram's indifference to the Christian edifices as merely their Jewish lack of enthusiasm for being superseded.

There are, however, two more interesting possibilities. The first is that they have missed a chance. They have gone on their hike for the sake of a recovery, a turning point; and the sheer physicality of what they are doing means that they feel their revival from breakfast and coffee. But transfiguration, a transition from sheer physicality, does not appear to them. They have given up too soon on their capacity for miraculous transformation in light of the divine. The second is that they have not missed a chance; they have made a tacit decision about Judaism, not Christianity. Messianism is the source of Israeli narrative poverty, its insistence on a single narrative with a single chosen protagonist, the messianic nation itself. But there are many mountains in view from this one. The Hebrew title of the novel is *Isha Borachat M'Bsora*, which primarily means "A Woman Flees a Message," or "A Woman Flees News," but might secondarily mean "A Woman Flees a Gospel." She might be fleeing it to tell a more polyvalent story.

What is clear, if the missing option really flickers, is that the apparitional choice is a meta-choice between irresistible chosenness and free choosing. And every choice in the book, at each of its binaries, is downhill from the Tabor meta-non-choice. Binaries are relentless in *To the End of the Land*. Ora has two boys; every time she focuses on one, she accuses herself of favoritism in her narrative investment. Each of the two fathers seems at times to prefer one of the two sons, often the son of the other father. That paternal chiasmus takes shape in part because the fathers are best friends, worried about the choice each has made for Ora over the other. As a newly ambulatory child, Ofer has to pick an inaugural destination defined as his parents against his brother, as if to choose his generational solidarity. On her own walk, Ora domesticates a half-feral dog that, at one forking path, must choose between Ora and Avram.

The most consequential choice of the novel, reconstituted several times in fragments, is the least consequential. Enlisted in intelligence in the 1973 war, Avram and Ilan telephone Ora to ask her to put their names in a hat and draw one. Ora is not told the meaning of the blind choice, though she silently speculates that she is picking one of them to return home. We are not told the name Ora picks (Grossman, *Land* 220–1).

We know the result: Avram winds up in an exposed stronghold near the Suez Canal, where he survives alone among his fellow soldiers. He is captured, tortured, and eventually repatriated in varying states of consciousness or unconsciousness. He is psychologically, physically, morally wrecked for the nearly three decades between his own war and the Second Intifada his son volunteers to suppress.

Has a choice in fact been made? The diminution of choice can be charted by this slope of significance: Ora seems to be choosing life or death for Avram and Ilan; Ora is not choosing life or death for Avram and Ilan, since death is not by necessity or in fact the result of her choice, nor is she choosing one or the other for a suicide mission, since she does not know the mission, nor is she choosing one or the other for anything, since she is kept in ignorance of the nature of what she has been asked to decide, nor is she preferring one or the other, because she does not know whether saying one name is favoring or disfavoring the person named. Perhaps the choice is merely to say one name rather than the other and determine retrospectively the meaning of it.

If this is all that survives of choosing, it seems hard to care about it, though the novel asks us to care about it repeatedly; we cannot easily determine whether the picking of a name from a hat is conceived as the demise of choosing or its hairbreadth rescue. What emerges is that Grossman has identified two halves of incomplete choosing in two books. Dov's choice of death for his mother rather than his father is without fatal consequences for either, but the choice is existentially critical for Dov—it binds his future as an Israeli to one pillar of his upbringing. Inversely, Ora's choice is largely or entirely aleatory, involves (so it seems) no preference on her part, yet has dire consequences for her two lovers. Both antithetical cases insert a caesura between the subject and object of a choice. The intention of the choice breaks in half; its import may be entirely on the side of the subject, or entirely on the side of the object.

Should we prefer living in a world where choices can flow smoothly from subjects to objects of intention? In both books, the (hypothetical) combining of wish and effect, adding an effect to a wish or a wish to an effect, would amount to a choice rather than a mortal chosenness on one side but a mortal chosenness rather than a choice on the other. "Being chosen"—as a person or a people—seems, in this sense, arbitrarily connected to the choosing: unearned, a perverse preference, the luck of the draw. If God, for example, freely chooses a people for salvation, He chooses others for extinction, unconnected to any possible justification, if He is free.

We are in the conceptual world of *The Underground Railroad*, in which the fatality of race is parodied by the arbitrariness of one's racial assignment. The structurally chronic binarisms of *To the End of the Land* reach their crisis in the blind choice between Ilan and Avram for sacrifice or survival, but the choices throughout the scenes of the novel are ugly and ideally unnecessary. The ugliness consists in the disproportion of their significance and their necessity. Must a man choose between love and friendship? Must a parent choose between two sons? That question echoes the central choice from *A Horse Walks into a Bar*: Must a son choose between two parents? (In the aftermath of a different country's catastrophe, Oskar Schell cruelly informs his mother that he would have preferred the survival of his father.) Must a son choose between a brother and parents? *To the End of the Land* goes so far as to wonder whether a woman must choose one lover over another. Must God prefer one nation? Not all choices kill or let live, but all choices in these two novels tend toward life or toward death, some degree of salvation or obliteration, for an object of the choice. If effectual choosing is existentially central to human life, is there a way of imagining it such that it is free and humane, not divine and fatal?

One way of putting the question not asked at Mount Tabor is whether the potential beneficence of free choosing—"can you be free without being cruel?" asks a protagonist in *Be My Knife* (Grossman, *Knife* 225)—might be better thought of as messianic or Utopian. Do Ora and Avram refuse to consider the possibility of messianic transformation because they are tacitly considering a Utopian freedom of adventure and conversational equality, as if they belonged to a Cavellian remarriage plot? Presumably, the question is not inevitable on Mount Tabor because the terms of the question are specifically Christian; yet all conventional messianisms promise transformation, which implies the reception of obligatory divine truth. "Who are these people," Grossman wonders about the nonfictional Gush Emunim settlers he visits in *The Yellow Wind*,

> who are able to pilot their lives with logic and clearheadedness into the very heart of doubtful reality and then, upon arriving at a barrier which seems to all others impassable, metamorphose themselves into some other realm of existence, execute a sort of instant takeoff with the help of an Uzi, crossing the Messiah with a vertically launched aircraft, enter into an apocalyptic trance, dance like kids on the hill-tops, shout ecstatic and ridiculous prophecies? (Grossman, *Wind* 49)

"Who are these people?" is not a rhetorical question. Grossman appears to have no quarrel with settler clearheadedness; elsewhere, he says that settlers "plan their steps with wisdom, in a calculated and pragmatic way. In this way they are utopian rather than messianic. They are not sleepwalking hallucinators but, rather, very practical people" (Grossman, *Wind* 47).

The crux is how it is possible for practical people to aim lives at the heart of doubtful reality. The dubiousness of the shape of reality is the condition of *To the End of the Land*: if God is a circle whose circumference is nowhere and whose center is everywhere, Israel is a circle with a mutable perimeter and a disputed capital. You do not know how to aim your life toward its center or away from it, because there is illusion and contestation throughout its topology. Or put it this way: if your walking toward the center of reality arrives at an impassable barrier, you were not clearheaded and logical about tracing the radius toward it. There was a mistaken calculation not simply in advance of ridiculous prophecies but entailing them. Messianic inspiration is not what miraculously appears when an impassable barrier is reached; messianism produces the impassable barrier.

We can approach why Grossman tricks us into accepting that one book on storytelling is about stand-up comedy, and another book on storytelling is about leaving home. One novel begins with a comedian before a comedy audience that thins throughout the course of the performance until only a few sympathetic listeners remain, most crucially the judge, an almost-lost friend; the other begins with a mother's flight from a last invasive maneuver of the army in the company of one old, dear, and (again) almost lost friend. The initial setting, in both cases, centers on a formulaic social discourse, comic or tragic, forsaken in one case (by a comedian facing a hostile audience on stage) and declined in the other (by a mother facing imaginary military representatives at the front door); the deviation from formulas makes possible contingencies of storytelling in which unpredictable formal choices are mimetic of life choices. In *A Horse Walks into a Bar*, a monologue is a dialogue in disguise; in *To the End of the Land*, a nearly interior monologue surfaces into conversation. The point of storytelling in real or imaginary dialogue with a lost friend is to recall a moment of narrative potential not before but within the mortality of the present.

Grossman's complementary nonfiction project, in *Writing in the Dark*, is to imagine the Utopian rather than the messianic politics of real choice, choosing against chosenness as the source of group reality. Grossman quotes Isaiah to the purpose: "nation shall not lift up sword against nation, neither shall they learn war any more." "And only at the end of days," Grossman reminds us that David promises Jerusalem, "will peace be within thy walls, and prosperity within thy palaces." These promises seem to be messianic, but Grossman tells us that in Israel they are categorized as Utopian: "There is hope and beauty," he writes, "in this affinity between 'peace' and 'the end of days,' yet because the end of days is usually perceived in Jewish-Israeli consciousness as an abstract, utopian, even unattainable point in time, peace too is seen as abstract, utopian, and unattainable: a horizon that grows ever more distant as one approaches it" (Grossman, *Dark* 89). The messianic claim of Jewish-Israeli life, guaranteed by its military in the present, means that peace is postponed to an indefinite future; and Utopianism, which is traditionally an approach to the horizon of perfection, is redefined in the process as hopelessly, unrealistically distant.

Grossman does not contest the categorization of peace in Jewish-Israeli mass consciousness as not a messianic but a Utopian ideal; his strategy is to embrace its secularity as its ecumenical advantage. "Perhaps," Grossman writes, "if we know a life of peace, we may let go of the obsessive need, shared by so many of us, for some artificial 'unity,' which is viewed as sacred and is usually meant to strengthen our standing against anything that may undermine our stability as a society and as a people" (Grossman *Dark* 92). It is assigning sacredness to unity that causes the secular disunity of the people, old immigrants against new immigrants, the rich against the poor, Israeli Jews against Israeli Arabs, and the meta-antagonism of religious Jews against secular Jews.

Peace, including peace between Jews and Arabs, is not one of the enumerated outcomes of Grossman's Utopianism but its formal condition; nevertheless, its substance is located in a specific Jewish potentiality. Ending the West Bank occupation, Grossman believes,

> can start to bring Israel back from the digressions it has taken from its own ethos. If this happens, there may emerge a new possibility for the creation of a fascinating synthesis between two fundamental models of the Jewish people: on the one hand, the Jewish Israeli living in his own land, embedded in the earth and the landscapes, the rooted man whose daily reality encompasses all the contradictory layers of reality; and on the other hand, the universal, cosmopolitan Jew who aspires to fulfill a spiritual, moral mission, to be "a light unto the nations," to be the voice of the oppressed everywhere.

Grossman refers to this hypothetical synthesis as "a choice that combined . . . the loftiest universal and Jewish ideals, together with a humane economic and social system" (Grossman *Dark* 105–6). It is, in short, a choice that does not choose between the great twentieth-century antitheses of universal and tribal loyalty.

Grossman grants that "these ideas sound utopian, perhaps even naive. But there is a shred of utopian thought and wishful thinking in everything I have said" (Grossman, *Dark* 106). It may be worth unpacking this frankness. Grossman does not quite admit the naivety of his ideals; he admits only that they sound utopian (first time through) and that they are partly utopian (second time). He seems to distinguish Utopianism from wishful thinking, yet they both exist as a thread. Why give two names to one thing, or why assign qualitatively distinct concepts the same quantity? What is the relation of Grossman's (Utopian) politics to his (wishful) escapism?

It is to appraise the nature of this Utopianism and its relation to escapism that I conclude with Grossman's early masterpiece, *See Under: Love*. The question is whether Grossman's Utopianism manages to avoid the serious escapism of American fiction that preserves some local and performative innocence against general corruption, enslavement, and death. This is not an idle or imposed question: it is the ultimate question of the book. Much of Grossman's future oeuvre is commentary on *See Under: Love*. It contains encyclopedia entries, which I'll imitate.

Escapist literature. *See Under: Love* employs the same technique and meta-technique as American escapist fiction in general, interpolating a fiction into its fiction, and specifically the technique of *Kavalier & Clay*, interpolating a fantasy-adventure narrative of its own invention. The protagonist of the contemporary and Israeli setting of the story, Shlomo Neuman, usually called by his childhood name, Momik, is preoccupied in childhood with his newly unearthed great uncle, Wasserman, who was an adventure storywriter in his young adulthood "Over There," Poland before the war. Wasserman had invented an international team of child superheroes called The Children of the Heart, who travel the world saving geniuses in trouble, such as Beethoven and Galileo, and peoples in trouble, such as Armenians and American slaves. In one adventure, their rescue takes a science fiction turn when they transport "Red Skins" to the moon. Suffering a spiritual crisis as an adult, along with his nation, Momik invents a comeback narrative for The Children of the Heart—made up of aging, diminished versions of their younger heroic selves, and complemented by "derelicts" known to Momik in Israel— that takes place at the Warsaw Zoo from 1939 to 1943 and is supposedly written by Wasserman while in a death camp. The story, after many twists, concerns whether The Children of the Heart can maintain, in the way of American escapism, from within their interpolated fantasy, the innocence of a foundling at the zoo, who inexplicably lives a life from infancy through age sixty-five in less than a day.

It is one thing to set out to preserve the innocence of a child in early twenty-first-century America, another in Warsaw during the Holocaust. If The Children of the Heart can do so, it will be a miracle exceeding American escapist translations of messianism to superheroism.

Messianism. The unadulterated messianic possibility is not immediately, regretlessly, absolutely renounced. Grossman's novel purports to make available a glimpse of Bruno Schulz's missing novel, *The Messiah*, in which the Messiah enters Schulz's Drohobycz in the body of a braying donkey. This is consonant with the view of Otto, leader of The Children of the Heart and director of the Warsaw Zoo: the zoo is akin to Noah's Ark, he declares, "only the other way around. Here the animals will save the people" (Grossman, *Love* 367). Schulz's theory is that only the repudiation of language will allow people to give up their "longing for the past" (compare *Everything is Illuminated*) and recognize that "there are no eternal values except for the value of creation itself, which is not a value but a biological drive" (Grossman, *Love* 175). This may be an impossible lesson for humans, and Schulz comes to understand

> that his first two books, and this third one, *The Messiah,* in which he had been drowning and floundering for the past four years, were merely the clumsy scaffold he had built with his own two hands around a creature unknown. . . . And so he was making his last escape. He was not afraid of the Germans or the Poles, nor was this a protest against the war. At last he was running away to meet something new. (Grossman, *Love* 94–5)

The historical Schulz was murdered in Drohobycz before completing *The Messiah*, but the fictional and ahistorical Schulz joins the ocean as a salmon, his "last escape," his "running away." Swimming in silence replaces drowning or floundering in language: Schulz knows what he is running from and toward, though what he is running toward must exist outside all books.

This may leave it to Neigel, the Nazi commandant of Wasserman's concentration camp, to save messianism for humans, for language users. The attack on messianism is led by Hannah, whose Children of the Heart superpower is that, despite being "an ugly old woman," she seems to everyone the most beautiful woman in the world (Grossman, *Love* 414). Hannah is convinced that the foundling Kazik is the Messiah, so when he arrives with great velocity at the appropriate age, she lures him into intercourse that becomes homicidal, saying with each thrust of her knife, "This is for love. And this is for hope. And this is for the joy of life. And this is for renewal. And this is for creation. And this is for the power to forget. And this is for faith. And this is for illusion. And this is for the damned optimism you implanted in us" (Grossman, *Love* 416). She tries to finish off both Kazik and her litany of complaints against life, but is dragged away. At the center of the indictment are creation and the power to forget, which are central to Schulz's inhuman messianism, in honor of which he performs his own counter-version of transfiguration, human to fish.

Thus, when the Nazi Neigel tries to save messianic hope from Hannah's attack by trying to revise the story of Hannah and Kazik as told to him by Wasserman, we cannot automatically dismiss his variation on the Messiah's advent as a perversion, though it is bizarre.

> The sky over Hannah lying on the ground opened up and a cloud was rent by a bolt of lightning, and . . . God's feet descend[ed], first one and then the other, to stalk the earth . . . and then God lay with the most beautiful woman in the world, and she, Hannah, was so dizzy with love and passion that she completely forgot her hidden knife. She was attuned solely to His love agony and His need for her. (Grossman, *Love* 418)

This scenario for the Messiah manages to proceed from God's rending lightning bolt to Hannah's forgotten knife, from God's stalking the earth to His sleeping with Hannah, from Hannah's murderousness to her love, from God's godliness to His neediness, from illumination to illusion.

What is going on? Perhaps this raving is Neigel's hysterical attempt, under Wasserman's influence within Wasserman's story, to fuse a Nazi and a Jewish messiah, a messiah of power and powerlessness, as if you could deify and consubstantiate Sauron and Frodo, or Trujillo and Oscar Wao, or Neigel and Wasserman. Why has this Frankenstein's messiah come to stand for the hope of salvation jeopardized by Hannah's itemization of despair? The answer would seem to be the failure to detach messianism from power altogether, in Momik's own era, which means that convicting Neigel's messianism as only a Nazi permutation would be comforting but obfuscating. It is Jews, according to Grossman, who are guilty of "crossing the Messiah with a vertically launched aircraft" (Grossman, *Wind* 49). Messianism has been occupied by the military, which is why it appeals to Neigel in retrospect, though Neigel to his credit is also captivated by Wasserman's story and the theme of agonized love.

Neigel's antinomy is not laughable because the salvation of the world seems to require power (even the salmon Schulz finds it impossible to abandon his own lust for power except by abandoning his shoal). This leaves two options: either to live with the degradation of language by power or abandon it. A novel cannot survive either surrender. One way out might be the project of Marcus, Child of the Heart, to invent words for minute, previously undetected increments of human emotions, such as those incoherent emotions felt by Ora in *To the End of the Land*. Language, if it is not to be renounced, might be expanded and refined (an intimate grammar might be sharable). An expanded language would serve the interests of Wasserman, who had become "a fugitive from human language to protect himself from all the words that cut his flesh" (Grossman, *Love* 283) but who returns to it to make contact with Neigel. The incoherence of an expanded language, a language that could contain antithetical truths, on behalf of fictions that can retain their contradictions (e.g., that you can be ugly and beautiful at once, or omnipotent and needy) and thus their nonfatal choices, would be in contrast with the divine unity of the word and its people.

Choice. It is defined twice in the novel. Wasserman defines it to Neigel:

> we are machine and automatons, only there is a trace of something else within us, I know not what to call it, and that is effort. Indeed, the effort we make on behalf of this particular woman, or this particular child, the evanescent spark that flashes between two evanescent creatures like us and no other two, ai, that same exuberance which brings us into each other's sphere I will call "choice." (Grossman, *Love* 241)

In his own encyclopedia entry, Momik, setting out the terms of Kazik's story, defines choice tautologically as the "voluntary selection of one possibility out of many" (Grossman, *Love* 312). On the one hand, Wasserman is unsure whether "effort" is the right term for the nonmechanical aspect of choice, perhaps because effort can only follow choice. Effort must be equivalent to the original spark, but the spark does not necessarily spiritualize the mechanics. Choice cannot choose itself into being. To avoid an infinite regress, choice must have one foot in chemistry and mechanics; but chemistry and mechanics are what choice is meant to transcend, so it must have one foot in will and effort. There must be a congruity of predetermination and determination.

On the other hand, the encyclopedia begs the question of the bifurcation in choice by clandestinely repeating the thing to be defined in the definition: What does "voluntary" mean? The tautology bows to the infinite regress of choice. But what has been opened up by the tautology is choice not between particular humans, where a spark determines the life or death of the chosen, but among potentialities that are not annihilated in actualities. Wasserman hopes that "Kazik would choose to be a human being." Neigel responds, "Perhaps the worthy doctor can teach me how one chooses to be a human being. I always thought one was born so, no?" Wasserman argues that one elects to become human "by choosing to uphold certain values and precepts." Neigel counters that that is precisely what he has done: "I 'chose' to start killing." Wasserman refuses the terminology: "One does not choose to begin killing, Herr Neigel, but continues to do so. . . . One must rather make the conscious choice not to kill" (312). In Grossman's work, making a binary choice is making a murderous choice, the using up of choice.

Insofar as choice paradigmatically entails life-and-death decisions, that is, existential decisions, a peaceful choice is impossible. But choice on this understanding is self-contradictory: you do not choose to submit to history, it chooses you; and what you are chosen for is terminating the choice of your enemy. Given the self-contradiction of choosing violence, the only real choice is peace; the circular problem is that peace is the condition of nonviolent choosing. The answer to the question of whether one should kill sounds Pauline. If not killing is actually a choice and not obedience to a commandment, it can only be that love forestalls it—except that there cannot be divine authorization for sublating divine law. The superiority of fiction to the Gospels is that it makes improvisations such as Neigel's possible, in which God's homicidal and Hannah's deicidal violence are interrupted by unreality, a deluding of God that constitutes the caesura between their life or death choices and the objects of those choices. Hannah's power to make ugliness appear as beauty represents fiction's. It takes Hannah's illusion within Neigel's myth in relation to Wasserman's story within Momik's fiction channeling Schulz's fiction within Grossman's fiction—not a divine illumination of everything—to protect the kind of choosing that is not killing.

At a library, Momik as a child looked at "pictures of a mother and father forced to choose between two children, to choose which one would stay with them and which one would go away forever, and he tried to figure out how they would choose" (Grossman, *Love* 67). Nations at war make this sort of choice all the time; that's messianic reality for the literal-minded.

Peace. The question of Kazik is Grossman's nearest approach to the question of Jack or Oskar or Toph or Little Igor in American literature: Is it possible to imagine innocence before experience, protected for a prolonged moment by adults, who are renewed in the escapist process? It is impossible in the Israeli society of Aron and Momik, where a sense of endangerment generated by the past or the present overwhelms children's innocence in proportion to their capacity for innocence. Innocence in Israel means *not* forgetting one's own mortality, as opposed to the messianic alienation of mortality to one's enemies. (This recalls Faulkner's Benjy's knowledge that whites are mortal, which his siblings deny.) That Kazik matures at several thousand times the normal rate means that his innocence can survive even his adulthood if he can stay uncontaminated by reality for about a day. That this baby, even more than most fictional or metafictional babies, exhibits signs of being imaginary increases the plausibility of his preserved innocence. The problem is that he is imagined to be the impossible child of an aging Jewish widower (an original member of The Children of the Heart), and he is being raised in Warsaw during the Holocaust.

That the raising of Kazik is a joint Jewish-Israeli and diverse cosmopolitan venture seems designed to evoke its Utopian potential. But it is in the nature of Kazik's accelerated life that his body begins to decay while he is still growing and being raised, before he can be prepared for it, and before the question of an exemplary future can arise. In agony himself, feeling precocious mortality within childhood rather than protracted innocence within adulthood, he demands to see unhappy life for himself; the Armenian magician Harotian tears "an opening in the cage bars," but "instead of the zoo, the opening revealed a view of Neigel's camp." This includes the "high, gloomy watchtowers and electrified barbed-wire fences, and the train station which leads nowhere but to death. And he smelled the smell of human flesh burned by human beings." The editor of the encyclopedia in which we are reading this fable (Momik) comments in brackets: "No wonder. The camp had always been waiting there" (Grossman, *Love* 428).

It is as if Grossman is determined to make an explicit rejoinder to the contemporary form of American escapism, which is impossible because the extermination camp had always been waiting for Kazik. There was no moment of innocence prior to that perpetual ambush; his innocence is his uncaged openness to that experience of encaged death.

The last words of the novel are spoken by Wasserman to the commandant: "Do you understand, Herr Neigel? We asked for so little: for a man to live in this world from birth to death, and know nothing of war" (Grossman, *Love* 452). It seems little to ask particularly if Kazik lives sixty-five years in about twenty-two hours, at a zoo, home of animals that seem to promise messianic protection for humans and a team of adults with superpowers imagined it seems to elicit that very protection. "We asked for so little" of whom? The wish takes the form of a prayer, but there is no messiah to receive it. Not only can Wasserman, Momik, and their creations not choose a future for Kazik or allow Kazik to choose a future; they cannot provide the single condition of nonbinary choosing—the only complete choosing that is not an antinomy—which is peace outside any messianic kingdom. Grossman's Utopianism gives birth to an escapist fantasy of reliving or living in the first place one's innocence in the innocence of a child surrogate, and it fails. It fails in the way of Kavalier's comic book fantasy of an anti-Nazi superhero who can punch Hitler in the face but cannot save a European child. What remains is not an adventure, as in American escapist versions of Utopianism or in Wasserman's prewar novels, a flight to Neverland or the moon, but a wish, which is a prayer to nowhere. Wishful thinking is the shred of Utopia preserved by Grossman's fiction.

Chapter 11

CATEGORICAL DENIAL

I. Before and After

On or about May of 1998, as Arundhati Roy almost explicitly puts it in *The Algebra of Infinite Justice*, the Indian nation changed, when it became a nuclear power. It was, of course, a Large Thing, a tremendous geopolitical event, but why, in Roy's view, was it the decisive one in the modern history of India, in the history of India as a nation? In India's "search for selfhood" (Roy, *Algebra* 27), the bomb guarantees forever, it seems, a version of Indian history in which it has a perpetual atomic rival in Pakistan, and a perpetual threat from Islam, as its unifying motive. India might otherwise have founded its identity on the basis not of its unity against alien or, in the case of its own Muslim population, alienated threats but on its constitutive hurly burly: "India's redemption lies in the inherent anarchy and fractiousness of its people and its political formations. . . . It's too diverse, too grand, too feral, and— eventually, I hope—too democratic to be lobotomized into believing in one single idea" (Roy, *Algebra* 213–14).

It happens that in May of 1998, just before the bomb, Roy was contemplating her redemption as a novelist. Her first novel, *The God of Small Things*, had been published a year before to critical and popular acclaim on several continents. A friend predicted that Roy's remaining life would be anticlimactic, suggesting (the friend's exact meaning isn't clear to Roy or me) that "the only perfect ending to the story would be death." Roy adds as partial clarification: "My death." But Roy concludes that she can survive, so long as she doesn't succumb to an addiction to fame (Roy, *Algebra* 14). Thus, the bomb explodes at a critical moment for Roy personally and artistically. Just when she needs something on the other side of celebrity to postpone her demise in some sense, India as a nation commits spiritual suicide: "Something had died but it wasn't me" (Roy, *Algebra* 17).

Or was it? It's worth quoting her declaration of independence from India at length because of how much, as early as 1998, she began inventing the terms of *The Ministry of Utmost Happiness*, her second novel, published in 2017. "If protesting against having a nuclear bomb implanted in my brain is anti-Hindu and anti-national, then I secede. I hereby declare myself an independent, mobile republic. I am a citizen of the earth. I own no territory. I have no flag. I'm female, and have nothing against eunuchs" (Roy, *Algebra* 21). But though *Utmost Happiness* ascribes Indian murderousness to maleness, and though one of the two female protagonists is transsexual (inhabiting for a while a home for hijras, a category that includes eunuchs) and the other declares her own independent nationhood, nevertheless its setting is inside India, within Indian impasses. It is not easy for Roy to separate her own fate from that of her homeland because her crisis is not entirely a matter of political affiliation. "To me," Roy writes, the bomb "signifies dreadful things": "the end of imagination. The end of freedom" (Roy, *Algebra* 2). This means that she may withdraw her allegiance to nuclear India, but doing so does not extract the bomb implanted in her brain.

How does a novelist, even one weaned from celebrity, survive the death of her nation's imagination? In May of 1998, when India was transformed, so was the direction of Roy's career. "Things can change in a day," Roy insists three times in *The God of Small Things* (164, 192, 339). If imagination was extinguished in May of 1998, at least it is true that a certain kind of imagination said so: the imagination of disaster; the imagination of self-destruction; the imagination of the Fall. (Rahel, one of Roy's surrogates in *The God of Small Things*, learns at Nazareth Convent that "depravity" means "the innate corruption of the human nature due to original sin" [Roy, *God* 16].) Roy's imagination always divides Before from After, even if what comes after is the death of imagination.

"The End of Imagination," on India's induction into the league of nuclear powers, is the first essay of Roy's first book of journalism. Subsequent essays have other views about the decisive turn in Indian history. In *Field Notes on Democracy*, Roy proposes a new lapsarian moment. "Let's mark the date: spring 2002. While we can thank the U.S. president and the Coalition Against Terror for creating a congenial international atmosphere for fascism's ghastly debut, we cannot credit them for the years it has been brewing in our public and private lives" (Roy, *Field Notes* 42). It is an a priori of Roy's perceptiveness that a boiling point must be marked, though fascism had been simmering. In Roy's analysis, the impunity of the Gujarat pogrom of 2002, in the wake of 9/11, is the precondition of the death of imagination that takes the form of passively accepting the world's division into two antagonists, and accepting that in the battle of civilizations, all virtues may be forsworn. "With each battle cry against Pakistan," Roy writes, with patriotic anti-nationalism akin to Grossman's Jewish cosmopolitanism, "we inflict a wound on ourselves, on our way of life, on our spectacularly diverse and ancient civilization, on everything that makes India different from Pakistan" (Roy, *Field Notes* 42–3). The world's options, like India's, diminish first to two, second to one.

Not until 2002? Roy gives us reason to surmise that the brewing had begun with the nuclear program of the late 1960s to 1970s, then the Emergency of 1975–7, then Operation Blue Star in 1984:

> It was Indira Gandhi who started the real slide. . . . She injected the venom into our political veins. . . . She showed us how to conjure enemies out of thin air, to fire at phantoms that she had carefully fashioned for that very purpose. It was she who discovered the benefits of never burying the dead, but preserving their putrid carcasses and trundling them out to worry old wounds when it suited her. Between herself and her sons she managed to bring the country to its knees. (Roy, *Algebra* 31)

If the country was brought to its knees between 1966 and 1984, with the Emergency making the degradation overt and official, how much lower could it debase itself in May of 1998 or spring 2002? India's imagination had already been reduced to Indira Gandhi's conjurations.

Yet blaming Indira Gandhi, in tandem with sons Sanjay and Rajiv, can't be exactly right. Indian statehood was not innocent of conjuring enemies and declaring war on them before her administration. Roy's counter-history of India is designed to make its bomb, fostered into existence by Mrs. Gandhi, appear as an inevitability of Indian nationhood. Roy credits the revolution of Mohandas Gandhi as "a sophisticated, magnificent, imaginative struggle"; his genius was to focus India's commotion on a single object. Once the common enemy was removed, however, the genie invoked by his genius was loosed. Gandhi took political fuel, wastefully consumed in internal political, social, and religious schisms, and brought it to a blaze; but "fires, when they're lit, race along any one of these schisms, and in the process, release tremendous bursts of political energy. Not unlike what happens when you split an atom." India has already experienced this metaphorical fission: "Yes," Roy grants, the harnessed genie "won us freedom. But it also won us the carnage of Partition" (Roy, *Algebra* 30). Indira Gandhi's secondary contribution was to make "the genie a permanent state guest" (Roy, *Algebra* 31). India had no national history, in effect, *prior* to the atomic bomb.

Despite the theological possibility of tracing India's fall from grace back from 2002 to 1998 to 1975 to its genesis in 1947, there remains a date that can be considered the year of the temptation and Fall. Roy specifies that the "starting gun" of her essays of 2002–8, *Field Notes on Democracy*, "is the year 1989, when, in the rugged mountains of Afghanistan, capitalism won its long jihad against Soviet Communism." "Within months of the collapse of the Soviet Union and the fall of the Berlin Wall, the Indian government, once a leader of the Nonaligned Movement, performed a high-speed somersault and aligned itself completely with the United States, monarch of the new unipolar world" (Roy, *Field Notes* 4–5). In this sudden globalization, "*Freedom* has come to mean *choice*," but "choice has less to do with the human spirit than with different brands of deodorant" (Roy, *Field Notes* 5). As opposed to Grossman's world of violent binarism, Roy's globe isn't even binary. In *The Shape of the Beast*, Roy christens the whole post-1989 epoch "the Age of Spurious Choice. Eveready or Nippo? Coke or Pepsi? Nike or Reebok?" (173).

Of all the dates that Roy proposes for the Fall, India's on behalf of the planet's, 1989 is the year that rings truest to her. The intermittent but persistent subject of the essays that divide her novel of 1997 from her novel of 2017 is the privatization of India, and every other aspect of contemporary Indian life that she decries follows from it. This entails uncovering the links between corporatization, a concealed, secular, international dispensation, and its spectacular, palpable consequence in on-the-ground, murderous Hindutva. First: inflaming religious passion provides a smokescreen for the privatization of India (Roy, *Algebra* 183, *Field Notes* 60–1). Second: inflaming religious passion sets the poor against one another, confusing any kind of anti-privatizing communal solidarity (Roy, *Field Notes* 47). Third: the imposition of "corporate globalization on to an almost feudal society . . . reinforce[s] inequality," which breeds "religious fascism" (Roy, *Beast* 82). By a fortunate circularity, corporate privatization causes the social disruptions that disguise its inroads. In light of this phenomenon, Roy's obsessions—the bomb, the dams, the religious persecution, the displacements and societal destruction, the decay of justice, democracy, and freedom—are epiphenomena. Whatever was cynical, hateful, and even genocidal in Indian life before 1989 has been retrofitted for a new use by neoliberalism.

Roy had not fully understood the significance of 1989 in *The God of Small Things*, though she had glimpsed it. She has grasped it by the time of *The Ministry of Utmost Happiness*, though it is another question whether she found a way to write a novel about invisible corporate profits behind spectacular Indian tribalism and suffering. We can investigate the before and after of her two novels for signs of the somersault of 1989, but we should not anticipate a literary redemption of India's fallen state in advance of, or as substitute for, its political redemption; Roy is not that sort of an escapist. Her imagination of the change in India tends to be fatalistic: she does not pretend to have a Utopian or messianic prescription for saving India from an eternity of neoliberalism. Her politics tend to be improvisatory and mutable, but history, on the darkest hypothesis, is not. "Is the last stop of every revolution advanced capitalism? Think about it—the French Revolution, the Russian Revolution, the Chinese Revolution, the Vietnam War, the anti-apartheid struggle, the supposedly Gandhian freedom struggle in India . . . what's the last station they all pull in at? Is this the end of imagination?" (Roy, *Beast* 225).

Roy has written two novels determined to work out the literary response to a nation (after India explodes its nuclear bomb) and a world (after the fall of Soviet communism) in which she fears that imagination—she does not make an ad hoc exculpatory distinction between political and artistic varieties—may be extinct. Put that starkly, the literary future is not promising. But the imagination of even catastrophic change is slightly more optimistic than the imagination of absolute eternal changelessness. If India has courted self-destruction in the phases of its self-creation in 1947, 1975, 1989, 1998, and 2002, it is also true, according to Roy, that India has never changed, that it is still enduring the consequences of its almost prehistoric caste antagonism, its "Love Laws," to use the kenning of *The God of Small Things*. The alternatives of that book are as follows: everything can change in a day; nothing changes. The unchangeableness of history is what *The God of Small Things* calls History. The question is whether the catastrophic fallenness of modern Indian history predicts a messianic return, a break in History, a rebirth of imagination.

II. Before

Everything can change in a day: in *The God of Small Things*, there are two days that support this claim. The first is the day on which Sophie and her mother, Margaret, arrive from England to Kerala on a visit. Sophie (aged nine) is the daughter and Margaret, the English ex-wife of Chacko, an Indian man educated at Oxford. Chacko is Ammu's brother and thus uncle of her children Rahel and Estha, the seven-year-old fraternal twins (sister and brother) who are the fractional protagonists of the book. The day that Sophie and her mother arrive in Kerala, the day after Estha has been sexually abused in a movie theater, Rahel sneaks away from the awkward welcoming to visit her older untouchable companion, Velutha, who is almost a contemporary of the divorcee Ammu; and Ammu herself exchanges an unmistakable look with the kind and charismatic Dalit. The second is the catastrophic, hysterical day, two weeks later, on which Ammu is imprisoned in her room for her incipient affair with Velutha; Estha, fearing he might be pursued to his home by his movie theater abuser, tries to escape to an evacuated villa across the river with Rahel and Sophie; and Sophie drowns. The consequences of that include the exiling of Ammu from her home and children, followed by her illness and death four years later; the exiling of Estha to his father's care in Calcutta, separating him from his inseparable twin; and the police execution of Velutha.

It is challenging to summarize how the destructive machine functions. Here is a power point account of how it kills Velutha. His execution is set in motion by an alliance of the local Communist organizer (for whom the Dalit represents a caste disturbance to workers' solidarity and hence his own ambition) with the local factory owner Chacko (himself a Marxist in theory) and the local police, in concert with Chacko and Ammu's aunt, the wretched Baby Kochamma, caretaker of the Ipe family's Syrian Christian caste privilege, and even Velutha's father, who betrays his son to protect relations with the relatively benevolent Ipes. Seven-year-old Estha, who has not inherited a caste, religious, or economic position he wishes to defend, is drawn into the decentered but cumulative conspiracy, persuaded by Baby Kochamma to testify against Velutha to protect his mother, Rahel, and himself. Velutha is killed not only by his caste and political enemies but also by his caste and political allies, not only by government officials but also by friends and family, not only by the past but also by the future.

What changes on the second day is the snuffing of the flickering hope that something might have radically changed on the first day, two weeks before. Though the novel makes mention of the Vietnam War and Armstrong's first steps on the moon, it is as if, by way of its Love Laws, India is fundamentally ahistorical. We can observe, as a first approximation, Roy's even-handed assignment of blame for the accidental and intentional homicides of her novel. The book is apolitical to the extent that it is ahistorical: if all Indian history conspires against change, politics is corrupt of necessity. Roy notes that her first novel was criticized by the Indian left and her second by the Indian right, and one can see why these turns are taken (Roy, *Beast* 11). In *Small Things*, all phases of Indian life—its domestic arrangements, social relations, and politics (its right and pointedly its left)—collude to defend the status quo.

This may seem to call into question the book's reason for existing. But like everything that Roy imagines, the novel has a before and after: twenty-three years after the events of late 1969, Estha, who has already returned from his exile in Calcutta to the family home in Ayemenem, is reunited with his twin sister Rahel, back from the United States. At this conjunction, the question of the book becomes: What is the relation of the early days of reunion and Terror, as the book calls it, and the later day of reunion and love? The book registers four main assaults on the Love Laws—the unfettered relations of Sophie and the twins, the twins and Velutha, and Velutha and Ammu in 1969; the incest of Rahel and Estha in 1993—and the question, rephrased, is what the final challenge has to do with the three prior challenges that had resulted in moral and medical death. How does a revolt against the Love Laws come back into play in the present, Benjaminian fashion, though at a microcosmic scale, given the ruthlessness of its suppression in all of history through 1969?

Begin with the relation of two challenges in 1969 to Love Laws preventing affection between Dalits and the touchable castes: the love between the twins and Velutha and the love between Ammu and Velutha. These challenges, carried out across the river, ought to be complementary. Ammu will "love by night the man her children loved by day. [She will] use by night the boat her children used by day" (Roy, *God* 44). Rahel and Estha adore Velutha as a charming, ingenious, solicitous older brother with qualifications as proxy father; Ammu loves Velutha as the sexual consummation of their outrageous emotions for each other. This would seem to be a workable division of labor, from a non-Hindu point of view. Ammu refers to Rahel and Estha's prior opening of intercaste affection with Velutha as midwifery to the birth of her own intercourse with him (Roy, *God* 336).

Yet the interference of the two relations is disastrous. On the day that Estha takes Rahel and Sophie with him on his escape across the river, fatal to Sophie, the twins try to find their mother, but she had been locked in her room by Baby Kochamma for the scandal of her affair with Velutha. Estha fears that the man who had abused him at the theater will find him at home; instead of reassuring her children, Ammu cries, "If it wasn't for you I wouldn't be here! None of this would have happened! . . . *You're* the millstones around my neck! . . . Why can't you just go away and leave me alone?" (Roy, *God* 253). She does not merely fail to comfort them; she adds a motive for their flight to the abandoned villa. Her words induce her children to feel unloved, though it isn't self-evident what she intends. Does "None of this would have happened" mean that without the twins there wouldn't have been a trail-blazing for her affair with Velutha? Or does "You're the millstone around my neck" mean that without the twins she would have been free to conduct her affair with Velutha away from familial meddling in Ayemenem?

The question to ask, however, is not which of these antithetical meanings Ammu intended, because, on the level of plot, she is lashing out at the only vulnerable objects of her rage. On the level of plotting, the question is why Roy uses Ammu to connect the accidental death of Sophie (whom she does not reject when momentarily rejecting her children at the locked door) to the assassination of Velutha (against whom she never conspires). Ammu is not directly complicit in either the accident or the execution, yet by virtue of her domestic incarceration for loving Velutha, which results in Velutha's death, she indirectly impels Sophie to her own death at almost the same time and place.

The answer, I think, is that Roy has an idea about how Velutha might turn out to be the messianic figure who overthrows the Love Laws on behalf of antinomian love, though she has not a complementary but a contradictory idea about how Sophie might do so. That Roy's or Ammu's personal, profane, syncretist Indian religion, Syrian Christian wing, requires a messiah is clear from Roy's arranging that Velutha would be "a carpenter with blood-red nails" (Roy, *God* 307). The nails in question are not those of a crucifixion (or of a carpenter, or of a crucified carpenter) but a carpenter's fingernails, which are red because Rahel has painted them. The blatancy of the verbal and visual punning may mean that Roy needs us not to miss her allegory, but it may also indicate that she does not fully believe in it. That is perhaps why she requires antithetical martyrdoms.

On the one hand, "biology designed the dance" (Roy, *God* 335): the rebellion against the virtually prehistoric hierarchical Love Laws is driven by primordial anarchic sex. This echoes Bruno Schulz's messianic vision in *See Under: Love*: to escape our "longing for the past," Grossman's Schulz proclaims, we must understand that "there are no eternal values except for the value of creation itself, which is not a value but a biological drive" (Grossman, *Love* 175). Sex may be the egalitarian prehistoric phenomenon that redeems history for both its victims and exploiters. Ammu has a dream of Velutha as "a cheerful man with one arm" who holds her close. She wonders: "Who was he, the one-armed man? . . . The God of Loss? The God of Small Things?" (Roy, *God* 217). "Loss" suggests incompletion—"If he held her, he couldn't kiss her. If he kissed her, he couldn't see her" (Roy, *God* 215). "Small Things" suggests the possibility of intercourse like Oscar Wao's, temporarily beneath the radar of law, nation, and history.

Yet we seem also to be in the realm of Madame Sosostris and her Tarot deck, in which the one-eyed man and the wounded Fisher King, among other auguries, make their appearance. In fact, Velutha, when he is not the divinity of small things, is a fisher king (he is a Paravan, the caste of fishermen) or vegetation god for the Indian Waste Land: he has on his back "a light brown birth mark, shaped like a pointed dry leaf," which (he tells Rahel) "made the monsoons come on time" (Roy, *God* 73). This is sexuality extrapolated to the rhythmic fertility of the seasons, the biological drive, as Schulz would have it, expanded to the scope of oceanic creativity.

Velutha is the God, it seems, of Large Things as well as Small, but in this aggrandized avatar, Velutha fails. Sophie is killed because of a storm out of season: "Though it was December, it rained as though it was June." The source as much as undoing of the antique Love Laws, primordial nature participates in the destruction of the potential for redemptive change. Not only does the storm kill Sophie; it also convinces Velutha's father to betray his son. "To a superstitious man, the relentlessness of that unseasonal downpour could have seemed like an omen from an angry god. To a drunk superstitious man, it could have seemed like the beginning of the end of the world" (Roy, *God* 254). He can imagine the end of the world more easily than he can imagine the end of castes. So much for the novel's hope that the Love Laws may be annulled, at long last, because they are unnatural. "Fear death by water," warns Madame Sosostris. Sophie's mother "had no prophylaxis, unfortunately, for Death by Drowning" (Roy, *God* 329). Sexuality in particular, like nature in general, can be as arbitrary and angry as it is a rhythmic and restorative god.

Against that tendency toward sublime largeness—against the adult presumption that even smallness needs a consummation and an apotheosis sufficient to restore the Waste Land—the instinctive disregard of Love Laws on the part of the children remains beautiful and small. They are sufficiently unlike that we may be unsure what to make of the narratological fact that the deaths of Velutha and Sophie occur in nearly the same place and time. What agency ordains her death, too?

Sophie's death seems a peripheral casualty of the cruelty of India, whose cynosure is Velutha. Her death is under-determined, in contrast with Velutha's, which is over- or omni-determined.

Their threat to the Love Laws is nonetheless profound in its smallness because, together, the three children represent not the deification of weakness (God of Loss, God of Small Things, the crucified God) but the humanization of power.

Sophie's purchase on humanness, despite her long-awaited descent from the sky enveloped in adoration, is established perversely. Rahel is killing ants; Sophie proposes that they "leave one alive so that it can be lonely"; Rahel ignores her and massacres them all (Roy, *God* 186). But Sophie in the course of a week pleases the twins in unexpected ways, conclusively when she "revealed herself to be human. One day the twins returned from a clandestine trip to the river (which had excluded Sophie Mol), and found her in the garden in tears, perched on the highest point of Baby Kochamma's Herb Curl, 'Being Lonely,' as she put it. The next day Estha and Rahel took her with them to visit Velutha" (Roy, *God* 189–90). This means retrospectively that Sophie's suggestion to preserve one lonely ant had been for the sake of an inter-species congregation of solitude. It is that access of humanness that brings her to the murderous river.

The contiguous challenges imaged by Velutha and Sophie to the Love Laws are dissonant. Power in Kerala fears Velutha's potential power; Sophie represents "power's fear of powerlessness" (Roy, *God* 308), which is a fear not of rebellion against the law but carelessness of it. Her solitude does not add a dimension to Velutha's sexuality. Her restored humanness contributes nothing to his wounded divinity. Though the twins bring Sophie to Velutha, we see nothing of what transpires because, presumably, nothing much can.

On the American model, Roy's book is not escapist, though Sophie possesses the requisite premature knowledge of death and grief, and Velutha the requisite protectiveness and playfulness. But Ammu's position in between, in her two roles as illicit lover and momentarily unloving mother, transmutes the intersection from renewed life for both to death for both. As lover of Velutha, she loses track of the absence of a father in the lives of her children and Sophie; it is the completion of their abandonment, and Sophie's plan to punish adults for it, that leads to her sacrifice in the flight across the river. "Sophie Mol had convinced the twins that it was *essential* that she go along too. That the absence of children, *all* children, would heighten the adults' remorse" (Roy, *God* 292, emphasis in the original). And it is Ammu's own imagination (stand-in for Roy's) of the necessity of a sacrificial procreative god that requires Velutha's death at the same time and place. The relations of adults and children are not redemptive because a re-parenting narrative, in which redemption occurs at the intersection of generations, cannot cohere in Ayemenem: Ammu cannot make what she wants from Velutha intersect with what the children need from Velutha and herself. (Dave Eggers's paranoid fantasies of what might occur when he leaves Toph to pursue his romantic life come true insofar as the dream of sexual fulfillment does not give way to the dream of shared sexual liminality.) The childrens' innocent Utopia does not chime with Ammu's corporeal messianism. It is left to the Love Laws to imagine in legalistic prurience the intersection of adulthood and childhood.

It is crucial that when, over two decades later, Rahel and Estha's incest poses the fourth and final threat of the novel to the Love Laws, their temporal status is ambiguous: "Not old. Not young. But a viable die-able age." They are thirty-one, the age when their mother died; the phrase had first registered that Ammu died not in her youth or old age, but too soon. Here it means that the twins encounter each other sexually within life and death at once (Roy, *God* 3, 327). The specific virtue of this incestuous affront to the Love Laws is that it is a reunion not merely of Rahel and Estha, but also of childhood and adulthood, that does not rely, in the American way, on the momentary coincidence of childlike adults and precocious kids, a momentary suspension of the contradiction between unawareness and knowledge of death. For *The God of Small Things* as a whole to work, the incest of Rahel and Estha must reiterate all the novel's affronts to the Love Laws, from the childhood side and the adult side at once, simultaneously within sex and death and childhood and innocence.

The process begins by associating the twins' incest with Sophie's burial. Though not miraculously resurrected, Sophie "was awake for her own funeral. She showed Rahel Two Things." The first is the dome of the funeral's church, "painted blue like the sky, with drifting clouds and tiny whizzing jet planes with white trails that crisscrossed in the clouds" (Roy, *God* 5). Insofar as the dome illustrates a cartoonish Heaven, Sophie seems not just awakened but enlivened by death, not so much rejuvenated as juvenile in the first place. The second is a bat baby that climbs up Baby Kochamma's leg until it reaches "the place between her sari and her blouse . . . . Baby Kochamma screamed and hit the air with her hymnbook. The singing stopped for a 'Whatisit? Whathappened?' and for a furrywhirring and a sariflapping." Sophie's celebration, though on the inside of her coffin, is a "secret cartwheel"

(Roy, *God* 6). She is reborn in her coffin as a mischievous child singling out a preferred adult antagonist, posthumous leader of a Children's Crusade against propriety.

Rahel and Estha's incest also extends the boundaries of life at the margins, to the special mortification, again, of Baby Kochamma. The first perception by Estha in reencountering his sister is that he is looking at his mother: "Still, he could see her. Grown into their mother's skin. The liquid glint of her eyes in the dark. Her small straight nose. Her mouth, full lipped . . . . Their beautiful mother's mouth, Estha thought. Ammu's mouth" (Roy, *God* 300). It is at that point of identification of Estha with Velutha and Rahel with Ammu that Estha and Rahel's incest begins: "Twenty-three years later, Rahel, dark woman in a yellow T-shirt, turns to Estha in the dark. . . . She whispers. She moves her mouth. Their beautiful mother's mouth" (Rahel, *God* 327).

It makes etymological sense that Estha seeks his mother's mouth and thereafter her womb on behalf of Velutha: incest = in + castus (impure). "Castus" reaches "caste" through Portuguese. But Rahel and Estha's incest has another dimension. Estha seeks unity with Rahel not symbolically entering but already fully within his mother's womb: "They had known each other before Life began," a kind of Aristophanesean unity. The cohabited womb before life and the rollicking coffin after it are inverse metaphors of innocent perversity.

Rahel and Estha's incest does not merely comprehend the challenges to the Love Laws as manifest in their friendship with Sophie, their friendship with Velutha, and Velutha's affair with Ammu. In those separate affiliations, childhood and adulthood do not synchronize; here they coalesce. The incestuous act does not merely set off suspicions of perversion; it brings into reality the full horror of what the Love Laws had imagined twenty-three years before. The intercourse of Rahel and Estha is perversion and salvation at once because incest, an act that could not have been illicit in the first instance if law was instituted to forbid it, makes it impossible to sort sin from grace. Rahel and Estha are adults violating a sexual taboo; they are prelapsarian fetuses. Though messianic and utopian visions fail in India because they attempt to redeem or direct history where history never moves, incest is yet more primordial than the Love Laws, the only thing that predates the prehistorical, the only thing with seniority even over unreliably regenerative and destructive nature because it precedes the distinction of natural and unnatural.

Incest conducts an experiment in defeating history and its politics by precluding them—Rahel and Estha's act has no public dimension, except by way of the novel. Their intercourse is a unity of withdrawals: what Larry McCaslin, Rahel's American ex-husband, cannot understand is that "the emptiness in one" (Rahel) is "a version of the quietness of the other" (Estha) (Roy, *God* 19–20). A recurrent trope of the books is "holes in the universe," invoked to represent both covert and departed things: black cats are "black cat-shaped holes in the Universe" (Roy, *God* 82), but Estha, bound for Calcutta, is an "Estha-shaped hole in the Universe" (Roy, *God* 156). In *Room*, Jack asks Ma the meaning of craters. "Holes where something happened," Ma tells him (Donoghue 24). In *Arcadia*, Bit thinks of his loss in 9/11 as "a hole in the sky" and of the loss of his wife as "a hole in his life where Helle had been" (Groff 207, 217). On this conceit, the overcoming of immortal Love Laws unites dead but revenant Sophie, Velutha, and Ammu with living but withdrawn Rahel and Estha.

The next unlikely project for overcoming Love Laws by way of the wedding of presence and absence would be uniting spectral author and haunted readers, readers who may be (as in my case, like Larry McCaslin's) white, male, middle-class, American adults, present, alive, and privileged. The novel makes extensive references to two other works of art, one Indian in origin and one American. At first glance, they represent antithetical East and West. *The Sound of Music* at the beginning of the novel represents for ingenuous Estha and Rahel the patriarchal order and pristine beauty of mythic Austria; the Kathakali performance at the end represents the messy familial horrors of the sacred myths of India. It would be simple to upend the hierarchy and prefer the dark truths of the dance to the whitewashing of the film. But Roy sets herself a more difficult challenge. We are told that the livelihood of the Kathakali actors now consists in abridging and bastardizing their sacred stories for indifferent tourists. Roy might have insisted on the purity of those stories and blamed invasive foreigners for their degradation, akin to blaming Nazis for Austrian degradation. The *Mahabharata* tale of Karna and Kunti would be her midnight "Edelweiss." That is the sort of simplification by which *The Sound of Music* became what *The God of Small Things* dubs it, a World Hit. Roy needs to avoid the escapism of a World Hit on the same basis; the novel's apparent desire to stay uncontaminated by a global audience must be prevented from becoming its selling point to a global market, nostalgic for ahistorical purity.

This obligation is performed by way of the novel's peculiar style. Style, after the publication of this book, while Roy works two decades as a political essayist, becomes one of her running preoccupations: Can her stylistic exuberance survive politics? Here the question is: Can her style survive apolitical popularity? Can it survive its own childishness, its claim, apparently, on a timeless, if unchaste, purity of its own?

The key is that the source of the style may be discovered at Sophie's funeral, which is described in nursery poem prose: "Sophie Mol was almost nine. She had a special child-sized coffin./ Satin-lined./ Brass handle shined" (Roy, *God* 4). (These last phrases are divided into poetic units.) The prose alliterates, assonates, and jingles: "The congregation gathered around the coffin, and the yellow church swelled like a throat with the sound of sad singing" (Roy, *God* 4). The nearly fulsome poeticizing of the prose is best conceived this way: something of Sophie's life, entombed and preserved in childhood forever, informs Rahel's verbal imagination, which in English never outgrows its susceptibility to the sounds of words prior to their meanings. At the funeral, Rahel hears English by way of an approximate syllabification: "Dus to dus" (Roy, *God* 7). This becomes a recurrent technique: lay-ter, bar nowel, No Locusts stand I.

When Roy's style seems most mannered, we should take it to be appropriate to the childishness of Rahel in the era of her first self-conscious relationship with the English language stunted by her identification with the English girl's death. At age seven, "Rahel thought that *boot* was a lovely word. A much better word, at any rate, than *sturdy. Sturdy* was a terrible word. Like a dwarf's name" (Roy, *God* 46). (Her idea of the names of the seven dwarfs comes from Disney.) Even at the moment she recognizes her adulthood, Rahel considers the eventuality as if a child coming upon language: "What a funny word *old* was on its own, Rahel thought, and said it to herself: *Old*" (Roy, *God* 92). Registering the signs of her advancing age, Rahel's imagery remains juvenile: "She had half-moons under her eyes and a team of trolls on her horizon" (Roy, *God* 155).

Roy's imagination is least self-possessed when most blatant: what seems like precious stylistic self-indulgence is actually a way of floating the consciousness of the book between ages and eras, chastity and unchasteness, life and death, remainder and loss. It survives the death of the imagination by securing death within the imagination, populated by Disney dwarfs and trolls.

Readers can feel the book's invitation in mature English to a language that refuses to grow up. The last word of the book is "Tomorrow," translated from the Malayalam word spoken ritually by Ammu and Velutha to each other, "naaley" (Roy, *God* 340). Thus, the book appears to end hopefully, though at the moment Ammu and Velutha had been briefly together in their private joy, the book's omniscient narrator had foreseen that torture and death would come "later," which is then syllabified, Rahel style, as "Lay Ter" (Roy, *God* 334). The book ricochets between escapology and the inescapable. By its language, the book seduces its audience and repels it, rejuvenating the escapism of a World Hit like *The Sound of Music* and encrypting it. This encryption makes possible the author's escape from us. The only advantage of a doomed Before and After over changelessness is that Before survives as what is missing from After. Caste freedom survives the killing Love Laws as an equality-shaped hole in the universe; this is the book's politics. The strategy of Sophie's rebellion all along had been to make "the absence of children, *all* children" the fullness of "adults' remorse" (Roy, *God* 292), but only readers are left to feel the guilt and grief of it. Mediators have vanished because we killed them.

III. After

In a 2001 interview, Roy, responding to an attack on the style of *The God of Small Things*, suggests that it is politics by other means: "My language, my style, is not something superficial, like a coat that I wear when I go out. My style is me—even when I'm at home. It's the way I think. My style *is* my politics" (Roy, *Beast* 11). This is certainly true for her first novel; insofar as the book's style floats between the linguistic imaginations of Rahel as child and Rahel as adult, it serves Roy's politics, which forms around the after-images or echoes of murdered potentials.

Yet when, toward the beginning of *The Algebra of Infinite Justice*, Roy justifies the necessity of reading "reports on drainage and irrigation" and any text that treats of "dams and why they're built and what they do," what must be set aside is "Joyce and Nabokov" and "Don DeLillo's big book" (Roy, *Algebra* 49). Postponing DeLillo means denying herself the company of a contemporary international novelist, one of whose books treats the responsibility of children to alert adults to the toxicity of their environment. Sidelining Joyce and Nabokov means temporarily demoting influences on the style of *The God of Small Things*. I take the first two sentences of that novel—"May in Ayemenem is a hot, brooding month. The days are long and humid" (Roy, *God* 1)—as homage to the beginning of "Spring in Fialta," another story of a truncated apotheosis, frustrated illicit love, and accidental death: "Spring in Fialta is cloudy and dull. Everything is damp" (Nabokov 13). More crucial to Roy's style is *Portrait of the Artist as a Young Man*, with its alertness to the sounds, prior to the meanings, of the colonizer's English; if Rahel judges that "sturdy was a terrible word" (Roy, *God* 46), it is because young Stephen Dedalus thinks that "suck was a queer word. . . . [T]he sound was ugly" (Joyce, *Portrait* 23). Roy also pays tribute to *Ulysses*, with its uncouth verbal amalgams, for example "the sea, the snotgreen sea, the scrotumtightening sea" (Joyce, *Ulysses* 9). In *Small Things*, green is almost never allowed its integrity as an adjective: its third sentence describes "mangoes in still, dustgreen trees"; later, the "grass looked wetgreen" (Roy, *God* 1, 10). Roy's classical oceanic alliteration imitates Joyce's grossness: "the sea was black," Roy writes, "the spume vomit green" (Roy, *God* 216).

Roy's commitment to style and her sacrifice of DeLillo, Nabokov, and Joyce are not necessarily contradictory: if the politics of *Small Things* centers on what has been lost, then possibly the sacrifice of style, at least in its more self-reflexive and flamboyant phases, is itself a stylistic choice that returns to politics. One hypothetical Indian family that fails to cohere, in *The God of Small Things*, consists of a Christian mother and a Dalit father, along with two fully Indian children and their half-British, half-Indian cousin. The voluntary world family that fails to cohere in *The Ministry of Utmost Happiness* may include the brotherhood of DeLillo, the fatherhood of Nabokov, and the grand-fatherhood of Joyce. The question is: In giving up that much of the genealogy of style, what remains for a writer who identifies style as the locus of her politics?

In the essays between novels, Roy frequently worries the issue of how to write fiction in a time of political crisis. One answer begins to appear at the outset of *Utmost Happiness*, which reads like a reprise of *Small Things* in a different key:

At magic hour, when the sun has gone but the light has not, armies of flying foxes unhinge themselves from the Banyan trees in the old graveyard and drift across the city like smoke. When the bats leave, the crows come home. Not all the din of their homecoming fills the silence of the sparrows that have gone missing, and the old white-backed vultures, custodians of the dead for more than a hundred million years, that have been wiped out. The vultures died of diclofenac poisoning. Diclofenac, cow aspirin, given to cattle as muscle relaxant, to ease pain and increase the production of milk, works—worked—like nerve gas on white-backed vultures. Each chemically relaxed, milk-producing cow or buffalo that died became poisoned vulture bait. (Roy, *Ministry* 5)

The first chapter that immediately follows this italicized headnote is entitled, "Where Do Old Birds Go to Die?" (Roy, *Ministry* 7). It is the question that had defined Sophie as a seeker of small wisdom in *The God of Small Things*; the itinerary of the dead is Roy's continuing obsession. But everything shifts at the word "diclofenac": Roy's prose makes acquaintance with that of Robert Newman in *The Fountain at the Center of the World*, which runs the passé appreciation of nature into the technical diction of industrial chemistry. Poetry—at least poetry in its lyric vein, even poetry in its elegiac mood—dies along with the sparrows and vultures. Style like the dead has the force of its departure.

It is an overstatement and an understatement to say that death is everywhere in *Utmost Happiness*. It overstates the matter this way: though the book implicitly travels to Gujarat for the pogrom of 2002, and though it explicitly travels to Kashmir to witness its executions and massacres, nevertheless most of the protagonists of the book survive and manage, in a couple of cases, to welcome and foster new generations of Indians.

Yet one might almost say that, as a qualitative rather than a quantitative matter, death is more than merely a frequent intermittent presence in the book. Or say that no longer a linear phenomenon, death adds dimensions along the book's plotline. In that sense, death survives where style had once lived. The vultures that die at the cemetery—the death of the guardians of death—are harbingers of the multidimensionality of death in Kashmir, which equals a qualitative revolution in death. Death leads to death, in the usual way of revenge (Roy, *Ministry* 233), but death also begets death in novel ways. The wife and child of Musa, one of the book's protagonists, are accidentally murdered at the funeral procession of an intentionally murdered rebel (Roy, *Ministry* 326). When the funeral turns into a massacre, the corpse of the rebel in question, reshot, is said to be "doubly dead" (Roy, *Ministry* 330). Writing to his dead daughter, Musa realizes that what used to be reality compared to the fairy stories she renounced seems now itself a vampire tale: "in our Kashmir the dead will live forever; and the living are only dead people, pretending" (Roy, *Ministry* 349). Musa shares a nom de guerre with a friend; when the friend is killed by mistaken identity, Musa half-jokes that he attended his "own funeral. I gave myself a twenty-one gun salute" (Roy, *Ministry* 395). He is later properly killed. Srinagar, summer capital of the former state of Jammu and Kashmir, comes "alive only when it had to bury its dead" (Roy, *Ministry* 392). Young Kashmiris become invincible "because they knew they were already dead" (Roy, *Ministry* 335). "Death was everywhere.

Death was everything. Career. Desire. Dream. Poetry. Love. Youth itself. Dying became just another way of living" (Roy, *Ministry* 320).

Once death has become an alternative life, when death does not replace poetry but *is* poetry, what precisely is left for a novelist to write, even a novelist who has treated absence in her previous novel as the only remaining hope, so long as it maintains a shape? At the end of the book, Roy does allow a moment of similarly muted hopefulness. Zainab, the foster daughter of the book's first heroine, the transgendered Anjum, marries a Dalit who pretends to be a Muslim (he takes the name Saddam Hussain [*sic*] to face humiliations or violence, as he believes Saddam Hussein faced death with courage). This scrambling of Love Laws includes a wedding journey to a mall, built on a field where Saddam's father had been killed by a mob. Anjum decides that Saddam's father needs to be reburied in the graveyard where she has lived and welcomed disparate desperate guests for some time (they buy a shirt at the mall for the sake of having something to bury); his "second funeral" prompts Anjum to bury the ashes of her mother, so the mother has "a second funeral too," the second second funeral of the day (Roy, *Ministry* 419). This is an attempt to return to the dead their individual dignity, so to speak their shape; by redoubling funerals, Anjum seems to sacralize the mass double dying in Kashmir. But it is not enough for Roy to continue to make a politics from the shape of absence; the inescapable point about death in Kashmir is its indiscriminateness, its disintegration, its formlessness, its sprawl. It requires a new poetics.

The Ministry of Utmost Happiness is willing to try out almost any literary strategy that leaves imagination its integrity within the black tide, the new spreading amorphousness of death. For the sake of artificially sorting the unsortable text, I will divide these attempts into three types, though each one evokes its own antithesis, each form its deformation.

1. The book begins with Aftab, a hermaphrodite whose preferred sex is female and who changes her name to the male or female "Anjum." She inclines to go much further in her insult to taxonomy: "Who says my name in Anjum? I'm not Anjum, I'm Anjuman [a group, a meeting]. I'm a *mehfil*, I'm a gathering. Of everybody and nobody, of everything and nothing" (Roy, *Ministry* 8). She resembles Borges's God in "Everything and Nothing," who resembles Shakespeare: "I dreamed the world as you, Shakespeare, dreamed your own works, and among the forms of my dreams are you, who like me, are many, yet no one" (Borges, *Fictions* 320). She shows promise of living as a metamorphic author writes. The first section of the novel is given over to Anjum in Delhi, before it is

given over mainly to a young woman named Tilo, in and out of Kashmir: the opening intention is to find a figure who can, as protagonist of a novel, embody the novel's creator's desire to oppose killing by opposing the masculinist binary on which it is based. Later, Tilo, though herself overtaken by binary choices, endorses the Anjum solution in a poem:

How
    to
    tell
        a
shattered
       story?
           By
           slowly
                  becoming
everybody.
        No.
        By slowly becoming everything. (Roy, *Ministry* 442)

In fact, the first sentence about Anjum reports that "She lived in the graveyard like a tree" (Roy, *Ministry* 7). Humans and parakeets (Roy, *Ministry* 24), and humans and electrical fans (Roy, *Ministry* 24), share qualities in the Anjum sections of the book.

The problem with centering this repudiation of the boundaries of animal and vegetable, animal and mineral, male and female, and life and death on Anjum is that Anjum is a particular character, idiosyncratic, willful, and self-interested. She is too vividly herself to be everything. She is waywardly headstrong: born with male and female sex organs, she determines to become a woman.

It requires some supplementing to keep Anjum plausible as representing an ecumenical India within the confines of her own character and body. When Anjum declares that she is a *mehfil*, she claims not merely to be a gathering but more appealingly a concert. "Myself am Utopia," she seems to assert, yet she has already moved into the Khwabgah, the House of Dreams, with other hijras who comprise a spectrum of nonbinary sexualities. There are hijras who are Muslim, Hindu, and Christian. The favorite song of their favorite film is "Pyar Kiya To Darna Kya" from *Mughal-e-Azam*, in which the son of the Mughal emperor Akbar (himself married to a Hindu woman and owner of the original House of Dreams) falls in love with a dancing girl; the son is supported in his Oedipal rebellion against his father's dynastic prejudice by a loyal Rajput friend. In one respect, the film resembles *The Sound of Music*: singing and dancing are more powerful virtues than military prowess and discipline, and have the capacity to upset rigidities. It seems to Anjum, when she first enters the house, that she is "walking through the gates of Paradise," which is Anjum and the novel's first attempt to locate Utopia somewhere within the potentialities of India (Roy, *Ministry* 24).

The House of Dreams fails to maintain a united front of subtly distinguished difference, though it disintegrates less spectacularly than Akbar's court. Better for that purpose is the Hazrat Sarmad Shaheed's dargah, a shrine devoted to a Jewish Armenian merchant who loved a Hindu boy, later converted to Islam, then rejected Islamic orthodoxy. His shrine, magnetic to both Hindu and Muslim pilgrims, proves effective in teaching the mother of Anjum, while he is still the pseudo-male Aftab, how to love him; and it proves effective much later when, from beyond the grave, Sarmad, "Saint of the Unconsoled and Solace of the Indeterminate," blesses the union of Zainab and Saddam (Roy, *Ministry* 421). *The God of Small Things* is a centripetal book around the deaths of Sophie and Velutha; *The Ministry of Utmost Happiness* is centrifugal, with a burgeoning cast of characters who come and go; when Tilo takes over from Anjum as protagonist of the book, the hope that a single person might gather Indian multiplicity comes to an end. The book must give itself over to dispersion, which means it must give up dreaming of a character who like her creator is "everything and nothing." The book sprawls in counter-imitation of the sprawl of death.

2. *The Ministry of Utmost Happiness* is centrifugal both spatially and temporally. It moves from Delhi to Kashmir with other locations along the way. It moves erratically in time, though eventually it zigzags from about 1955, when Anjum is born, until about 2015. It is most disinterestedly centrifugal when it follows the career of Amrik Singh, the notorious military torturer and killer of Kashmir, to Clovis, California, where he commits suicide. Such digressions allow Roy to heed warnings to herself from the time of her essays, between novels: "a lazy utopia and a flawed sense of justice will have consequences that do not bear thinking about. This is not the time for intellectual sloth or a reluctance to assess a situation clearly and honestly" (Roy, *Field Notes* 181–2). "I think," she tells an interviewer, "we all are just messing our way through this life. People, ideologues who believe in a kind of redemption, a perfect and ultimate society, are terrifying" (Roy, *Beast* 195). Roy's decentered novel protects her anti-Utopianism, her anti-messianism, her impure, improvisatory political art.

Roy also tells an interviewer that she "would not want to write a book 'about' Kashmir. I hope Kashmir will be in all the books I write" (Roy, *Beast* 203). She fulfills this promise in *Utmost Happiness*: the Tilo phase of the book radiates out from the Kashmiri dystopia, but it is mainly not located there. The book begins and ends in Delhi and registers events all over India, by way of its multiplicity of stories and reportage. The omniscient reportorial voice surfaces from time to time, so that we register the most important themes from Roy's career as an essayist as they are manifest all over India: Coca Cola consumerism (Roy, *Ministry* 17); the murderousness of dams and mass dispossessions (Roy, *Ministry* 100–1); mining and the uprooting of the Adivasis (Roy, *Ministry* 427); the Emergency (Roy, *Ministry* 38–9); the relation of 9/11 to Hindutva (Roy, *Ministry* 45–6); Modi and the Gujarat massacres (Roy, *Ministry* 47–50, 108–9); the Union Carbide catastrophe in Bhopal (Roy, *Ministry* 114–15); the misrepresentations of the tourist and Bollywood industries (Roy, *Ministry* 94–5, 378); the decay of democracy. At some points, material from the essays is more or less directly transposed.

Roy-as-novelist and Roy-as-journalist seem sometimes to vie for the narrative voice; at other times, Roy surrenders the narration to her characters. Of those surrogates, Tilo resembles Roy in biography and attitude. But much of the narrative is ceded to a weakly liberal government employee whose benefit to the novel is that he loves and protects Tilo, and with partial success keeps track of her for us. In this dispersal of narrative authority, the book itself seems to take over the political hope represented by its initial protagonist Anjub, then by the Khwabgah, then Sarmad's dargah: to serve as the emblem of all that cannot be reconciled but must coexist in a polymorphous Indian culture. (*Lincoln in the Bardo*, also centered at a cemetery, similarly takes over from Lincoln himself the project of reflecting jagged coexistences.) The novel features a chapter entitled "The Ministry of Utmost Happiness," but so far as I noticed, the phrase does not appear in the prose; Sarmad, to whose shrine the novel proceeds at its beginning and end, is referred to as the Hazrat (saint or prophet) of Utmost Happiness. But after the book concludes, its Acknowledgments include thanks to "Reverend Sunil Sardar, whose insights are somewhere in the foundations of The Ministry" (Roy, *Ministry* 447). This seems to mean that *The Ministry of Utmost Happiness* attempts an administering of utmost happiness, itself.

That would entail thinking of the book not as centered on the taxonomy-unfriendly Anjub but as radically decentered; the novel would have to take the risk of its centrifugal aspiration, which is not for happiness as a subjective individual affect but rather as the horizon, the largest circle, of community. The risk is not merely aesthetic. Just as the attempt to center the book on Anjub leads to the necessity of supplementing her with other gods or goddesses of difference until the book is almost totally commotion, so does the expansiveness of the novel produce a disturbing reduction, which is the bathetic fate of all novelistic hyperbole.

The risk is that in following leads all over India, the novel must simplify rather than complicate its political account. Roy is for nonspurious choosing, but political choosing does not entail infinite possibilities: at the end of one essay, she writes, "We're standing at a fork in the road. One sign points in the direction of 'Justice,' the other says 'Civil War.' There's no third sign, and there's no going back. Choose" (Roy, *Field Notes* 201). Subtler demarcations, such as the calibrating of sexual identity by the inhabitants of the Khwabgah, which might have displayed above its door a third sign in the directives of gender, give way to a binary choice here. Nor, in the case of the war between privatization and the people, is there any subtlety in where justice lies. "The minute armed struggle becomes a strategy," Roy tells an interviewer, "your whole world shrinks and the colours fade to black and white." But in the face of India's recalcitrance to justice, Roy recognizes that "to be ineffective is to support the status quo . . . . And being effective comes at a terrible price. I find it hard to condemn people who are prepared to pay that price" (Roy, *Beast* 224).

The declension here is as follows: in the politics of division, the infinitesimal subtlety of personal choice reduces to the blunt disjunction of justice vs. civil war. But insofar as justice, even within that stark opposition, can discriminate shades of gray, political effectiveness might need to reject it for the purity of black and white; and Roy is not fully capable of disavowing even that reduction. In an essay, she writes, "With all due respect to President Bush, the people of the world do *not* have to choose between the Taliban and the US government" (Roy, *Algebra* 246). This sort of choice is what Roy always condemns as the death of imagination. How close to presenting that kind of fatal nonchoice, as in Grossman, does Roy come in *The Ministry of Utmost Happiness*?

Rather close. The heroine of the larger part of the novel, Tilo, is protected, adored, and pursued by three men from 1984 onward, when they met during a college theatrical production; one becomes a reporter of variable morality and commitment, one a government official of weak liberal sentiments, and one a Kashmiri freedom fighter. Of the three, Tilo loves only the freedom fighter, Musa. They are this novel's version of Rahel and Estha at the time of their incest. "He [Musa] was the same age as her [Tilo]. Thirty-one. The silence between them swelled and subsided like the bellows of an accordion playing a tune that only they could hear. He knew that she knew that he knew that she knew. That's how it was between them" (Roy, *Ministry* 359). By this echoing, *Ministry* performs a political revision of the private rebellion of *The God of Small Things*. In viable, die-able Kashmir with Musa, Tilo is radicalized by its saturation in death. Sameness stands for difference here because justice for self and others is self-identical; objective clarity overwhelms distinctions.

Utmost Happiness is frank about the brutality of Kashmiri men, including freedom fighters, toward Kashmiri women; about the savagery of their revenge; about their infighting, which will lead to an internal bloodbath if they ever win independence. But the novel comes close to arguing that choice has dropped out of Kashmiri politics; that in the interest of justice, only one side can be supported; that choice itself is not an option. Tilo appropriates an abandoned baby, whose mother is allowed a nine-page posthumous letter, gradually winning the attention of the apolitical Anjum. After detailing the horrors of her life, the baby's mother writes:

My Party is my Mother and Father. Many times it does many wrong things. Kills wrong people. Women join because they are revolutionaries but also because they cannot bear their sufferings at home. Party says men and women are equal, but still they never understand. I know Comrade Stalin and Chairman Mao have done many good things and many bad things also. But still I cannot leave my Party. . . . So I am returned to Dandakaranya to live and die by my gun. (Roy, *Ministry* 431)

When the reading of the letter is completed, Anjum says, "LAL SALAAM ALEIKUM," which, Roy hypothesizes about her character and, by extension, her own fiction, "could have been the beginning of a whole political movement, but she had only meant it in the way of an 'Ameen' after listening to a moving sermon" (Roy, *Ministry* 432). An impulse of the novel has approached an explosion for half a sentence and been defused. The mother has been allowed to make a transfixing apology for disregarding the complexity of her own side's moral grayness. (The grayness includes her choice of the party's parenthood over her own motherhood.) Her choice against complexities seems the death of imagination in light of the hopelessness that anything besides local violence can resist the juggernaut of national violence backed by international finance. "This is the worst part of the Occupation," Musa himself says, "This reduction, this standardization, this stupidification" (Roy, *Ministry* 377).

At the end of a commitment to imagine—to represent, even to embody—all India in its profusion of religions, sexualities, and political persuasions, the novel considers participating in the death of imagination. Its Realpolitik takes the form of escapology in reverse: the joining of a movement to die in.

3. Is there an alternative to the failures of unity and multiplicity, is there perhaps an Agambenian conjoining of Chronos and Kairos, dispersing and gathering, in the book's zigzag temporality? The book's first baby with time-of-the-end vibrations is Zainab, the foundling adopted by Anjum.

> Zainab's real passion, it turned out, was animals. . . . She wanted to free all the half-bald, half-dead white chickens that were pressed into filthy cages and stacked on top of each other outside the butcher shops . . . . She would not listen when she was told that dogs were unclean—*najis*—for Muslims and should not be touched. (Roy, *Ministry* 40–1)

Zainab seems ideally raised to become the messianic Indian who will destroy all privilege at once, on behalf of not just everyone but everything. Yet she falls victim, in effect, to the book's determined recognition of the desultoriness of time, its Chronos aspect. Zainab breaks Anjum's heart by preferring a younger, hipper member of the Khwabgah as a substitute mother. And though that familial story turns out happily when Zainab marries Hussain, Zainab by this time is no longer a candidate for savior: she is described as "a plump eighteen-year-old now, studying fashion design at a local polytechnic" (Roy, *Ministry* 308).

Meanwhile, in Kashmir, Miss Jebeen, the daughter of Musa, who demands reality rather than fairy tales for her bedtime stories (Roy, *Ministry* 322), is killed along with her mother as collateral damage in the assault on a militant's funeral. Later, Tilo is impregnated by Musa but gets an abortion. Thus, when a new foundling is appropriated by Tilo and then Anjum, and is called Miss Jebeen the Second, she seems conjured to gather and redeem three figures whose promise was destroyed at three discrete stages of incompletion: the fetus of Tilo and Musa; the infant of Musa; and the foster child of Anjum, grown into mediocrity.

The fanfare for Miss Jebeen the Second is biblical. The first section ends this way:

> Anjum waited to die.
> Saddam waited to kill.
> And miles away, in a troubled forest, a baby waited to be born . . . .
> (Roy, *Ministry* 96, ellipsis in the original)

The next chapter is entitled "The Nativity," and though "no angels sang, no wise men brought gifts" to the prophesied baby, nevertheless "a million stars rose in the east to herald her arrival" (Roy, *Ministry* 99). The book has had several moments of Before and After transformation, but none qualifies like this one as an Indian BC and AD. Miss Jebeen the Second is every baby's second chance: as against the doubling of death in Kashmir, this is a doubling of birth in Delhi. As against the doubling of funerals, the promise here is not to individuate dying but to redeem living, by a communal nurturing.

After Anjum responds to the baby's mother's posthumous story with her faux political cry of "Lal Salaam Aleikum," all the listeners "close ranks around Miss Jebeen the Second like a formation of trees, or adult elephants—an impenetrable fortress in which she, unlike her biological mother, would grow up protected and loved" (Roy, *Ministry* 432). The comparison to elephants is apt at a graveyard that has been "turned . . . into a zoo—a Noah's ark of injured animals" (Roy, *Ministry* 405). It seems like a version, perhaps a quotation, of *See Under: Love*, in which the foundling Kazik is conjured into the world to be protected by a team of derelict superheroes at a zoo, who stake their own salvation on their ability to save the child.

The final words of Roy's novel are prophetic: "Things would turn out all right in the end. They would, because they had to. Because Miss Jebeen, Miss Udaya Jebeen, was come" (Roy, *Ministry* 444). Thus, the book arrives at the limit of escapism, messianism devolving on a child without qualities. Our impression is that it is not merely the world, but also the book hopelessly within the world, that is being escaped by this good news. Yet it is the book itself that takes responsibility for this climactic, prophetic language in a peculiar tense, and we look to the book to determine whether the turn in Roy, at long last, on the last page of her latest work, from the past or past-ridden present to the future, equals the turn from the death to the rebirth of imagination, victimized once by the atomic bomb and neoliberalism and jeopardized a second time by the requirements of opposing these enormities and their downstream tribal effects.

The last we see Miss Jebeen the Second, she has been taken on a tour of Delhi by Anjum from the graveyard in which they, along with Tilo and many others, are domiciled. Anjum and friends have developed their cemetery living space into a shelter and a local business: Jannat Guest House and Funeral Services. The business takes care of funeral rites for those who have been refused burial elsewhere. Anjum's cemetery complex also treats injured animals and includes a school, vegetable garden, and swimming pool, empty as yet. Men, women, hijras, children, animals, vegetables, and minerals flourish among the dead. Tilo, grieving for Musa, is nonetheless able to "write to him regularly and visit him often enough through the crack in the door that the battered angels in the graveyard held open (illegally) for her" (Roy, *Ministry* 443). It is the Utopia that Anjum once located in herself alone, then at the House of Dreams—a gathering of shattered stories. It seems preordained that any Utopia created by Roy would include the dead on equal terms, a uniquely messianic aspect. ("Jannat" means Paradise.) You can accept the hospitality of the guesthouse forever.

It is the least likely and most convincing Utopian space in all the novels I've looked at, the only one that is sustainable, because imperfection, decay, and death are inside it. Groff's Arcadia has death on the inside of it, but it comes as a surprise and insult to the undertaking. The internalizing of death in Roy's novel means that it posits a Utopian escape with a messianic escapology underwriting it. The graveyard, however, is not enough; it holds its own against the cemeteries of Kashmir but does not transcend them. Miss Jebeen the Second "embarked on her brand-new life in a place similar to, and yet a world apart from where, over eighteen years ago, her young ancestor Miss Jebeen the First had ended hers. In a graveyard. Another graveyard, just a little further north" (Roy, *Ministry* 311).

Miss Jebeen the Second, not defeating but temporarily escaping the cemetery with Anjum on their midnight exploration of Delhi, needs to "soo-soo," and once that is accomplished, she "marvel[s] at the night sky and the stars and the one-thousand-year-old city reflected in the puddle she had made. Anjum gathered her up and kissed her and took her home" (Roy, *Ministry* 444). Jebeen redux ex-creates a no-since, an overcoming of logic and temporal linearity; she makes an objectivity of her abjectivity, a pool descended from Alice's tears. Her soo-soo reflects the stars that had heralded her birth, though (in the absence of magi and angels) not her birth uniquely. If *The Ministry of Utmost Happiness* plays Revelation to *The God of Small Things*'s Gospels, the type of this scene is the passion of Velutha: "Police boots stepped back from the rim of a pool of urine spreading from him, the bright, bare electric bulb reflected in it" (Roy, *Small Things*, 320). The potentially messianic girl resurrects the quasi-messianic man to save the world, finally, from masculinity and its binaries. Whether Roy's novel is the precise minimum of escapism, a hope based on no evidence that Utopian adults can save a particular messianic child to save themselves by extemporaneous re-parenting, or whether the novel abandons us instead, like orphans, to an inescapable unimaginable world, unimaginable because the imagination has been executed by it, depends on whether we believe in that doubling of Heaven on Earth, that Chronos mirroring that Kairos, that reflection of the celestial in the excremental, that profane millennial typology, that returning to the home of the surviving and the dead.

Part IV

PREQUEL

Chapter 12

THE TUNNEL OUT

I want to use William H. Gass's masterwork, *The Tunnel*, published in 1995 after twenty-six years of writing, as a prequel to twenty-first-century escapism. (Gass's book makes reference to Bernhard Kellermann's popular novel of 1913, *Der Tunnel*, about an idealist who promotes a trans-Atlantic tunnel that is outmoded by air transport at its completion in twenty-six years. William Kohler, the narrator of Gass's book who digs a tunnel out of his own cellar, is no doubt named and conceived from Kellermann's name and novel. What mode of flight has replaced Gass's *Tunnel*?) *The Tunnel* is something like 300,000 words long; I'll make several points about it, in a pseudo-philosophical numbering method that Professor Kohler scorns, as resistance to his sensibility.

1.1. The book, narrated by a historian of Nazi Germany with some sympathy for Nazis, begins with the implicit claim of being the least escapist novel ever written, though it makes several equivocal allusions to *Peter Pan* and *Alice in Wonderland*. Here is a passage that might be taken as a refutation, before the letter, of *Life is Beautiful*, imagining a death camp scene:

> A father speaks earnestly to his son and points at the heavens where surely there is an explanation; it is doubtless their true destination. . . . So the son is lied to right up to the last. Father does not cup his boy's wet cheeks in his hands and say, You shall die, my son, and never be remembered. . . . Only our numbers will be remembered—not that you or I died, but there were so many of us. (Gass 34)

Thus, Roberto Benigni's heroic clowning is an extravaganza of falsity, and the truth is the obliteration of all that is individual about the individuals who are killed, including their love, creativity, and humor. Truth-telling about the impossibility of escape, even the escape of individual death, of holes with shapes, would seem to be the simple opposite of escapism.

1.2. Kohler's thesis about Nazism is expressed in his work-in-progress, *Guilt and Innocence in Hitler's Germany*; the novel we are reading is an apologia written by Kohler while he is trying to write an introduction to that study and digging his tunnel. The thesis is that Hitler was a "petty little twerp" (Gass 455) and that the Final Solution was the responsibility of those millions of Germans who enacted his pathetic fantasies. In this light, Kohler's apologia is also a confession. Kohler is aware that his own bigotry, his own small-scale and mainly verbal loathsomeness, arises from the same disappointments as those of the Germans who comprised "Hitler's Germany." Kohler's life, in his reading of it, has consisted of the following: a bullying father; an alcoholic mother; childhood companions incapable and unworthy of friendship; a depression-era Midwestern environment (tornados, Dustbowl, a plague of grasshoppers); a wife who is his mortal enemy; loveless children; women who resist him; lovers who tire of him; colleagues in the History department of a Midwestern state university who torment him; the dreariness of being a historian who might have been a poet; an unsatisfactory body. He identifies with Germans who, in comparable throes of frustration and loneliness, wanted to be masters for once.

1.3. Kohler's identification has this complexity: he identifies with Jews so identifies with Nazis. This can be put less paradoxically: because he feels what it is to be a victim, he determines to feel like a killer. (In Don DeLillo's *White Noise*, the narrator, a Professor of Hitler Studies, is advised by a friend to take up killing to evade dying.) It is for this reason that Kohler, studying in Germany, may have thrown a brick through a window on Kristallnacht, and writes books that try to grasp the spirit of Nazism from inside. But the pure paradoxical form of the identification is the most accurate one, for reasons that will be seen.

2.1. The first explanation for why Kohler digs his tunnel from his basement is his own: "My tunnel is my quarrel with the earth" (Gass 182). This is equal, on Kohler's own interpretation, to fear of being buried alive, prefigured by Jews on the edge of their mass grave, slaughtered by machine gun fire, who "worry only that the earth will cover their open eyes" (Gass 34).

2.2. The problem with this self-explication is that by digging his tunnel, Kohler causes a cave-in and "nearly buried himself alive" (Gass 493). If Kohler digs to prevent his burial alive, why does he invite it by digging? In case we miss the metaphor, he wonders on the next page: "what transgression would be handed the harsher judgment: . . .

my tunnel or this text?" (Gass 494). The text seems as much cave-in as tunnel.

3.1. Or say that Kohler's metaphysical horror is not earth but the abyss, which Kohler spends two pages defining and philologizing. It is not Hell, because Hell has a bottom. "The abyss is honest absence; . . . it is true not-being-there. . . . [I]t is the utter absence of significance; it is the world as unread and unreadable" (Gass 185). One might have thought that his profession as professor of history would make the world legible.

3.2. But Kohler's final judgment as a historian is that history is "empty as an empty pantry" (Gass 11). So is biography: intrigued by his grandmother's steamer trunk—"perhaps it was full of Gran's memories"—Kohler discovers it to be "unoccupied darkness," a container of empty space (Gass 590). Kohler nearly locks himself in the trunk, almost burrowing himself alive. If one's mission is to flee nothingness, the least effective method may be to enlarge one's nihilistic autobiography while enlarging the hole of one's basement.

3.3. The lived experience of absence and emptiness for Kohler is his almost perfect solitude. When Kohler decries the dinginess of his tunnel and figures out how to bring light into it, he arrives at this puzzle: "why must one bring the world into the tunnel, when the tunnel is supposed to be the way out?" (Gass 155). Though Kohler populates his memoir with descriptions of colleagues, his wife, a named and an unnamed son, three or so lovers, a charismatic teacher in Germany, fellow students in Germany, and literary heroes, his tunnel does not bring him to the world or from it; it is a vacancy for his vanity.

4.1. Or say the tunnel is a confrontation not with the earth or the abyss in their distinct identities but with the Real: Lacan's term for what cannot be distinguished. What Kohler excavates is not elemental like earth, nor does he dwell there in a purity of nothing like the abyss. "I see slime as our world's most triumphant substance, slowly slime is covering the earth, more of it every day" (Gass 435). "You could scarcely call the clay dirt, it was something else, yellow pencil shavings, the petrified puke of ages past" (Gass 499). History and biography may now be "buried beneath this dung-like slag" (Gass 650), which, because of his own digging, comes also to include the excrement of his family cat. Slime is the currency of the irredeemably nonredemptive past. Perhaps with psychoanalytic precision, Kohler claims to be excavating a "realm in the Real" (Gass 503); loosely imitating Žižek, you could divide the Real into three phases, earth, abyss, and slime.

4.2. I refer neutrally to Kohler's confrontation with the Real, rather than his quarrel with it, to put his endeavor in plausible intimacy with

Badiou's idea of the basic motive of the twentieth century, its *"passion for the Real"* (Badiou, passim). Badiou argues that the twentieth century did not transcend the Real, that all its commitment to form was a method for making contact with it, as a sculptor might form marble or clay, or a mathematician formalize the infinite, not to contain them but to feel their stony or squishy or abyssal resistance. Or not quite to feel that resistance but to minimize toward zero their distance from it. This is called by Badiou "subtraction," the nonviolent aspect of the craving for the Real (Badiou 54 ff.). Kohler considers the horrors at the center of the century in the subtractive mode; and the variations of his formality (his endless rhymes, alliterations, and puns, his nonlinear page designing) are form-fitting masks of the formless Real.

4.3. Badiou's concern is with the theorists of the twentieth century: mathematicians like Cantor, poets like Pessoa, playwrights like Brecht, painters like Malevich, revolutionaries like Lenin, thinkers like Freud. Kohler, for all his bluster, identifies with the losers of the century, who like his father rage against their entrapment in failing bodies and families, or like his mother drink against their subjugation; those who are buried alive or whose immersion in the world's slime or sense of their infinitesimal smallness enflames their own bigotry, hatred, and violence. These are not the great figures of their century whose genius is to subtract toward the Real; these are the nonentities who dwell there. Kohler experiences in his tunnel an unexpected affinity with Mark Spitz leaving Fort Wonton or with Paul D in his underground cage. With respect to the disgust and enticement of dissolution, he resembles both a slave and a member of the *Freikorps*.

5.1. Perhaps we can think of the tunnel as self-excavation, Kohler's digging into his own past, personality, and psyche. "I'm going into my own mine," he writes, a pun that seems to repeat the selfsame thing three times (Gass 299). "I go down into the depths of myself and fool around in hidden holes" (Gass 266).

5.2. For what purpose? Is the project to emerge from the womb and rebirth canal into a new life? Two alternative projects seem to replace the motive of rebirth with the desirability of prebirth. First, Kohler wishes to reverse time: "Why grow painfully past puberty in order to be imprisoned, married in order to be made a eunuch, and to have lived . . . so that such a weary round be replicated?" A more radical Peter Pan, Kohler prefers to return as if to his own womb to rediscover "the acres of Edens inside ourselves" (Gass 651). Is the wish for a prehistoric paradise or for preorganic death, in the manner of Freud's death drive? "Some darks may be boundless, stratospherical, pure, but I prefer mine circumscribed as a corset, and where, if I had a soul, it would be squoozen, and where, when I'm found, I'll be identified as the remains of a child, doubled over, waiting to be born" (Gass 635). The play, in advance, on the escapist novel is precise: the child—squoozen is the remnant of a faux naïf, even prenatal vocabulary—who stands for the adult writer's desire to retreat in time is aborted or miscarried. The child-man and man-child do not share a space, as in escapism proper; child-adults do not meet incestuously, perverse and prelapsarian at once, in the womb, as in Roy; the unborn adult in the womb commits the suicide of the child desiring birth.

6.1. The point is not a pointless deconstruction of each of Gass's Kohler's explanations for why he is digging, or to reiterate that the Real reveals and is revealed in symbolic fractures. The point is to summarize the aesthetics of escapism, its trinity of escape, escapism, and escapology, by way of a book that types much of the relevant literary past and future. The *escape* of escapism in *The Tunnel* is from the Midwest, from its mediocrity and meanness, though Kohler like Eggers is "not even Jewish," let alone an escaping slave fleeing through Indiana on a literal underground railroad. As a matter of physical escape, it is not clear in what direction his tunneling tunnels; he knows he is tunneling *from* his domestic and professional life, but not what he is tunneling *to*.

6.2. *The Tunnel* is nearly pure *escapology*. Insofar as Kohler decides simply to flee his wife, his domesticity, his town, and his work, he could walk out the front door, like Hawthorne's Wakefield. By making an art of subterranean escaping, Kohler, on Gass's behalf, turns the book itself into escapology, the study and performance of resurrection, though it fails.

6.3. Thinking of the "pain which pleasure is accused of covering up" (Gass 576), Kohler writes that "it won't be enough if you can't chuck your work, and besmirch your honor, enclose your cock in a candy wrapper; if you can't break a window with a brick or board" (Gass 577). Covering up pain is the simple purpose of pleasure—all pleasure is escapist pleasure—and giving pain is its method. "No pleasure but meanness," as Flannery O'Connor's Misfit puts it, but Kohler turns it into a fantasy. The reversal of escape and escapism is an outcome threatened in *The Amazing Adventures of Kavalier & Clay*, in which an American Nazi is a fan of The Escapist. Escapism as pseudo-messianism suffers from the lack of a church to distinguish Christ from anti-Christs; what *The Tunnel* lacks, as a twentieth-century rather than a twenty-first-century novel, is a child to shoulder the sloughed messianic burden.

7.1. "[T]he Führer unintentionally teaches" two lessons, according to Kohler: "That Mankind is not redeemable" and that "Utopias are foolish" (Gass 454). By his example, Hitler teaches the two lessons of escapism. Every attempt to dig out of the book's slimy grave threatens burial alive. Every attempt to carve out a space in the abyss of the book increases the vacuity. Every hope of revenge on the infinitesimal potential of life is petty. Every rebirth requires sui-abortion. Freedom is toward Nazi Germany and away from family discord, an inversion of *The Sound of Music*, in which freedom is away from Nazi Austria and toward family harmony. So much for a direction of history. That is the good news: it means that freedom *cannot* be achieved by walking out the front door, as if it were a strait gate. No need to attempt it. Escapology is the artifice of real risk, the miming of redemption. It treats death as the thing that can be evaded by mere surviving, as opposed to the politics of one's life or world, which cannot. "Nothing more exhilarating," Oscar Wao says after his failed suicide, "than saving yourself by the simple act of waking" (Diaz 201). The postponement of death turns bathos into an endeavor, a salvaging of saving.

7.2. The epigraph of *The Tunnel* is from Anaxagoras, addressing a man who fears dying in a foreign land, "*The descent to hell is the same from every place*" (Gass 3). No use leaving home or returning. The motive of escapism today is the difficulty of telling the direction of freedom from enslavement, or salvation from preterition, so long as one dwells on the flattened surface of a sphere. Make a Frisbee of it and wing it.

ACKNOWLEDGMENTS

I would have a more respectable Acknowledgments page if I had been braver about showing this book to colleagues when it was a manuscript-in-progress. Nevertheless, I let Chris Pye know enough about the project to prompt his suggesting Todorov's *On Fantasy*, which ended up teaching me how to diagram my disparate predicates of escapism. Shyla Foster quickly grasped the essential argument and knew that I should discuss Emma Donoghue's *Room*, which came to occupy a central position in the study, where escapism begins to unravel. Louise Glück, Anita Sokolsky, and Steve Tifft made useful remarks about chapters of my book and would have helped it immeasurably more if I had let them. Frances Restuccia has been the book's only running commentator. On two occasions, she deposited relevant books for me to buy while I was standing in line (smugly satisfied with my purchases) at bookstores; she was right about that, and more. The theoretical aspect of the book will not meet her standards, but it wouldn't have existed at all if she had not insisted on its pertinence. I taught a lovely class on escapism at Williams College and owe much to its acuteness. Many thanks to Haaris Naqvi at Bloomsbury for his judgment and encouragement. Many thanks to the two distinguished readers he found for the manuscript, Michael Szalay and Deak Nabers, whose criticism was precise and convincing, in at least one case homing on the same deficiency, which forced me to improve the book in important ways. Only the fear of invidious omissions keeps me from listing the teachers, colleagues, friends, and students whose critical voices echoed in me as I wrote, encouraging me at times but usually warning me away from the simplicities of conception and evasiveness of phrasing that I am prone to.

REFERENCES

Agamben, Giorgio. 1999. *The End of the Poem: Structure in Poetics*. Ed. Werner Hamacher and David E. Wellbery. Trans. Daniel Heller-Roazen. Stanford: Stanford University Press.

Agamben, Giorgio. 2005. *State of Exception*. Trans. Kevin Attell. Chicago: University of Chicago Press.

Agamben, Giorgio. 2005. *The Time That Remains: A Commentary on the Letter to the Romans*. Trans. Patricia Dailey. Stanford: Stanford University Press.

Agamben, Giorgio. 2010. *Nudities*. Trans. David Kishik and Stefan Redatella. Stanford: Stanford University Press.

Agamben, Giorgio. 2018. *The Adventure*. Trans. Lorenzo Chiesa. Cambridge, MA: MIT Press.

Agamben, Giorgio. 2018. *Pulcinella or, Entertainment for Kids in Four Scenes*. Trans. Kevin Attell. New York: Seagull.

Anderson, William. 1998. *The World of the Trapp Family*. Singapore: Anderson.

Augustine. 1993. *Confessions*. Trans. F.J. Sheed. Indianapolis: Hackett.

Badiou, Alain. 2007. *The Century*. Trans. Alberto Toscano. Cambridge: Polity.

Badiou, Alain. 2012. *In Praise of Love*. With Nicolas Truong. Trans. Peter Bush. New York: New Press.

Barrie, J.M. 2015. *Peter Pan*. New York: Random House.

Baudrillard, Jean. 1991. *Simulacra and Simulation*. Trans. Sheila Faria Glaser. Ann Arbor: University of Michigan Press.

Baudrillard, Jean. 1995. *The Gulf War Did Not Take Place*. Trans. Paul Patton. Bloomington: Indiana University Press.

Baudrillard, Jean. 2010. *America*. Trans. Chris Turner. London: Verso.

Bellamy, Edward. 2007. *Looking Backward 2000–1887*. New York: Oxford University Press.

Benjamin, Walter. 1969. *Illuminations: Essays and Reflections*. Ed. Hannah Arendt. Trans. Harry Zohn. New York: Schocken.

Berlant, Lauren. 2008. *The Female Complaint: The Unfinished Business of Sentimentality in American Culture*. Durham: Duke University Press.

Borges, Jorge Luis. 1998. *Collected Fictions*. Trans. Andrew Hurley. New York: Putnam.

Butler, Octavia E. 1979. *Kindred*. Boston: Beacon.

Butler, Octavia E. 2005. *Bloodchild and Other Stories*. 2nd. ed. New York: Seven Stories Press.

Butler, Octavia E. 2005. *Fledgling*. New York: Grand Central.

Callenbach, Ernest. 1975. *Ecotopia: The Notebooks and Reports of William Weston*. New York: Random House.

Carroll, Lewis. 2002. *Alice's Adventures in Wonderland and Through the Looking Glass.* New York: Random House.

Carver, Raymond. 1981. *What We Talk About When We Talk About Love.* New York: Knopf.

Carver, Raymond. 1989. *Cathedral.* New York: Random House.

Cavell, Stanley. 1981. *Pursuits of Happiness: The Hollywood Comedy of Remarriage.* Cambridge, MA: Harvard University Press.

Chabon, Michael. 2000. *The Amazing Adventures of Kavalier & Clay.* New York: St. Martin's.

Chabon, Michael. 2004. *The Final Solution.* New York: HarperCollins.

Chabon, Michael. 2007. *The Yiddish Policeman's Union.* New York: HarperCollins.

Chabon, Michael. 2008. *Maps and Legends: Reading and Writing Along the Borderlands.* New York: HarperCollins.

Chabon, Michael. 2012. *Telegraph Avenue.* New York: HarperCollins.

Chesterton, G.K. 2013. *St. Francis of Assisi.* Brewster: Paraclete Press.

Ciabattari, Jane. "The 21st Century's 12 Greatest Novels." January 19, 2015. www.bbc.com.

Claeys, Gregory and Lyman Tower Sargent, eds. 2017. *The Utopia Reader.* New York: New York University Press.

Crouse, Timothy, introd. 2010. *The Sound of Music: The Complete Book and Lyrics of the Broadway Musical.* New York: Hal Leonard.

Dancer in the Dark. 2000. Directed by Trier, Lars von. Paris: Canal+.

Derrida, Jacques. 1976. *Of Grammatology.* Trans. Gayatri Chakravorty Spivak. Baltimore: The Johns Hopkins University Press.

Derrida, Jacques. 1994. *Specters of Marx.* Trans. Peggy Kamuf. New York: Routledge.

Díaz, Junot. 2007. *The Brief Wondrous Life of Oscar Wao.* New York: Penguin.

Donoghue, Emma. 2010. *Room.* New York: Little, Brown.

Douglass, Frederick. 1963. *Narrative of the Life of an American Slave.* New York: Doubleday.

Dyer, Richard. 1992. *Only Entertainment.* New York: Routledge.

Eggers, Dave. 2000. *A Heartbreaking Work of Staggering Genius.* New York: Random House.

Eggers, Dave. 2006. *What is the What: The Autobiography of Valentino Achak Deng.* New York: Random House.

Eggers, Dave. 2012. *A Hologram for the King.* New York: Random House.

Eggers, Dave. 2014. *The Circle.* New York: Random House.

Eggers, Dave. 2016. *Heroes of the Frontier.* New York: Random House.

Fanon, Frantz. 2008. *Black Skin, White Masks.* Trans. Richard Philcox. New York: Grove.

Faulkner, William. 1990. *Go Down, Moses.* New York: Random House.

Foer, Jonathan Safran. 2002. *Everything is Illuminated.* New York: Houghton Mifflin.

Foer, Jonathan Safran. 2005. *Extremely Loud and Incredibly Close*. New York: Houghton Mifflin.

Foer, Jonathan Safran. 2016. *Here I Am*. New York: Farrar, Straus and Giroux.

Fordin, Hugh. 1995. *Getting to Know Him: A Biography of Oscar Hammerstein II*. New York: Da Capo.

Foucault, Michel. 1975. *Discipline and Punish: The Birth of the Prison*. Trans. Alan Sheridan. New York: Random House.

Freud, Sigmund. 1930. *Civilization and its Discontents*. Trans. James Strachey. London: Hogarth.

Friedman, Thomas L. 2007. *The World Is Flat: A Brief History of the Twenty-First Century*. New York: Farrar, Staus and Giroux.

Gass, William H. 1995. *The Tunnel*. New York: Dalkey Archive.

Gilman, Charlotte Perkins. 1979. *Herland*. New York: Random House.

Greenblatt, Stephen. "The King of the Bitter Laugh." *New York Review of Books*, April 20, 2017, 46–48.

Groff, Lauren. 2015. *Arcadia*. New York: Hachette.

Grossman, David. 1988. *The Yellow Wind*. Trans. Haim Watzman. New York: Farrar, Straus and Giroux.

Grossman, David. 1994. *The Book of Intimate Grammar*. Trans. Betsy Rosenberg. London: Jonathan Cape.

Grossman, David. 2002. *Be My Knife*. Trans. Vered Almog and Maya Gurantz. London: Bloomsbury.

Grossman, David. 2008. *Writing in the Dark*. Trans. Jessica Cohen. New York: Farrar, Straus and Giroux.

Grossman, David. 2010. *See Under: Love*. Trans. Betsy Rosenberg. New York: Random House.

Grossman, David. 2010. *To the End of the Land*. Trans. Jessica Cohen. New York: Random House.

Grossman, David. 2017. *A Horse Walks Into a Bar*. Trans. Jessica Cohen. New York: Knopf.

Hamacher, Werner. 2001. "Now: Walter Benjamin in Historical Time." In Friese, Heindrun, ed. *The Moment: Time and Rupture in Modern Thought*, 161–96. Liverpool: University of Liverpool Press.

Hamid, Mohsin. 2017. *Exit West: A Novel*. New York: Random House.

Hammerstein, Oscar Andrew. 2010. *The Hammersteins: A Musical Theatre Family*. New York: Black Dog and Levanthal.

Heller, Joseph. 1961. *Catch-22*. New York: Simon and Schuster.

Jameson, Fredric. 1973. "The Vanishing Mediator: Narrative Structure in Max Weber." *New German Critique*, Winter 1, 52–89.

Jameson, Fredric. 2005. *Archaeologies of the Future: The Desire Called Utopia and Other Science Fictions*. New York: Verso.

Jameson, Fredric. 2016. *An American Utopia: Dual Power and the Universal Army*. New York: Verso.

Joyce, James. 1991. *Portrait of the Artist as a Young Man*. New York: Putnam.

Joyce, James. 2015. *Ulysses*. Dublin: O'Brien.

The King and I. 1956. Directed by Lang, Walter. Los Angeles: 20th Century Fox.

Knapp, Raymond. 2005. *The American Musical and the Formation of National Identity*. Princeton: Princeton University Press.

Langdon, Margaret. 1944. *Anna and the King of Siam*. New York: John Day.

Lawrence, D.H. 2003. *Studies in Classic American Literature*. Cambridge: Cambridge University Press.

Lerner, Ben. 2014. *10:04*. London: Granta.

Levinas, Emmanuel. 2003. *On Escape*. Trans. Bettina Bergo. Stanford: Stanford University Press.

Limon, John. 2000. *Stand-up Comedy in Theory, or, Abjection in America*. Durham: Duke University Press.

Lyotard, Jean-François. 1984. *The Postmodern Condition: A Report on Knowledge*. Trans. Geoff Bennington and Brian Massumi. Minneapolis: University of Minnesota Press.

Mailer, Norman. 1967. *Why Are We in Vietnam?: A Novel*. New York: Random House.

Marin, Louis. 1984. *Utopics: The Semiological Play of Textual Space*. Trans. Robert A. Vollrath. New York: Humanity.

More, Thomas. 2005. *Utopia*. Trans. Paul Turner. London: Penguin.

Morrison, Toni. 1987. *Beloved*. New York: Knopf.

Morrison, Toni. 1993. *Playing in the Dark*. New York: Vintage.

Most, Andrea. 2004. *Making Americans: Jews and the Broadway Musical*. Cambridge, MA: Harvard University Press.

Nabokov, Vladimir. 1969. *Nabokov's Dozen*. Freeport: Books for Libraries.

Patterson, Orlando. 2018. *Slavery and Social Death: A Comparative Study*. Cambridge, MA: Harvard University Press.

Pearce, Joseph. 1998. *Tolkien: Man and Myth*. San Francisco: Ignatius.

Phillips, Adam. 2002. *Houdini's Box: The Art of Escape*. New York: Random House.

Rawls, John. 1999. *A Theory of Justice Revised Edition*. Cambridge, MA: Harvard University Press.

Roy, Arundhati. 1997. *The God of Small Things*. New York: HarperCollins.

Roy, Arundhati. 2002. *The Algebra of Infinite Justice*. London: Random House.

Roy, Arundhati. 2008. *The Shape of the Beast*. London: Random House.

Roy, Arundhati. 2009. *Field Notes on Democracy: Listening to Grasshoppers*. Chicago: Haymarket.

Roy, Arundhati. 2017. *The Ministry of Utmost Happiness*. New York. Random House.

Saunders, George. 2017. *Lincoln in the Bardo*. New York: Random House.

Serres, Michel. 1982. *Hermes: Literature, Science, Philosophy*. Trans. Susan Willey, Suzanne Guerlac, et al. Baltimore: The Johns Hopkins University Press.

Shepard, Jim. 2015. *The Book of Aron*. New York: Knopf Doubleday.

The Sound of Music. 1965. Directed by Wise, Robert. Los Angeles: 20th Century Fox.

Speer, Albert. *Inside the Third Reich*. Trans. Richard and Clara Winston. New York: Simon and Schuster.

Stein, Gertrude. 1990. *Selected Writings of Gertrude Stein*. Ed. Carl van Vechten. New York: Vintage.

Stiglitz, Joseph E. 2019. *People, Power and Profits: Progressive Capitalism for an Age of Discontent*. New York: Norton.

Theweleit, Klaus. 1987. *Male Fantasies. Volume 1: Women, Floods, Bodies, History*. Trans. Chris Turner, Carter Erica, and Stephen Conway. Minneapolis: University of Minnesota Press.

Tokarczuk, Olga. 2017. *Flights*. Trans. Jennifer Croft. New York: Random House.

Ward, Jesmyn. 2017. *Sing, Unburied, Sing*. New York: Scribner.

Wheeler, Hugh. 1956. "Quantum Mechanics by the Method of the Universal Wave Function." Ph.D. diss. Princeton University.

Whitehead, Colson. 1999. *The Intuitionist*. New York: Random House.

Whitehead, Colson. 2011. *Zone One*. New York: Random House.

Whitehead, Colson. 2016. *The Underground Railroad*. New York: Random House.

Whitehead, Colson. 2019. *The Nickel Boys*. New York: Random House.

Wilderson, Frank B. 2020. *Afropessimism*. New York: Liveright.

Wynter, Sylvia. 2015. *On Being Human as Praxis*. Ed. Katherine McKittrick. Durham: Duke University Press.

INDEX

www.ingramcontent.com/pod-product-compliance
Ingram Content Group UK Ltd.
Pitfield, Milton Keynes, MK11 3LW, UK
UKHW020733280225
455688UK00012B/630